# Maimonides and the Merchants

JEWISH CULTURE AND CONTEXTS

Published in association with
the Herbert D. Katz Center for Advanced Judaic Studies
of the University of Pennsylvania

Steven Weitzman, Series Editor

A complete list of books in the series
is available from the publisher.

# MAIMONIDES AND THE MERCHANTS

## Jewish Law and Society in the Medieval Islamic World

Mark R. Cohen

PENN

UNIVERSITY OF PENNSYLVANIA PRESS

PHILADELPHIA

Published by
University of Pennsylvania Press
Philadelphia, Pennsylvania 19104-4112
www.upenn.edu/pennpress

Printed in the United States of America on acid-free paper
1 3 5 7 9 10 8 6 4 2

Library of Congress Cataloging-in-Publication Data
Names: Cohen, Mark R., 1943– author.
Title: Maimonides and the merchants : Jewish law and society in the medieval Islamic world / Mark R. Cohen.
Other titles: Jewish culture and contexts.
Description: 1st edition. | Philadelphia : University of Pennsylvania Press, [2017] | Series: Jewish culture and contexts
Identifiers: LCCN 2016055419 | ISBN 9780812249149 (hardcover : alk. paper)
Subjects: LCSH: Jewish merchants—Islamic Empire—History—To 1500. | Commercial law (Jewish law)—History—To 1500. | Partnership (Jewish law)—History—To 1500. | Maimonides, Moses, 1135-1204. Mishneh Torah. | Islamic Empire—Commerce—History—To 1500. | Islamic Empire—Ethnic relations—History—To 1500.
Classification: LCC DS135.L4 C65 2017 | DDC 296.3/677—dc23
LC record available at https://lccn.loc.gov/2016055419

*For Linda*

# Contents

# Notes and Abbreviations

All references to the Talmud are to the Babylonian Talmud, unless otherwise indicated. Transcriptions of Judaeo-Arabic follow classical Arabic conventions and use the system in the *Encyclopaedia of Islam*, except that *dj* and *ḳ* are replaced by *j* and *q*, respectively. Hebrew transcriptions follow a simplified format, omitting the macron for long vowels. I have used the edition of the Mishneh Torah of Shabse Frankel, which is generally considered the most reliable printed edition. For the English translation of passages from the Mishneh Torah, I have consulted and generally relied upon *The Code of Maimonides*, 14 vols. (New Haven, CT: Yale University Press, 1949), making changes where I deemed them necessary.

| | |
|---|---|
| AIU | Alliance Israélite Universelle Geniza Collection, Paris |
| AJS | Association for Jewish Studies |
| APD | Arabic Papyrology Database |
| Bodl. | Bodleian Library Genizah Collection, Oxford |
| CUL | Cambridge University Library Genizah Collection |
| ENA | Elkan Nathan Adler Geniza Collection, Jewish Theological Seminary, New York |
| FGP | Friedberg Genizah Project |
| JNUL | Jewish National and University Library (now NLI National Library of Israel) |
| Mosseri | Mosseri Genizah Collection, currently undergoing conservation at Cambridge University Library |
| NS | New Series |
| PGP | Princeton Geniza Project |
| TS | Taylor-Schechter Genizah Collection, Cambridge University Library, Cambridge |

# Introduction

Research for this book began unexpectedly, with my study of poverty and charity in the Jewish community of medieval Egypt.[1] That work is based primarily on documentary evidence from the Cairo Geniza about the poor and those who came to their relief—whether through private charity or communal institutions. For the normative stance of Jewish law (halakha), I consulted Maimonides' Code, the Mishneh Torah—specifically, the section "Laws of Gifts for the Poor" (*Hilkhot mattenot 'aniyyim*). Maimonides' Laws of Gifts for the Poor represented the first attempt to draw together and systematically codify all the rabbinic teachings about charity, assembled from rulings scattered throughout the Bible and the Talmudic and post-Talmudic literature.[2] To my surprise, I discovered that several enigmatic rulings about charity in the Code over which some medieval commentators had puzzled could be explained by drawing on Geniza evidence of how charity operated "on the ground."[3] I hypothesized that other subjects in the Code relating to daily life could be similarly illuminated using the same methodology. Commercial law seemed an obvious candidate for further inquiry.

## 0.1 Jews and Jewish Law in the Commercial Economy of Medieval Islam

The Mishna and its commentaries, the Palestinian and Babylonian Talmuds, put heavy emphasis on agrarian life, and it is certain that most Jews in pre-Islamic Palestine and Babylonia engaged in farming. This does not mean that Jews were not to be found in urban areas. The situation was quite the contrary, especially in Palestine. The many craftsmen mentioned in rabbinic texts probably dwelled in towns, as did many farmers. The merchants we encounter in the Mishna, the Tosefta, and the Gemara of the two Talmuds seem to have operated mainly in local or regional markets connected with farming and handicrafts: the merchants of Jerusalem (*tagarei yerushalayim*); the merchants of Lydda (*tagarei lod*); the Gentile merchants (*tagarei ummot ha-'olam, tagarei goyim*); and the merchants who (unlawfully) sold produce grown in the sabbatical year (*soḥarei shevi'it*). Long-distance commerce was exceedingly rare.

To be sure, one can point to those Jewish members of the triad of adventurous itinerant "Syrian, Jewish, and Greek" merchants, who traversed the western reaches of the Roman Empire and its Germanic successor states in late antiquity and the early Middle Ages. Or one can cite those Middle Eastern Jews who plied the ancient spice-trade route to southern Arabia; or those rabbis and other Jews who traveled from Babylonia to Palestine and sold silk imported from the Far East.[4] But these were exceptions proving the rule: Talmudic society rested firmly on an agricultural base. Reflecting the predominantly agricultural character of Jewish society in eastern Roman and Sasanian late antiquity, neither the Palestinian nor the Babylonian Talmud has a well-developed commercial law or maritime law. The Mishna, the foundational text of both Talmuds, assumes a predominantly agrarian economy even in its discussions of commercial exchange.[5] It is only in the Gaonic period that we begin to find responsa and other legal texts that deal in detail with commercial matters. This was, in large part, a result of the Islamic conquests.

### *0.1.1 The Islamicate Commercial Revolution*

The advent of Islam in the seventh century brought profound economic changes to the Middle East and to the Jews living there. Beginning with the Qur'ān and the precedent of the Prophet's own mercantile activities, and building on the extensive trade of pre-Islamic Arabia, Islam showed itself to be more favorably disposed toward commerce and the accumulation of wealth than either pagan Roman or early Christian society.[6] The unification through Islamic conquest of the formerly warring great empires of Byzantium and Persia opened up vast territories for long-distance trade and exchange of goods within a single realm. Accelerated urbanization accompanied a monetized "commercial revolution," to borrow a term used to describe similar economic developments in medieval Europe that began only centuries later. With minimal restrictions, passage through the huge "Domain of Islam," stretching from Spain to Transoxiana, was open to resident merchants of all faiths, though non-Muslims paid heavier commercial taxes than Muslims, in addition to the discriminatory poll tax, the *jizya*. Non-Muslim foreign merchants might remain for a year without being required to accept the status of *dhimmī* ("protected people") imposed upon native Jews and Christians and a few other groups.[7]

The territories of the empire possessed extensive resources that fueled this commercial revolution. Access to gold, particularly in conquered lands of West Africa and Nubia, provided abundant currency for the monetized economy. Waterways—the Persian Gulf, the Mediterranean Sea, the Red Sea, the Indian Ocean, as well as many long, navigable rivers—facilitated mid-range and long-distance trade, independent of the slower and more cumbersome overland caravan routes.[8] Merchant practices long entrenched in the ancient Near East took off in new directions in the train of Muslim traders. The predominantly agrarian Jewish economy was utterly transformed by these developments.[9] Emblematic of this radical change are the Rādhānite Jewish merchants of Babylonia described in Arabic sources from the ninth century, who traded as far as western Europe, at one end, and South Asia and the Far East, at the other.[10]

The expansion of commerce was accompanied by and benefited from demographic changes affecting the Jews. Some Jews doubtless joined the waves of migrations from the Islamic East to the western provinces at the time of the conquests. They moved west in large numbers later on, during the breakup of the Abbasid Empire into successor states in the late ninth and tenth centuries, establishing new Jewish settlements in the Mediterranean lands and thickening others that were already there. Many of these migrants sought their livelihood in long-distance trade.[11]

Already in the very early period of Islamic rule, mercantile customs that were hardly known in the Talmud came to the fore. Partnerships for international trade became more complex. A form of commercial agency, likely stemming from the pre-Islamic trade of Arabia but unimagined in the Talmud, became widespread. Shared by all traders regardless of confessional adherence, these forms of business collaboration gave the Islamicate marketplace a truly interdenominational character.[12] Islamic law, particularly the Ḥanafī school, originating in Islamic Iraq in the eighth century (the Iraq of the Babylonian Geonim), Baber Johansen writes, considered "commercial exchange . . . open and accessible to everyone whose rational capacities qualif[ied] him for the calculation of profit and loss, [and] everybody ha[d] access to the bazaar."[13]

The Babylonian Geonim, the post-Talmudic halakhic and communal authorities and heads of the yeshivot, or academies of learning, in Islamic Iraq, who dominated rabbinic leadership from the seventh to the eleventh centuries, responded to the new prominence of merchants in Jewish economic life through their responsa, through *taqqanot* (new legal rulings), or by considering custom as a source of law. Through the lens of the Geniza documents pertaining to commercial life and with an eye on his own responsa, the present book will show that Maimonides (1138–1204) went beyond the Geonim, adapting the halakha to accommodate the new economy through codification in his Mishneh Torah. The present study, therefore, uncovers an aspect of originality and creativity in Maimonidean legal thought that has not hitherto been recognized.

## 0.2 The Mishneh Torah

Completed around 1178, the Mishneh Torah was unique in the history of Jewish codification.[14] In fourteen volumes, it encompassed all of Jewish law, from the Bible through the Mishna, the two Talmuds, and the opinions of the post-Talmudic teachers in the Islamic period, the Geonim and the Talmudists of al-Andalus. In its scope, form, and structure, Maimonides' Code departed from all earlier efforts to codify Jewish law. Maimonides assembled halakhot that were diffused throughout the classical legal corpus, including laws that would come into force only in the messianic era, and arranged them topically. To make the work even more "user-friendly," he devised new, rational categories to make it possible to access rulings on specific subjects easily—rulings that, in the Talmuds, are found associatively in a variety of not so obvious places. To make it accessible to all, including those who could not understand the abbreviated Aramaic style of the Talmud, he composed the Code in the lucid Hebrew of the Mishna.[15] Further breaking with precedent, he included a basic summary of Jewish beliefs, founded on philosophical principles. In an even more radical departure from the method of classical halakha and that of the Geonim, Maimonides did not identify his sources in rabbinic law.[16] Finally, and particularly important for the present study, whereas the Talmud is notably deficient in the field of commercial law, Maimonides established a firm place in the halakha for such subjects as partnership, agency, sale, leasing, and credit, consolidating disparate Talmudic statements on these subjects and, as we shall see, adjusting business law to adapt to the ways of the Islamicate marketplace.

The study of the Code goes back to the author's own lifetime.[17] Its early dissemination evoked questions about its contents from students and other readers.[18] The work was the object of particular scrutiny by later medieval and early modern commentators. A selection of important commentaries surrounds the text in the standard printed editions, but the total quantity of premodern and modern commentaries numbers in the hundreds. Many of the commentators' efforts were devoted to uncovering and citing the sources underlying individual rulings.

In modern research, the most influential work on the Code is Isadore Twersky's *Introduction to the Code of Maimonides*, which appeared in 1980.[19] In seemingly exhaustive manner, Twersky described the form, scope, classification, language, and style of the work, as well as the revolutionary inclusion of a philosophical credo in a book of halakha. One aspect missing from his study, however, is a social-historical analysis of the Code in the context of everyday Jewish life in the Islamic world. Such an analysis is undertaken in the present book, made possible thanks to the documents of the Cairo Geniza.

## 0.3 The Cairo Geniza

The extraordinary evidentiary value of the Cairo Geniza for the present study results from the circumstances of its creation and from its contents. Following an ancient Jewish custom practiced by traditional Jews to this day—and by Muslims as well—pages of religious writings no longer in use are "buried," usually in a cemetery (Islamic practice varies in this regard), and left to decompose on their own, rather than violating their sanctity by physically destroying them.[20] Originally, a geniza was designated to accommodate only holy writings, such as torn sections of a Torah scroll or pages from books of the Bible that had become separated from their original codices—this is true of "Islamic geniza" as well, for pages of the Qur'ān.[21] Later, the practice was extended to anything written in the Hebrew alphabet.

The Cairo Geniza, discovered in the latter half of the nineteenth century, was "buried" not in a cemetery but in a storage room of a medieval synagogue in Old Cairo (Fustat), the house of worship known today as the Ben Ezra Synagogue.[22] Different reasons have been suggested for this seemingly atypical form of geniza,[23] but, whatever the reason, the anomaly worked to our good fortune because the contents of the Geniza were all the easier to retrieve, once it was discovered. Moreover, because Egypt has an arid climate, the paper and inks have survived largely intact, even though the fragments are often torn. With careful reconstruction and conservation of damaged portions, the writing is almost as readable today as it was at the time it was written, as long as 1,000 years ago, when the bulk of the earliest dated or datable manuscripts was composed.[24]

The Cairo Geniza trove numbers (at latest count) some 330,000 folio pages.[25] Of these, the vast majority are literary texts. Genres represented include Bible, late antique and medieval Hebrew poetry, midrashic and halakhic works, philosophical treatises, magical and mystical texts, prayer books, and even fragments of Arabic belles lettres and Islamic literature, including pages of the Qur'ān transcribed into Hebrew letters. The rest, probably 20,000 or more self-contained items, are materials from everyday life, which we would call "secular."[26] They date mostly from the eleventh to mid-thirteenth centuries, the so-called classical Geniza period, which includes the years that the Maimonides family lived in Egypt, after arriving there from the Islamic West in 1166. Small amounts of "secular" material date from later times—as late as the end of the nineteenth century.

This "documentary Geniza," as it is called, following Goitein, includes letters, court records, marriage contracts, deeds of divorce, wills, documents concerning pious trusts, business contracts, merchant accounts, book lists, lists of recipients of charity, and registers of gifts for charitable purposes, and more. Though many of them are in Hebrew or Aramaic, most of them are written in Judaeo-Arabic, that is, Arabic in Hebrew characters, a form of Middle Arabic containing many vernacular features as well as lexical meanings not found in dictionaries of classical or modern standard Arabic. Filled with realia about real people and daily life, these sources reveal aspects of economic, social, and family life, as well as of material culture and individual mentalities that were previously completely unknown.[27] With the benefit of the documentary Geniza, we have direct and relatively unmediated access to these realia and a basis on which to evaluate Maimonides' codification.

## 0.4 Responsa and Legal Monographs

Legal sources apart from the Code play an essential role in this study as well. They exist primarily in the vast reservoir of Jewish responsa from the Islamic world. A responsum (Heb., *teshuva*), like an Islamic *fatwā*, is a legal opinion written by a jurisconsult—in Arabic, a *muftī*—in answer to a question often arising out of litigation in a court.[28] The responsa of the Babylonian Geonim, preserved in editions of medieval manuscripts or retrieved in the form of loose leaves from the Geniza, emanate from Iraq of the eighth to eleventh centuries, before the time of Maimonides. Many, if not most, of them, however, respond to queries from outlying Jewish communities in the Mediterranean, as far away as Spain. Thus, they shed light on commercial life in the geographical area of primary interest here and, importantly, during the centuries for which the Geniza provides no documentary remains.

Other relevant responsa include those of Maimonides' predecessors in al-Andalus—notably, the illustrious R. Isaac Alfasi (d. 1103), who came to Spain from North Africa and taught in the yeshiva of Lucena, and his equally brilliant disciple and successor, R. Joseph ibn Migash (d. 1141). The latter was the teacher of Maimonides' father, and through his father, the son absorbed the teachings of that great sage and of Alfasi himself. Maimonides was thus familiar with both the Gaonic and the Andalusian traditions, which need to be taken into account in any study of his Code.

Complementing the responsa of the Babylonian Geonim, another important source emanating from their academies are their legal monographs, most of them written in Judaeo-Arabic. These cover a variety of subjects, many in the realm of civil law. They include treatises on divorce, inheritance, gifts, buying and selling, partnership, preemption, bailment, suretyship, debts, oaths, judicial procedure, and methods of acquisition, as well as formularies for composing different types of legal documents.[29] Gaonic legal monographs consolidate rules governing everyday life and represent a sphere of intellectual creativity that took place against the background of the formation and systematization of Islamic law in Iraq and elsewhere. With the exception of the few monographs that were translated into Hebrew in the Middle Ages, most of them are preserved, if at all, in a fragmentary state, including hundreds of small or larger scraps from the Geniza. Robert Brody notes that these Gaonic monographs "practically disappeared from view as the center of gravity of the Jewish world shifted to Christian Europe, beginning in the twelfth century."[30] Like the responsa, however, they are relevant to a socio-legal study such as the present one. A particularly important Gaonic monograph for the subject at hand, partially reconstructed and recently published by Brody from Geniza fragments, is Saadya Gaon's "Book of Bailment." This mini-code illustrates how Saadya attempted to accommodate within the halakha the form of commercial agency alluded to above. Saadya's halakhic step places in bold relief Maimonides' own and different attempt to assimilate this same merchant custom into Jewish law.[31]

Of particular importance for this study are the hundreds of extant responsa written by Maimonides himself, most of them "published" in medieval manuscript collections and edited, most recently, by Joshua Blau.[32] Many individual responsa, some with Maimonides' own handwritten answer, were discovered among the manuscripts of the Geniza or elsewhere. Since Maimonides' responsa date from the twelfth century, their historical value is nearly equivalent to that of the Geniza documents.[33] A considerable number of them deal with economic affairs, and, as we shall see, it is sometimes possible to detect nuances in the Code that are illuminated by responsa that he issued.[34] Their significance is enhanced by the fact that most of them preserve the original Arabic in which they were composed.

## 0.5 Historical Versus Comparative Legal Study

The large question that guides this study—the relationship between Jewish law and society in the medieval Islamic world—has, in recent years, been addressed from another angle by Gideon Libson in illuminating research on comparative Jewish and Islamic law.[35] His findings, which I will have frequent occasion to cite, have brought to light striking evidence of the relationship between Jewish law and Islamic law in the Gaonic and post-Gaonic periods. Libson shows that halakhists like Samuel b. Ḥofni Gaon (d. 1013) and Maimonides were aware of Islamic law and adopted some of its approaches and rulings in their own legal works.[36] He also shows that the Geonim adopted judicial procedures that were prevalent in Islamic *sharīʿa* courts but inconsistent with Talmudic halakha; and that Maimonides, in his Code, showed awareness of these departures from the Talmudic norm.[37] Y. Zvi Stampfer has applied the comparative approach to Samuel b. Ḥofni's treatise on the laws of divorce.[38] Amir Ashur has pointed to similarities (as well as differences) between stipulations in Jewish engagement, betrothal, prenuptial, and marriage contracts in the Geniza and stipulations in cognate Islamic documents.[39]

Deeply familiar with Islamic as well as Jewish law, Libson argues convincingly that, in many cases, the Geonim absorbed material directly from Islamic law as custom, employing the principle of halakhic jurisprudence that custom can serve as a source of Jewish law.[40] For Maimonides, Libson looks in the first instance to Shāfiʿī law, which was prominent in Egypt even when it was ruled by the Ismāʿīlī Fatimids (969–1171), and even more so during Maimonides' time. Libson finds Shāfiʿī legal parallels in the Mishneh Torah as well as similarities in theoretical approach.[41] While Libson's scholarship in all these matters centers on a legal-historical reading, focusing on the influence of Islamic law on Jewish law in the realm of prescriptive texts, he properly understands the process of borrowing as a response to socioeconomic forces in the Islamic world. Central to his thesis is his taxonomy, drawing a distinction between "borrowed custom," a custom "lifted directly from Islamic law," and "responsive custom," which "stemmed from the Geonim themselves in response to the general economic and existential needs of the time."[42]

The present study puts primary emphasis on the economic aspect itself, foregrounding documentary evidence from the Geniza and in the responsa of economic realities in the Islamic world that are reflected in and responded to in Maimonides' Code. Through a careful analysis of a broad selection of halakhot dealing directly or indirectly with commercial law and practice, this case study in Maimonidean codification strengthens the conclusion about the relationship between Jewish law and society arrived at through comparative legal study. At the same time, it points to an aspect of originality in the Code that has hitherto gone unnoticed.[43]

## 0.6 Islamic Legal Change

In order to situate Maimonides and his predecessors in their general intellectual milieu, it is instructive to consider what contemporary scholars of Islamic law consider to be the traditional Muslim view on legal change. Subhi Mahmassani explains that Muslim jurists place restrictions on making changes in ritual law. Concerning "worldly transactions," however, some Muslim jurists adopt a more flexible policy. They take the context of legal rulings into account and allow for changes in the law to conform with changing circumstances.[44] Summarizing the relationship between law and society, Mahmassani adds that "some caliphs, *imāms*, and jurists . . . endorsed the possibility of change in the explanation or interpretation of texts, because of a change in their causes or in the customs upon which they were based, or in answer to necessity and public interest."[45] Frank Vogel explains the situation as follows: "Practice also reveals vital aspects of law going beyond substantive doctrine, such as the workings of morality or revealed precepts outside of law and the formal legal system (in our sense) and various methods of responding to social and economic circumstances and changes without overt change of doctrine, such as contingently justified gradations, variations or exceptions in doctrine, fictions, artifices, or court procedures."[46]

Hossein Modarressi notes the Qur'ānic principle that "[n]o one can change [God's] words" but goes on to explain what he calls "the principle of discretionary judgment in Sunnī law": "The interests of the community and individual welfare do not remain constant but rather change over time and from place to place, in accordance with changing social circumstances. The law legislated on such a changing basis must inevitably change too; and it is held to be the function of the jurists to modify the interpretation of the laws to conform with new social conditions and the requirements of the time."[47]

Wael Hallaq's view on legal change in Islam runs along a similar path. "Muslim jurists were acutely aware of both the occurrence of, and the need for, change in the law, and they articulated this awareness through such maxims as 'the fatwā changes with changing times' (*taghayyur al-fatwā bi-taghayyur al-azmān*), or through the explicit notion that the law is subject to modification according to 'the changing of the times or to the changing conditions of society.'"[48] A maxim cited in the Ottoman Meçelle (Article 39) sums this up succinctly: "There is no disputing that rules of law vary with the change in times" (*lā yunkar taghayyur al-aḥkām bi-taghayyur al-azmān*).[49]

Thus, despite the fact that custom is technically not accepted as a source of law in Islam, historically it has played an important role in legal evolution. The early nineteenth-century Ḥanafī jurist Ibn ʿĀbidīn sums up the maxim about changes in the law with changes in the times: "Since the *muftī* must follow custom even if it contradicts the written text in the established reports, is there a difference between general custom and special custom, as in the first part [of the treatise], that is when custom contradicts the textual rule? I say: there is no difference between them except that general custom establishes general rules and special custom establishes a special rule. In conclusion, the rule of custom applies to all people, whether custom is general or special, within general custom in all countries applying to people in all countries, whereas a custom special to one area applies only to this area."[50]

The Geonim and Maimonides lived, therefore, in a society in which custom played a significant role in juristic theory and practice, especially in commercial law—the area, probably more than any other, where practice influenced legal norms. In seeking to understand Maimonides' method of codification, it is useful to consider Wael Hallaq's discussion of the relationship between the jurisconsult and what he calls the "author-jurist." Hallaq proposes that the principal device effecting legal change in Islam was the *fatwās* (responsa) issued by *muftīs* (jurisconsults) and, in turn, transformed by "author-jurists" into changes in normative law.[51] By the very nature of his profession, fielding questions arising from daily life, the *muftī* knew, better than most people, where the discrepancies between law and society lay. Maimonides, who was both a Jewish *muftī*, writing hundreds of responsa—*muftī al-milla*, "*muftī* of our religious community," in the words of one Jewish seeker of legal guidance[52]—and at the same time an author-jurist, compiling a comprehensive code of Jewish law, belonged, therefore, to a cultural milieu shared with his Muslim counterparts.

## 0.7 Structure of the Book

To guide readers of this book, I present here a brief summary of its chapters. Chapter 1 discusses codification and legal change. I introduce two legal scholars who have raised the question of the relationship between the two. One of them is Maimonidean scholar, Gerald Blidstein; the other is Alan Watson, scholar of legal history and theory. Periodically in the book, I will return to these scholars, linking their views to the discussion at hand. In Chapter 1, I also review one of Maimonides' most discussed *taqqanot*—a reform in the synagogue service—to demonstrate how he took daily life into account in his legal decision-making in the Code, even in the realm of ritual.

Chapter 2, "Halakha and the Custom of the Merchants," makes the case that the Babylonian Geonim and Maimonides were attuned to the ways of the Islamicate marketplace. The Geonim called this (in Arabic) *ḥukm al-tujjār*, "the custom of the merchants." I show how they accommodated merchant practice and other exigencies of the new mercantile economy with *taqqanot*, through their responsa, or by adopting new commercial practices, employing the legal maxim that custom can override the halakha. I include a discussion of the rabbinic concept of the "custom of the mariners," illustrating the importance of the custom of the surrounding society for Jews, even in Talmudic times.

In contrast to the Geonim, Maimonides responded to the new commercial economy through codification. I establish the place of the custom of the merchants in the Code by closely analyzing one halakha from his *Hilkhot sheluḥin ve-shutafin*, "Laws of Agents and Partners." Unlike the Geonim, Maimonides, who elsewhere freely uses the term "custom of the mariners," does not employ the actual phrase "custom of the merchants," a translation of the Gaonic *ḥukm al-tujjār*. Rather, writing in Hebrew and using Mishnaic language, he chooses a traditional rabbinic phrase, *minhag ha-medina*, "local custom," to clothe the new reality in ancient garb.

Chapter 3, "Updating the Halakha," presents several examples from the Code (charity, Sabbath observance, marital relations, and others), where Maimonides incorporates the element of commerce into a ritual law of the Talmud where it is absent, in order to "update" the halakha to fit the mercantile economy.

Chapter 4, "Partnership," discusses forms of commercial collaboration popular among Jewish merchants of the Geniza period. These include institutions of partnership recognized by the Talmud. A non-Talmudic form of partnership that seems to be an Islamic precursor of the later European *commenda* was acknowledged by Islamic law and practiced by Muslims and occasionally by Jews. Especially important in this chapter is the section on partnership with a Muslim, which responds to the reality of interfaith business relations in the Geniza world.

Chapters 5 and 6 go together. Chapter 5, "Commercial Agency (*Ṣuḥba*)," describes a completely new institution of commercial collaboration practiced by Jews. Actually a form of commercial agency, it was first identified by S. D. Goitein and called "formal friendship"; I refer to it as *ṣuḥba*-agency. Geniza letters reveal that *ṣuḥba*-agency was twice as popular a means of doing business as all other forms of long-distance trade combined. In *ṣuḥba*-agency, merchants did not invest together or share profits and losses, as in a partnership. Rather, they compensated one another by doing reciprocal business favors. This informal procedure mimicked a form of commercial agency called *ibḍāʿ*, practiced by Muslims and enshrined in Islamic law. Arabic letters written by Muslim traders confirm that Jewish traders followed the custom of the Muslim merchants. Because it was unknown to the Talmud, *ṣuḥba*-agency lacked a means of enforcement in Jewish courts, a defect that Maimonides, preceded by Saadya Gaon in the tenth century, sought to remedy in his Code (here in Chapter 6, "*Ṣuḥba*-Agency in the Code"). In Chapters 5 and 6, I also discuss the controversial theory of Stanford economist Avner Greif concerning the special way in which Geniza merchants enforced agency relations. Chapter 7 is devoted to an institution of agency that the Talmud recognizes—

proxy legal agency, equivalent to our power of attorney. Here we find Maimonides staunchly rejecting a Gaonic reform that had been designed to accommodate the transition from Jewish landownership in Iraq to commerce, following the Islamic conquest. However, as I shall show, Maimonides was not out of step with an economic reality that the Geonim had attempted to address. Rather, he was conscious of facts on the ground in Egypt and in his native Andalusia that rendered the Gaonic "fiction" unnecessary.

Chapter 8 discusses Maimonides' ruling on buying and selling, the cardinal components of exchange in any commercial society and a constant form of activity in the daily lives of Geniza merchants. Maimonides stridently opposes selling or acquiring property by any other means than the ones prescribed by the Talmud. I hypothesize that his purpose was to discourage Jewish traders from employing the Islamic method of "offer and acceptance." At the end of the chapter, I explicate a halakha about writing contracts that exemplifies Maimonides' effort to adapt the halakha to accommodate the technological innovation represented by the production and use of paper in the Islamic world, replacing papyrus or other writing surfaces assumed by the Talmud.

In Chapter 9, I review the question of the status of Jews (and non-Muslims in general) in Islamic courts, both the position of Islamic law on the matter and the evidence of Jewish (and Christian) recourse to Islamic courts. This was a major and abiding problem for Jewish leadership (as for Christian religious elites). I offer my opinion that much of Maimonides' updating and reform of Jewish commercial law in the Code can be explained by his concern over this challenge to Jewish communal autonomy. I suggest that he wanted to provide Jewish merchants with an alternative and comparable Jewish equivalent to the Islamic legal system.

The Conclusion to the book discusses the question of originality in Maimonides' legal thought, a subject that the book raises from a new angle. In closing, I compare my approach to legal change in Maimonides' Code with Haym Soloveitchik's approach to law and society in medieval Ashkenazic Europe.

# Chapter 1

# Codification and Legal Change

## 1.1 Codification and Legal Change: Two Views

In "Where Do We Stand in the Study of Maimonidean Halakhah?," published over a quarter of a century ago, the eminent Maimonidean scholar Gerald Blidstein wrote: "Though law is a notoriously conservative aspect of culture, legal systems do reflect changing economic and social realities." With specific reference to the Code, he adds: "The economy of the medieval East was, in certain ways, a continuation of that dominant in Talmudic times; but certain realities had of course changed. The Islamic East was urban and mercantile." He then asks the intriguing question: "Does Maimonidean law reflect this shift? Or does it—the responsa aside—remain firmly fixed within the Talmudic reality, both in its resources, rulings, and attitudes? Do we find extrapolations from Talmudic law to the new situation—or perhaps more than that, or less?"[1] Blidstein raises here, but does not answer, the question of legal change in Maimonides' treatment of commercial law, the question that animates the present book.

The distinguished legal historian Alan Watson addresses legal innovation in regard to Roman and English law in his classic *Society and Legal Change*. He points to the inertia of private law, its resistance to change—what Blidstein terms its "notoriously conservative aspect." Watson is even more categorical in his negative assessment of the capacity of law to adapt to changes in society. "The argument of this book," he writes, "is that in the West, rules of private law have been and are in large measure out of step with the needs and desires of society and even of its ruling elite; to an extent which renders implausible the existing theories of legal development and of the relationship between law and society."[2] He asks, however, in an important aside, whether "codification," especially original codes, can "remove the significant divergence between law and society and . . . abolish legal scaffolding." By "legal scaffolding," he means an encrustation of legal rules meant to modify the existing laws but that, in fact, makes them more complex than necessary.[3]

In a later iteration of his thesis, Watson registers an exception to the rule of inertia in private law. Mercantile custom, he writes, is particularly susceptible to what he calls "transplant bias," referring to his book *Legal Transplants: An Approach to Comparative Law*.[4] He explains: "What is borrowed is international mercantile law based on what merchants do. To a very large degree, this law is received because the merchants' business would otherwise be directly disadvantaged." It is received, moreover, "without the merchants' having much knowledge of law."[5] Applying Watson's formulation to the present case, we may imagine a process whereby Jewish merchants in the Islamic world adopted mercantile practices current in the marketplace without necessarily knowing the Islamic law that supported those practices. They would, however, have been exposed to the legal basis for these customs when, as commonly happened, they turned to Islamic courts to draw up and register contracts or when they appeared before a *qāḍī* to adjudicate disputes. How a jurist like Maimonides confronted, from a traditional Jewish perspective, these new norms of the marketplace—and how he accommodated them in his Code—will occupy us throughout this book.

### *1.1.1 Codification and Legal Change in Maimonides' Code*

Addressing Blidstein's query about the historical context of Maimonides' Code and bearing in mind Watson's question about codification and legal change, I examine aspects of commercial law in the Mishneh Torah to determine whether—and, if so, how—Maimonides responded through codification to economic realities of his time and place. These realities are revealed especially in the documentary treasures of the Cairo Geniza but also in the responsa of the Islamic period.

Others have noticed echoes of life "on the ground" in the Code but not with reference to the evidence of the Geniza documents.[6] Though not without precedent in the history of Jewish codification—as already noted, the Babylonian Geonim compiled dozens of legal monographs on specific subjects, including a number of limited general codes[7]—Maimonides went a giant step further. He constructed a code that meets the criteria for the kind of compilation envisioned by Alan Watson.[8] By breaking the halakha into discrete units, each classified in a rational way that liberated the law from the complexity of Talmudic discourse, it minimized the "legal scaffolding" that Watson describes in connection with Roman and English law. Like the "original" codes envisaged by Watson, Maimonides' opus can be said to have represented a new "canon" of the halakha.[9] It is my considered opinion, and I hope to make the case effectively in this book, that much, if not most, of the enhancements to the commercial law that I have detected in the Code represent Maimonides' conscious and—from our perspective, at least—original effort to close the gap between the law of the Talmud and the practice of contemporary Jewish merchants, giving Jewish courts a competitive edge in deterring Jewish merchants from recourse to Islamic courts.

If Maimonides' innovative response through codification to current mercantile practice has not been appreciated, it is partly because Maimonides went to great lengths to assert the conservative nature of his work and partly because scholars have not thought to apply the Geniza evidence to the subject at hand. In his Introduction to the Code, Maimonides proclaimed that it contained nothing new. It was simply a "repetition of the Law," a phrase generally assumed to echo the term *mishneh torah* in Deut. 17:18 but perhaps referring to its postbiblical content.[10] It consists of a compendium of postbiblical, binding rulings, the latest link in a continuous chain of halakhic writings. It subsumes the Mishna (and its parallel, the Tosefta), Sifra and Sifre (the most legalistic of the halakhic midrashim), the Mishna and Gemara of the two Talmuds, and the legal writings of the post-Talmudic Geonim, as well as his Andalusian teachers. In his Introduction and in other writings, he modestly called the Mishneh Torah his *ḥibbur*, which he defined as a collection of halakhot without accompanying dialectical examination, similar to the Mishna.[11] With this in hand, users would have no need to consult any of those works. While Maimonides' professed deference to tradition was in keeping with a fundamental principle of codification in the Jewish conception,[12] his unprecedented method of omitting sources, coupled with his unambiguous statement that the Code made consultation of prior halakhic literature unnecessary, opened the door to suspicion that he had departed from traditional legal norms.

Maimonides must have anticipated that his method of codification would leave many readers puzzled, if not perplexed. Indeed, this kind of criticism began during his own lifetime in Egypt. When challenged in a letter from Pinḥas ben Meshullam, the judge of Alexandria, to explain halakhot in the

Code for which the judge could find no source in the rabbinic corpus, Maimonides insisted sharply that he had not deviated from the tradition and chastised his correspondent for failing to locate the relevant sources on his own. If here and there, he had "originated" a ruling, he said, he had marked it clearly as his own.[13] He wrote, further, that he had intended to publish a work explaining his treatment of difficult halakhot—for instance, halakhot based on the Palestinian Talmud, which was not well known to most students and scholars in his time, but he had not found the time to complete that project.[14]

The omission of sources in the Mishneh Torah unleashed a torrent of commentaries seeking to anchor its rulings in Talmudic literature. Most of the time, the commentators found something. Occasionally, they did not, or they differed with one another, raising suspicions that something was not quite right.

Modern scholars have generally taken Maimonides at his word and accepted the Code as simply a summa of received Jewish law, though the innovative aspects of the Code uncovered in recent years by such scholars as Gideon Libson and Sarah Stroumsa should prepare us to find other features of originality in Maimonides' great halakhic opus.[15] Maimonides' denial of his originality notwithstanding, it is reasonable to ask, with Blidstein, whether the work responds in some way to everyday life and, with Watson's question in mind, whether he used codification to reconcile Talmudic law with the custom of merchants in the Islamic world.[16] Thanks to the Geniza, we are in a position to answer both questions in the affirmative.

### *1.1.2 Maimonides in His Society*

Maimonides did not live cloistered in a rabbinic academy. He was intimately involved with society, as head of the Jewish community for many years and as jurisconsult, answering questions of Jewish law arising from daily affairs—a "man of action," to borrow the title of one of Goitein's essays.[17] In economic matters, especially, Maimonides was fully aware of the gulf that separated the world of the Talmud from the world of the Geniza merchants. Though known to us primarily as a philosopher, legist, and physician, his younger Muslim contemporary Ibn al-Qifṭī (1172–1248), who lived in Cairo until 1187, reports credibly in his biographical dictionary of philosophers, scientists, and other learned men, *Ta'rīkh al-ḥukamā'*, that Maimonides, upon his arrival in Egypt, "made a living by trading in jewels and suchlike."[18] We know from the

Geniza that his brother, David, engaged in trade between Egypt and India. Maimonides, furthermore, had passed the early years of his life in the commercial milieu of Muslim Spain, then in the North African trading hub of Fez, before settling in Egypt, the pivotal point in the East-West Mediterranean and Indian Ocean trade. Reading the Code in the light of Geniza documents from everyday economic life as well as in the light of Maimonides' own responsa, we shall see that, despite his disclaimers in the Introduction and in his letter to the Alexandrian judge, in commercial law, Maimonides used codification, in Watson's words, to "remove the significant divergence between law and society," namely, traditional Jewish law and his own Islamicate society.

## 1.2 The Method

New emphases in the Code, new taxonomies of halakhic content, subtle changes of wording, reorganization of Talmudic material, or additional material not found in the Talmudic corpus, all responding to changes in the economic order of the Islamic world, illustrate Maimonides' method. Taken as a whole, the evidence, often difficult to discern, sheds light from an unexpected angle of vision on the question posed by Watson and by Blidstein about the relationship between law and society and reveals a creative feature of the Code that has not previously been recognized.

To be sure, in bridging the gap between law and society, Maimonides did not operate in an intellectual vacuum. In his attitude toward custom, for instance, he, like the Geonim before him, accepted the rabbinic approval of custom as a valid source of law. Twersky took note of this, but all the examples of local custom that he cites—usually specifically flagged by Maimonides himself as "custom"—belong to the realm of personal, family, and ritual law. Moreover, Twersky asserts that Maimonides was selective and discerning when it came to customs having universal (as opposed to local) validity.[19]

In his comprehensive review of Twersky's *Introduction* to the Code, Blidstein contends that the claim, implicit in Twersky's work, that the Mishneh Torah shows no signs of the impact of immanent historical, social, and economic forces in the non-Jewish (Islamic) environment, needs further scholarly consideration.[20] To this, we may add the following. Twersky discusses "the problem of contradictions" in the Code, "troublesome features" such as statements apparently disagreeing with the Talmud, or with one another, or even statements lacking Talmudic antecedents entirely. He explains them as part of a well-thought-out method with its own logic, rules, and purpose.[21] But this fails to take into consideration that, in affairs of the marketplace, Maimonides often diverged from the ancient halakha because that halakha was geared to an economy quite different from the commercial economy of the Islamic world. As we shall see, in commercial law, he made adjustments to the halakha to accommodate customs of the merchants, customs that were deeply entrenched among Jewish merchants. These are revealed in rich and colorful detail in the Geniza documents. In this light, Maimonides' retort to the judge of Alexandria, like his insistence in the Introduction to the Code that he was simply compiling laws from classical Talmudic and post-Talmudic sources, sounds like a disclaimer intended to ward off criticism that he was, in some cases, overstepping the bounds of traditional Jewish jurisprudence.

### *1.2.1 Criticism of the Method of the Code*

The perplexed judge of Alexandria was far from Maimonides' only critic. One of his contemporaries, the Babylonian Gaon Samuel b. Eli, protested strenuously against the Code, which, in his view, undermined the teaching of the Talmud and, by extension, detracted from the importance of his Talmudic academy in Baghdad.[22] The harshest critic was R. Abraham b. David of Posquières in southern France, although Twersky argues that his biting criticisms were in keeping with acceptable rhetoric of the times.[23] Maimonides' defenders, particularly his son and successor, Abraham, went to great lengths to refute accusations leveled against the Code.[24]

The vast majority of medieval and early modern commentators approached the Code with a more reverent attitude. They searched for Maimonides' sources in classical rabbinic texts or in works of his predecessors in the Islamic period. Their goal was not to challenge the Code but rather to rehabilitate it. When they failed to find a reasonable underpinning for a ruling on commercial law in the Code, it was often because they did not fully understand the economic realia of Maimonides' time.

## 1.3 Maimonides' Reforms of Synagogue Practice and Their Relationship to the Code

To illustrate the interplay of law and society in Maimonides' thought, I review here his well-known reform of the synagogue service—particularly, how he translated almost surreptitiously what was an ad hoc *taqqana* into a permanent change in the halakha in the Code. If Maimonides was willing to institute reforms in the sensitive area of religious practice in his Code, we should not be surprised to discover that he instituted changes in the less controversial domain of commercial law.

### *1.3.1 The* Taqqana *Abolishing the Silent Recitation of the 'Amida on Sabbath and Festivals*

Sometime after his arrival in Egypt around 1165, Maimonides promulgated an "ordinance" (*rutba* in the Arabic original of Maimonides' responsa, translated as *taqqana* by the editor, Joshua Blau, and so referred to in the scholarly literature)[25] abolishing the silent recitation of the Eighteen Benedictions, also called the 'Amida prayer (lit., "standing") because it is recited while erect. Traditionally, during the morning and afternoon prayers on the Sabbath and festivals, the 'Amida was recited first by the congregation praying silently along with the cantor, after which the cantor repeated the prayer aloud. The purpose of the repetition was to enable congregants who did not know the prayers by heart to fulfill their liturgical obligation by listening as the cantor repeated each blessing and by responding "amen." During the evening prayer, the Eighteen Benedictions were recited only once, silently, because that prayer was originally considered optional and therefore no obligation fell upon congregants to recite it.

Maimonides explained his action as a response to indecorous behavior during the service. During the reader's repetition, members of the congregation who had already fulfilled their obligation by praying silently with the cantor were in the habit of getting up from their places during the cantor's repetition, stepping outside, talking to one another, blowing their noses, spitting on the floor, and, in the process, turning away from the direction of prayer—which Maimonides, like other Jewish writers before him, calls *qibla*, employing the Islamic term for the direction of prayer toward the holy city of Mecca.[26] This lack of decorum was not peculiar or new to Maimonides' time and place. A responsum of the Babylonian Gaon R. Naṭronai b. Hilai (Gaon from 857/858 to 865/866) reprimands Jews who sit in the courtyard outside the synagogue during services, talking and making light of the sanctity of the prayers.[27]

Maimonides notes that the disrupters set a bad example for others, who imitated their gauche behavior. Consequently, the cantor's repetition on their behalf fell unheeded, and the blessings that he chanted were for naught (*berakha le-vaṭala*). In addition, the people for whom the repetition was intended ended up failing to fulfill their obligation to at least *hear* the prayer. Maimonides was especially disconcerted by the prospect that Muslims, who "observe this with their own eyes" (*yashhadūnahu*), would think that, for Jews, prayer was "for fun [*la'b*] and mockery [*huzu'*]," quoting the very words that the Qur'ān ascribes to the People of the Book when they mock Islam (Sura 5:57). We may imagine that Muslims passing by the synagogue during daylight hours overheard and even observed the chaotic spectacle inside the synagogue compound and ridiculed it. The reform, Maimonides asserted, limiting the 'Amida to a single, public recitation led by the cantor with all congregants praying along or answering "amen," aimed at removing a stain on the reputation of the Jews in Muslim eyes, a "profanation of the name of God" (*ḥillul ha-shem*), as he writes, citing a general rule.[28]

We learn about Maimonides' reform from his responsa, which portray the *taqqana* as an expedient and as a response to an immediate problem. Such changes in the halakha were normally time-bound, enacted to address an urgent situation. They were justified by the principle that one may "violate" the law (*haferu toratekha*)[29] when the alternative—leaving the law as is—would have dire consequences. This was a perfect case, then, for applying the *haferu toratekha* rule, which Maimonides invokes explicitly in explaining his action.[30]

### *1.3.2 Echoes of the* Taqqana *in the Code*

In the Code, which was meant to serve all future generations, Maimonides adhered to the status quo ante, codifying the halakha in accordance with ancient practice, leaving the initial silent recitation of the 'Amida intact.[31] Nonetheless, we hear echoes of the *taqqana* in the Code in directives calculated to achieve the same end. In the halakha about the recitation of the Eighteen Benedictions, for example, Maimonides rules that, following the silent recitation, when the cantor begins chanting the prayer aloud, "everyone must stand and listen and answer 'amen' after each blessing, *both those who have not yet fulfilled their obligation and those who have already fulfilled theirs.*"[32] I take this phrase to be aimed at those very people who disturbed the decorum during the cantorial reprise. Maimonides instructs them to adhere to proper conduct after they have finished their silent devotion in order to avoid *ḥillul ha-shem.* In this way, he achieved the goal of the reform within the context of the existing halakha.

Another echo of Maimonides' concern about synagogue decorum may be found in a halakha recommending that people clean out their nose and mouth before praying, a practice not required in the Talmud but reminiscent of the Islamic custom of purifying the body before engaging in prayer. This practice would minimize the nose-blowing and expectoration that Maimonides singles out as an embarrassment in the face of Muslim onlookers.[33] In short, while Maimonides left the silent recitation of the Eighteen Benedictions on Sabbath and festivals "on the books," he instituted rules in the Code meant to eliminate the very behavior that had brought him to issue the *taqqana* in the first place.

An additional reverberation arising from Muslim ridicule of synagogue decorum seems to lurk behind another halakha in the Code. It concerns the seating arrangement during the prayer service.[34] In Maimonides' day, congregants seated themselves haphazardly, facing one direction or another, with no apparent order. This rankled Maimonides' rationalistic bent—his passion for systematization in all things. Doubtless, too, he worried that Muslims would contrast this unfavorably with the more reverent way of sitting in parallel rows in the mosque on Friday, the day of congregational prayer. And so he sought to change the way things were done.

The reform is enveloped in an ancient halakha from the Tosefta, giving it the sanction of rabbinic tradition. In the Laws of Prayer and the Priestly Blessing, Maimonides draws upon the language of the Tosefta but adds his own twist. He rules that people should sit in straight rows in the synagogue, one row behind the other, everyone facing the holy ark, while the elders sit facing the congregants.[35] This pattern recognizably models itself on the orderly positioning of worshipers during the Friday congregational prayer in the mosque. As in the case of the *taqqana* eliminating the silent recitation of the 'Amida, Maimonides' ruling in the Code on seating arrangements responded to a contemporary problem—much as the rulings of the Geonim had done in their day—bringing synagogue practice more into line with the dignified prayer service of the mosque, with its straight, parallel rows of worshipers facing the *qibla*. If the stories in Arabic sources of Maimonides' outward conversion to Islam in Spain during his youth at the time of the Almohad persecutions are true, as scholars, including me, are increasingly coming to believe, he would have had direct experience of the mosque service, though even without conversion to Islam, he would have been aware of the orderly pattern of seating in the Muslim house of worship.[36]

Though his synagogue reform arose from an immediate concern about entrenched patterns of behavior requiring emergency intervention in the form of a *taqqana*, Maimonides found ways of addressing the problem for the long term in the Code. This amounted to a sub-rosa change in the halakha of Jewish prayer. Similarly, his halakhic adaptations in the realm of commercial law represented a response to deep-seated norms of marketplace practice stemming from the "custom of the merchants" and were meant as permanent adjustments to the halakha.

Chapter 2

# Halakha and the Custom of the Merchants

## 2.1 The Babylonian Geonim and the Custom of the Merchants

Maimonides' predecessors, the Babylonian Geonim, were quick to recognize the transformation in Jewish economic life that followed the Islamic conquest and, in particular, the role that merchant custom—some of it inconsistent with Talmudic halakha—played in Jewish business affairs.[1] With unabashed transparency, they introduced modifications in Talmudic law, without having to call upon the Talmudic principle of *dina de-malkhuta dina* ("the law of the state is law").[2]

A prime example is the order of payment known as the *suftaja*. Muslim long-distance traders widely employed this fiscal instrument, and Jews themselves may have begun using it as early as the mid-eighth century.[3] It is abundantly attested in merchant letters from the Geniza for the eleventh to early thirteenth centuries. In a typical example, person A needed to transfer money to a distant addressee, person C. To avoid the risk of loss of specie, through brigandage, or shipwreck, or other cause, he would send a *suftaja* in that amount with person B to the addressee, who would cash the *suftaja* through a local person holding money on behalf of person A. The avoidance of loss due to the danger of transporting specie was considered a benefit to person A, hence a veiled form of interest. For that reason, some Islamic legists objected to the device, and it was problematic for the Geonim as well.[4]

Queried about the halakhic permissibility of the *suftaja*,[5] an unnamed Gaon authorized its use, even though the Talmud (Bava Qamma 104b) ruled against employing a similar device, called *diyoqne* (*diyuqne*), a word taken from the Greek and betraying its origins in the pre-Islamic, Greco-Roman period.[6] The responsum is significant, not only because it illustrates realistic rabbinic adjustment to economic change but also for its specific use of the term "custom (or law) of the merchants." "Our halakha [*fiqh*] does not support the sending of a *suftaja*, as our rabbis said: 'One may not send money with a *diyoqne*, even if witnesses have signed it.' However, when we saw that people use it in doing business with one another, we began admitting it in court, lest trade among people cease. We sanction it, no more and no less, in accordance with the 'custom (or law) of the merchants' [*ḥukm al-tujjār*]. Such is the law and nothing should be altered in it."[7] The occurrence of the concept *ḥukm al-tujjār* in a Gaonic legal opinion—in a Geniza court record from 1141, it is referred to as *al-ʿāda bi-Miṣr bayn al-tujjār fī l-sharika*, "the custom in Fustat among the merchants concerning partnership"[8]—sanctioning a practice frowned upon by the Talmud but essential in the monetized economy of the Islamic world, is telling. It is reminiscent of the Latin term *lex mercatoria*, "law merchant," in medieval Europe, used to describe a body of marketplace customs peculiar to and shared by merchants, and which A. L. Udovitch long ago suggested had a counterpart in what he called "the 'law merchant' of the medieval Islamic world."[9] Leaving aside the contentious debate about the merchants' law in Europe—whether such a corpus of laws really existed; and, if it did, where it first appeared; whether these customs originated with merchants or with legislation by the "state"; whether they represented the common, "transnational" practice of merchants everywhere; and how these customs were transplanted from place to place[10]—it is clear that the Geonim were aware of and concerned about merchant customs that contradicted Talmudic halakha. Their solution was to let custom override the halakha[11] and sanction the *suftaja*, as they said, "lest trade among people cease." Saadya Gaon (d. 942) expressed the Gaonic rationale with similar resignation: "In all transactions of the merchants, *diyoqna'ot* [plural of *diyoqne*] are not acceptable according to strict law, *but the merchants have disregarded* [*the prohibition*] *in order to facilitate their transactions.*"[12] This comment and the remark "*We saw that people use it in doing business with one another*," in the responsum on the *suftaja* indicate that Jewish merchants followed well-established customs of their economic class, adhering to norms that were not always consistent with the Talmudic legal system but that had been inscribed in Islamic law during its formative period. The Geonim certainly knew that if they did not accommodate the use of the *suftaja*, in any dispute concerning this device Jewish merchants would simply resort to Islamic courts, where the commercial instrument was recognized.[13] Gaonic sanction of the *suftaja* meant that Jewish merchants could bring litigations involving this financial device before the Jewish *beit din*, rather than seeking resolution in the court of the Muslim judge. In the wake of the Geonim, the *suftaja* gained codified status as a valid "custom followed by the merchants" in the *Halakhot* of R. Isaac Alfasi and, later on, in Maimonides' own Code, in the name of "my teachers" in al-Andalus.[14]

Other Gaonic adjustments reflect their awareness of the new mercantile economy as well. In a *taqqana* from the second half of the eighth century, they ruled that widows claiming the money promised them in their marriage contract and payable upon the death of their husbands, as well as general creditors claiming repayment of a debt, could collect what was owed them from the deceased husband's movable property. The Talmud stipulated that they could place a lien only on his real property. A responsum attributed to an early ninth-century Gaon explains the reason for the *taqqana*: "Here [in Babylonia], most people [i.e., Jews] do not own land."[15] The new rule had the dual purpose of protecting women's postmarital livelihood and keeping credit flowing in an economy that very much depended on credit in the purchase and sale of commodities.

In conforming Jewish law to the needs of the Islamicate marketplace, the Geonim faced a greater challenge than their Muslim counterparts. The formative period of Islamic law coincided with the Islamicate commercial revolution. In a seminal article, "The Rise of the Near Eastern Bourgeoisie in Early Islamic Times," S. D. Goitein showed that most of the early Muslim jurists were themselves merchants, or at least au courant with merchant custom.[16] Joseph Schacht had already shown that customary commercial law of pre-Islamic Mecca, echoed in commercial terms in the Qur'ān, entered Islamic law in its formative period.[17] These customs, like the *suftaja*, were therefore absorbed into Islamic law as early as the eighth century. The most flexible and "liberal" of the law schools (*madhhabs*) in this respect, the Ḥanafīs, named after their founder, Abū Ḥanifa (d. 767), and, to a lesser extent, other legal schools incorporated these practices into Islamic law as it took shape.[18]

In contrast, the formative period of Jewish law had long passed when the Islamicate commercial revolution arrived. The Geonim had a huge corpus of halakha from the pre-Islamic, Talmudic period to contend with, and this corpus served an agrarian society, not a highly commercialized, monetized society in which long-distance trade and credit figured prominently. Like the examples cited above, they accommodated these transformations through their responsa, through *taqqanot* (though they seem rarely to have resorted to this halakhic tool), through what they called "the custom of the yeshiva,"[19] and through rulings incorporated into mini-codes, many of which deal with commercial law.

## 2.2 "Custom Overrides the Halakha" and *Qinyan Siṭumta*

The Geonim had a juristic tool at their disposal that they could deploy when faced with discrepancies between Talmudic law and contemporary merchant practice recognized by Islamic law. This was represented by a rabbinic maxim, *minhag mevaṭṭel halakha*, "custom overrides the halakha," analogous to an Islamic legal maxim, *al-ʿāda muḥakkima*, "custom is legally authoritative."[20] The Jewish maxim appears in the Palestinian Talmud.[21]

The Talmudic precedent for this concession to daily economic affairs occurs in connection with transfer of ownership (Heb., *qinyan*). Recognizing the necessity for flexibility when buying and selling, the Talmud validates a procedure called *siṭumta* (meaning "a seal"), which, if it conformed with local custom, could substitute for one of the methods of acquisition dictated by the Talmud, such as physically pulling the object (*meshikha*) or lifting it up (*hagbaha*). The example given by the Talmud is wine. The medieval commentator Rashi, thinking of the importance of wine as a commodity in his own time and place in eleventh-century France, explains the notion as follows. When a retailer purchases barrels of wine for his shop from a winemaker, he does not take all of them at once but leaves some in the seller's wine cellar to be claimed later, as needed. He marks the kegs with a *siṭumta* to identify them as his own. This procedure signifies proof of purchase and substitutes for "pulling" the object.[22] As summed up by R. Solomon b. Adret (Rashba; thirteenth-century Spain), "we learn from this that custom overrides the halakha [*minhag mevaṭṭel halakha*] as well as in any similar matter. *In all monetary matters, one may buy and sell in accordance with custom*. Therefore, one may complete a purchase in whatever way it is customary for merchants to do so."[23] Rashba's rule echoes, further, an axiom of economic history: mercantile custom typically evolves out of the needs of the marketplace, in contexts connected with trade, rather than in schools of law.[24]

## 2.3 Trade and the "Custom of the Mariners"

The importance of custom in Jewish economic life is attested in the Talmud in a concession to practice in the surrounding society that was to prove essential for long-distance trade during the Islamic period. I refer to what the rabbis call *minhag ha-sappanim*, the "custom of the mariners."

Classical rabbinic literature, it has been observed, contains a paucity of nautical terms.[25] While the Mishna, the Tosefta, and the Talmuds contain occasional discussions of legal issues relating to sea travel, which some have argued represent traces of an indigenous Jewish "admiralty law,"[26] these scattered fragments do not bespeak a widespread phenomenon of long-distance trade by ship that would have required detailed halakhic regulation.[27] Stories in rabbinic texts about arriving in or traveling to *medinat ha-yam*, literally, "the land of/by the sea," apparently originally meant not across the high seas but rather the Mediterranean coastal district of Palestine. Only later did this term assume the meaning of beyond the shores of the Land of Israel, namely, the lands of the Hellenistic diaspora at the eastern end of the Mediterranean.[28]

When Jews did travel by ship, for study, to visit family, to find a wife, or occasionally on business, they followed the custom of the mariners, a set of practices devised and put into practice by seafaring people in the society in which Jews lived. Classical rabbinic law mentions this concept once, in the Talmudic tractate Bava Qamma 116b, with a parallel in the Tosefta. Notably, the case regarding sea travel is preceded by an example concerning overland transport by donkey caravan, where the concept of the "custom of the mariners" is replaced by the "custom of the ass-drivers."

> [1] Our Rabbis taught: If a caravan traveling in the desert was attacked by armed men threatening to plunder it [*le-ṭorfah*], they reckon [the contribution to be paid by each merchant to buy them off] according to the monetary value [of the goods of each merchant] but not according to the number of souls. But if they hired a guide to go ahead of them, they also reckon [compensation for the loss] according to the number of souls [in the caravan]. They must not deviate from the custom of the ass-drivers. . . . [2] Our Rabbis taught: If a ship traveling on the sea was hit by a storm threatening to sink it, so that they jettisoned some of the cargo [lit., "lightened its weight"], they reckon [indemnification for the

> loss] according to the weight of the cargo and not according to its monetary value. They must not deviate from the custom of the mariners.[29]

The case in the Talmud recalls the rules of jettison and general average (equalized division among all merchants of responsibility for overall loss through jettison) in the ancient Roman law of the sea. This law was summarized later in Justinian's Digest (sixth century) and elaborated subsequently in the Nomos Rhodion Nautikos (Rhodian Sea Law), thought to have been compiled between 600 and 800 C.E.[30] Boaz Cohen, the eminent scholar of comparative Jewish and Roman law, pointed to the similarity between the maritime law of salvage in the classical rabbinic sources and in Justinian's Digest.[31]

In an important book comparing the Rhodian Sea Law with Islamic maritime law as reflected in Islamic *fatwās* and in the Arabic *Kitāb akriyat al-sufūn wa'l-nizā' bayna ahlihā* ("Treatise Concerning the Leasing of Ships and the Claims Between [Contracting] Parties"), Hassan Khalilieh argues that these rules from the late Roman Empire were mediated into Islam by local, Greek-speaking non-Muslims and "Islamicized" to conform with Qur'ānic and prophetic principles.[32] An example from Islamic maritime law would be the requirement that all shippers share in losses incurred when jettisoning cargo.[33]

The regulation in the Talmud that apportionment of loss among the travelers should be determined by weight and not by the monetary value of the jettisoned items addresses one of the basic issues in ancient and medieval legal discussions of jettison, though in Justinian's Digest and in virtually all medieval laws of jettison, the preference is for calculation by monetary value rather than by weight. Logically, weight was the primary consideration at the moment of jettisoning, though monetary value took center stage when merchants came to settle accounts later on.[34] In a parallel halakha, the Palestinian Talmud (Bava Meṣi'a 6:4, Venice edition 11a) stipulates that apportionment of loss is by both weight and value, evidently reflecting the dual consideration that operated in cases of jettison.[35]

The great diversity of rulings on jettison in ancient and medieval legal sources led Olivia Constable to surmise that "they must have reflected local practice and a common understanding of the basic principles of general average." She illustrates this with diverse opinions in Islamic maritime laws about how to assign value to goods cast overboard.[36] The Talmudic statement "they must not deviate from the custom of the mariners," supports her assumption that customs varied from place to place and shows that, in the absence of halakhot covering maritime law, the rabbis of the Talmud and, in this respect, Maimonides as well, recognized and enforced customary practice current in the surrounding society.[37] This precedent later informed the halakhic "policy" recognizing non-Jewish shipboard law when Jewish merchants traveled with their goods on ships owned by non-Jews, usually Muslims.[38]

With the coming of Islam, many new commercial customs came to the fore that required juristic attention and accommodation in the halakha. This process was begun relatively early by the Geonim, chiefly by granting commercial customs practiced in the Islamicate marketplace the force of law, exemplified by their legalization of the *suftaja*.[39] Maimonides, who inherited the legal tradition of the Geonim and of his teachers in al-Andalus, expanded on the foundation laid by his predecessors, carrying their work of responding to the realities of the marketplace to a new level of attainment through the process of codification in the Mishneh Torah.

## 2.4 The Custom of the Merchants in Maimonides' Code

Maimonides is likely to have been exposed to the custom of the merchants already during his youth, growing up in the commercial milieu of Muslim Spain and North Africa.[40] Upon his arrival in Egypt, as we know from Ibn al-Qifṭī, he was engaged in trade in precious gems.[41] He was intimately familiar with merchant custom from his India trader brother and from the legal queries about merchant activities that he regularly received. It should come as no surprise, therefore, to find Maimonides acknowledging and giving normative standing to the custom of the merchants in his Code.

A key text marking the place of merchant custom in the Code is found in the lead halakha of chapter 5 of *Hilkhot sheluḥin ve-shutafim* (Laws of Agents and Partners). Notably, however, the codifier does not use the phrase "custom of the merchants." Here, as elsewhere in the Code, for the custom of the merchants, he uses the Hebrew phrase *minhag ha-medina*, literally, "custom of the land" or "local custom," a locution that occurs in the Mishna, the Tosefta, and the Talmuds in relation to both ritual and civil law. He might have employed a neologism, *minhag ha-soḥarim*, translating the Gaonic term *ḥukm al-tujjār* and parallel to his own use of *minhag ha-sappanim*. His choice of the old, Tannaitic Hebrew expression *minhag ha-medina* suggests that he wished to anchor the custom of the merchants in his own time to the ancient halakha.

> If a person forms a partnership with another without indicating stipulations [*bi-stam*], he may not deviate from local custom [*minhag ha-medina*] as regards that kind of merchandise. Nor may he travel to another place, or form a partnership with others with the same kind of merchandise, or deposit it with others as a bailment, or trade in any other merchandise. He shall not sell on credit except that which it is always the custom to sell on credit—unless [both partners] stipulated this at the outset or [the itinerant partner] acted with the other's knowledge. If he deviates and acts without the other's knowledge and afterwards tells him "I did such-and-such" and [the stationary partner] consents to this, then the former is not held liable. None of these matters requires ratification by *qinyan*. Oral agreement alone is sufficient.

The standard commentators could find no precise source for this halakha in its entirety in a classical rabbinic text. For the statement "or trade in any other merchandise," R. Joseph Caro (d. 1575 in Safed, Palestine) in his Kesef Mishneh, one of the major commentaries on Maimonides' Code, cites a baraita in the Tosefta (Bava Meṣi'a 4:12 in the Lieberman edition), which is also cited by R. Isaac Alfasi in his epitome of the Talmudic tractate Bava Meṣi'a. The core text in the Mishna (Bava Meṣi'a 4:5) concerns a person hired to tend a shop. If he is a craftsman, the Tosefta adds, he should not practice his craft while on duty, lest he fail to pay attention to the customers. In Beit Yosef, Caro's commentary on another great work of codification, the Ṭur, by Jacob b. Asher (d. 1340 in Toledo, Spain) (Ḥoshen Mishpaṭ 176:10), the author speculates that Maimonides is analogizing from that case to a partner, who should devote all his attention to the partnership at hand, lest he be distracted by other business. In fact, as we know from the Geniza letters, merchants dealt in a myriad of different types of merchandise, often merchandise belonging to partnerships that they held at one and the same time with different merchants, and it was easy to lose track.

The topic sentence, "If a person forms a partnership with another without indicating stipulations, he may not deviate from local custom [*minhag ha-medina*, lit., "custom of the city or region"] as regards that kind of merchandise," warrants special attention. It calls to mind a principle expressed in

Islamic jurisprudence with respect to hire: "Whatever is not stipulated explicitly [*ghayra mashrūṭ*] in the contract is treated in accordance with the custom of each city."[42]

The phrase "local custom" (*minhag ha-medina*) is, indeed, key to contextualizing the halakha in question. It reflects aspects of everyday commercial practice in the Islamic world known to us from the Geniza and other Jewish sources from the Islamic period, particularly business arrangements concluded without drawing up formal, written contracts, which will be discussed in detail in chapters to come. The final sentence in the halakha makes this explicit: "Oral agreement alone is sufficient."

The phrase "[n]or may he travel to another place . . . unless [both partners] stipulated this at the outset or [the partner in question] acted with the other's knowledge" reflects the concern expressed in many Geniza letters or contracts and in a responsum of R. Isaac Alfasi that partners or agents keep to their prescribed itinerary, and it resonates with geographical restrictions that could be imposed upon an active party in an Islamic *commenda*, a type of business collaboration that we will discuss in Chapter 5.[43] Violation of an agreement about trading destinations, along with infringement of other conditions, often ended up in court or on the desk of a jurisconsult like Maimonides. One of his responsa, for instance, describes a dispute that arose in a *commenda*, called by its Arabic name, *muḍāraba*, in the query. The active merchant was supposed to proceed to a certain city, sell the merchandise belonging to the stationary investor, take his portion of the profit, and turn the capital sum plus the investor's earnings over to a specified person in that place. However, as is typical of so many informal arrangements between Geniza merchants, the traveling party and the investor had not recorded the stipulations in a contract; rather, they had agreed about this orally in front of the active partner's two brothers, who happened to be his designated heirs.

The traveling merchant sold the investor's merchandise but failed to deliver the latter's money as directed. Instead, be purchased other goods with the proceeds and departed for another destination by sea. When the ship on which he was traveling capsized, he lost his life, and only a portion of the goods that he was transporting could be salvaged. The investor demanded that the man's heirs pay him the entire original capital and all his profits because their brother had violated the conditions agreed to in their presence. Because there was no written contract, the case came before the Jewish court and ultimately was submitted to Maimonides for his opinion. He ruled that the truth about the agreed conditions could be ascertained only by the heirs taking an oath, the typical method of resolving disputes in both the Jewish and the Islamic courts in the absence of third-party testimony.[44]

The provision in halakha 5:1 about credit and the custom of the merchants reflects problems that could, and often did, arise when partners failed to stipulate whether merchandise could be sold on credit. Islamic schools of law discuss and disagree about whether a partnership contract needs to specifically stipulate permission to trade on credit.[45] Gaonic opinions were divided on the matter as well, but the power of merchant custom driving the commercial economy, in which credit was an essential tool, overcame compunctions in the Jewish, as it did in the Islamic, case.[46]

A responsum of the Babylonian Gaon Samuel b. Ḥofni (d. 1013) relates the story of a merchant-traveler who engaged in credit transactions. His action was challenged by the stationary partner, who claimed that he had not granted the man permission to extend credit to customers. The Gaon supported the active partner's actions because the man was putting his own money in jeopardy as much as that of his partner and because the stationary partner had not formally stipulated in advance that the other person should not sell on credit. The former, moreover, could not invoke the Talmudic rule expressed in the contract clause, "I sent you for my benefit, not to my detriment," because the active party was neither an agent nor a paid employee but rather a partner.[47]

Sale on credit was always potentially problematic because of the effort needed to collect what was due. Understandably, many stationary investors instructed their active partners to avoid such transactions. An example from the Geniza is a partnership contract among four investors in which the single, active partner agreed explicitly not to sell on the basis of "deferred payment" (*ṣabr*), meaning at a higher price, a way of circumventing the prohibition against taking interest among Jewish coreligionists.[48]

Maimonides' ruling on credit transactions in halakha 5:1 acquires particular significance in light of the extensive use of credit in the world of the mobile Geniza traders. In a situation where instructions about credit are not specified, Maimonides rules that everything depends on local merchant custom. The itinerant partner may not "sell on credit except that which it is always the custom to sell on credit—unless [both partners] stipulated this at the outset or [the active partner] acted with the other's knowledge. If he deviates and acts without the other's knowledge and afterward tells him, 'I did such-and-such' and [the stationary partner] consents to this, then the former is not held liable."

The remainder of halakha 5:1 prescribes basic rules that had to be followed by an active partner in the absence of written stipulations. Since these were dependent on merchant custom—custom, to underscore again, that was general and not specific to Jews—they did not need to be ratified by the formal Jewish method of *qinyan* (symbolic confirmation of mutual agreement, typically by grasping either end of a piece of cloth or scarf and similar to a handshake). Rather, as Maimonides closes, "oral agreement alone is sufficient." One may perhaps see here an allusion to a type of partnership attested in the Geniza, termed *mu'āmala*, that could be established without the formal requirements of Talmudic law.[49]

Seeking a parallel for Maimonides' ruling in the halakha in question, R. Joseph Caro (Kesef Mishneh ad loc.) quotes Maimonides' older contemporary R. Isaac b. Abba Mari of Marseilles in southern France, and later of Spain (ca. 1120–ca. 1190). In his digest of laws, *Sefer ha-'iṭṭur*, R. Isaac cites a responsum of the Babylonian Gaon Kohen Ṣedeq (Gaon 926–935), stating that an active partner may sell on credit even without the investor's permission if this is the "way [or custom] of the merchants," *orḥa' di-tagarei*, an Aramaic locution not found in the Talmud.[50] Like Arabic *ḥukm al-tujjār*, the Aramaic phrase describes the very same "custom of the merchants" that both the Geonim and Maimonides acknowledged as the extra-halakhic practice of the merchants.

### *2.4.1* Minhag Yadua' *and the Custom of the Merchants*

A more general and sweeping statement about the importance of the custom of the merchants—though again, not using the literal term—underlies a halakha in the Laws of Sales (*Hilkhot mekhira*). The halakhot at the end of chapter 26 there deal with local custom with regard to the designation of articles by an established name. Halakha 26:8 states: "It is an important principle in all business dealings that we follow the language of people in that place and [local] custom. In those places, however, where no recognized custom [*minhag yadua'*] exists or specific names for objects, but rather some people call this object one thing while others call the same object by another designation, then we do as the Sages have expounded in these chapters."

The phrase "recognized custom" (*minhag yadua'*) includes one of the adjectives, *yadua'*, used by the Geonim when referring to "custom."[51] Unknown in the Tannaitic and Talmudic corpus, it has the appearance of an Arabism, translating a word like *ma'lūm* or *ma'rūf* ("known" or "recognized"—the

Arabic term for custom is *'urf*).[52] These words are found together in a formula regarding custom in Islamic law.[53] In Maimonides' language, *minhag yadua'* and *minhag ha-medina* are functional equivalents, an equivalence that may be Andalusian usage.[54] Maimonides explains that local custom applies in the present case precisely because every Jew "recognizes" its existence as an alternative to the received halakha.[55]

* * *

In commerce, then, two realms existed side by side, according to Maimonides, as to the Geonim. First there was the realm of normative Jewish law (the halakha), as established in the Talmud; second was the realm of commercial custom. Jewish merchants in the Islamic world were thoroughly integrated into the wider commercial economy. In order to make a profit, in order to minimize risk, they were obliged to follow practices shared by all merchants, regardless of religion.

Under the rabbinic rubric of *minhag ha-medina*, Maimonides made room in his Code for this custom of the merchants—even if he did not always employ the term—in much the same way that early Islamic lawyers accommodated customs of the merchants in the developing Islamic legal canon during its formative period. Some of Maimonides' adaptations to accommodate mercantile practice were minimal, entailing no fundamental challenge to basic Talmudic norms. They simply updated Talmudic language to fit the needs of the Islamicate marketplace. Other adaptations, often imperceptible, went further, actually expanding the halakha to fit the custom of the merchants. The most startling of these instances is the creation of an enforcement mechanism for the new economic institution of informal commercial agency (see Chapter 6). On occasion, as we shall see, Maimonides attempted to regulate a legal reform to make it conform with Talmudic norms. The outstanding case of this is his rejection of the Gaonic legal fiction designed to facilitate proxy legal agency in the post-agrarian Islamic world (see Chapter 7).

## Chapter 3

# Updating the Halakha

### 3.1 Incorporating Long-Distance Commerce into the Code

The merchants we hear about in the Talmud operated primarily in local or regional markets connected with local or regional trade.[1] Commerce requiring travel over great distances was rare. The Islamic world, by contrast, knew a clear distinction between local (or regional) trade and long-distance trade, for each of which it had a specific Arabic term, *tijāra ḥāḍira* and *tijāra ghā'iba*, respectively.[2] With the coming of the Islamic conquests, Jews themselves entered long-distance trade for the first time, and in a big way.

In the Code, Maimonides often expands on Tannaitic (Mishnaic) or Amoraic (Talmudic) rulings, adapting them to the customary practice of the Geniza merchants, especially the world of partnerships and long-distance trade. Examples of this "updating" to be discussed in this chapter come from disparate corners of the halakha: the laws of charity; the laws of *'eruv*; laws concerning rest on the intermediate days of the festival; a halakha about commerce and the Sabbath; regulations concerning a husband's conjugal duties; and finally, a halakha regarding the impotent husband. These alterations, sprinkled throughout the Code, constitute strong evidence that Maimonides had his eye on the realities of post-Talmudic, Islamicate trade and the custom of the merchants when he compiled the Code. He wrote commerce, especially long-distance trade, into the halakha in places that did not originally deal with that aspect of Jewish economic life. While precedents for some of these modifications can be found in Gaonic or Andalusian writings, taken as a whole they illustrate Maimonides' original and concerted effort to narrow the distance between law and society in this important domain of human activity, recalling for us Alan Watson's hypothesis about the possible role of codification in reconciling law with society, as well as Blidstein's query suggesting the possibility of finding modifications in Jewish commercial law in Maimonides' Code.

## 3.2 Commerce and Charity

A subtle but typical example, already mentioned in a previous publication, occurs in Maimonides' laws of charity, Gifts for the Poor (*Hilkhot mattenot 'aniyyim*).[3] The halakha in question (7:14) states: "If a person travels *for commerce* [*bi-sḥora*] to another town and is assessed for [*pasqu 'alav*] charity by the inhabitants of the town he went to, he must contribute to the poor of that town. If [the merchant travelers] are many and they are assessed for [*pasqu 'alayhen*] charity, they should pay it, and when they leave they should bring the money back with them to provide sustenance for the poor of their own town. If there is a scholar [in the other town], they should give [the money] to him to distribute it as he sees fit."

Two Sephardic commentators, whose commentaries surround the Maimonidean text in the standard printed editions—R. David ibn Abi Zimra (Radbaz, d. 1573), chief rabbi of Egypt in the first half of the sixteenth century; and R. Joseph Caro (d. 1575), who lived in Safed, Palestine—found precedent for this halakha in tractate Megilla 27a–b in the Babylonian Talmud. The Talmudic statement there is virtually the same as that of Maimonides, save for the word *bi-sḥora*, "for commerce." It does not take much imagination to hear in this gloss an echo of the highly mobile commercial society of the Islamic Mediterranean in which Maimonides lived, a society whose contours are so familiar to us from the legal literature of the Geonim and the Andalusian sages, from the responsa of Maimonides, and, above all, from the Geniza records. The addition of the word *bi-sḥora*, one example of many such "updates" in the Code, epitomizes Maimonides' effort to adapt Jewish law to the medieval Islamicate economy. It is worth noting, too, that Maimonides reverses the order of the discussion in the Talmud, placing an individual traveler before a group, perhaps to focus attention on travel by individual merchants, which was so prevalent in his day and age.

It is likely that Maimonides was familiar with a responsum of R. Naḥshon Gaon (871–879), who lived in Abbasid Iraq, explaining a different Talmudic passage. The Talmud (Bava Batra 8a) quotes a baraita explaining that a visitor who stays in a town for at least thirty days is obligated to contribute to local charity. Naḥshon specifies that this refers to a person who is traveling "for commerce" (*bi-sḥora*) and who stays at an inn. This describes perfectly the situation of merchants in the Islamic world, who arrived in a town, did their business in the local marketplace, and lodged at an inn (*funduq*) or caravanserai.[4]

It is even possible that Maimonides meant to specify that the obligation to give to charity when visiting a foreign city applies *only* to individuals traveling for commerce[5] but not, for instance, to the itinerant poor. According to the Talmud (Giṭṭin 7b), indigents living off charity are themselves obligated to donate at least a small sum to charity. This was an ideal, and Maimonides codifies the Talmudic rule earlier in the same chapter of the Laws of Gifts for the Poor (7:5). But in the Geniza world, huge numbers of indigent travelers from near and distant parts of the Islamic domain and even from Byzantium and Latin Europe traveled from city to city, where, as the Geniza poor lists from Fustat copiously illustrate, they were entered into the local dole and were even expected to defray some fraction of their poll tax.[6] It was unrealistic to expect them to contribute to charity as well. Merchant travelers, on the other hand, were financially more able to give, and we may imagine that, when they attended a local synagogue while on a business trip, they were solicited for charity. The Geniza documents for Egypt describe how this so-called *pesiqa* system worked (the verbal form *pasqu* is used by Maimonides in the halakha in question): people in the synagogue made pledges either for a general fund or a specific, needy person, often a newcomer to town.[7]

The term "for commerce" is absent in the epitome of the Talmud compiled by Maimonides' Andalusian predecessor, R. Isaac Alfasi (d. 1103) (Megilla 8b in the pages in the printed Talmud). R. Asher b. Yeḥiel (Rosh, ca. 1250–1327) similarly omits the addition in his own code (Megilla 4:5). On the other hand, Maimonides' gloss on the Talmud was accepted by Rosh's son, Jacob b. Asher (d. 1340 in Toledo, Spain) in his Ṭur (Yoreh De'a 256), as well as by Joseph Caro in both his commentary on the Ṭur (Beit Yosef, Yoreh De'a 256:6), and his own code, the Shulḥan 'Arukh (Yoreh De'a 256). When Caro chose Maimonides' updated ruling on the obligation of a traveling merchant to contribute to charity in another town, he put the final stamp of approval on a change that Maimonides, building on a Gaonic precedent, had codified in the twelfth century in an effort to harmonize an ancient halakha with the economic realities of the medieval Islamic world. Per Watson, we may say that he was attempting to bring law and society into greater harmony. The adaptation fit Caro's own sixteenth-century economic milieu

(Safed in his time was a major trading crossroads in Ottoman Palestine), a fact that may have encouraged him to accept Maimonides' gloss "for commerce." Normally, Caro followed the ruling of the majority among his three authorities, Alfasi, Maimonides, and Rosh; but in this case, he ignored Alfasi and Rosh, both of whom simply quote the Talmud, and adopted Maimonides' update instead.

## 3.3 Commerce and the *'Eruv*

The gloss "commerce" (*seḥora*) appears in the Code in connection with the Sabbath *'eruv*, a symbolic device meant to enable people to carry items on the day of rest from a private dwelling to the common courtyard (Hebrew, *ḥaṣer*; Arabic, *dār*) and between disjoint living units in a common courtyard; or between disjoint courtyards opening onto a common alleyway (Hebrew, *mavoi*). The rabbinic solution was to symbolically aggregate separate domains into one so that people could move about freely, carrying items outside their private dwellings. This was accomplished by having all neighbors deposit an item of food in one of the living units.

One means of doing this is stipulated in Mishna 'Eruvin 6:5 (and discussed in the Talmud, 'Eruvin 71a): "If a householder is a joint owner [*shutaf*] with his neighbors, with one of them in wine and with the other in wine, they need not prepare an *'eruv*. But if with one it is wine and the other, oil, they must prepare an *'eruv*. R. Simeon says: In neither case do they need to prepare an *'eruv*."

Maimonides (*Hilkhot 'eruvin* 5:1) retains the structure of the halakha but embellishes it with some revealing changes in the language. "If residents of an alleyway [*mavoi*] hold some article of food jointly for commercial purposes [*shittuf le-'inyan seḥora*], for example, having bought wine, oil, honey, or the like in partnership [*shutafut*], they need form no additional token joint ownership [*shittuf*] for the Sabbath but may rely on their commercial joint ownership [*shittuf shel seḥora*]. The item in which they are partners [*shutafin*] must be the same type and contained in one vessel, but if one of them is partner [*shutaf*] with one person in wine and another in oil, or in oil alone but in two separate vessels, they must prepare an additional jointly owned [*shittuf*] item for the Sabbath [*'eruv*]."

These alterations do not occur in any earlier reiteration of the Mishnaic ruling, including Alfasi's abridgment of the Talmud. Maimonides' modifications, considerably elaborating on the Mishna, are steeped in significance. They demonstrate his effort to update classical rabbinic law in the light of the commercial realities of his time.

The rabbinic term for aggregating living units (apartments or whole courtyards) is *shittuf*, a word that is related to *shutafut*, "partnership." Maimonides, who follows the Talmudic commentary and understands the Mishna to refer to the aggregation of multiple courtyards opening onto a common alleyway, infuses the text with the meaning of commercial partnership by adding the word *seḥora*. He also uses the Hebrew term for commercial partnership, *shutafut*, to explain how the jointly owned articles of food were acquired. Along the same lines, in his Commentary on the Mishna, Maimonides defines *shutaf* in ʿEruvin 6:5 as *sharīk*, the Arabic term for "partner," typically applied to commercial or craft partnerships (*sharika*). To further strengthen the contemporary connotation, he specifies "commercial joint ownership" (*shittuf shel seḥora*). Finally, he amplifies the Mishna by adding "honey" to the original list, a commodity, in addition to wine and oil, in which, according to the Geniza documents, people in the Mediterranean traded.[8]

I submit that these are not accidental or incidental modifications of the classical rabbinic text. They illustrate Maimonides' careful choice of language, adapting an ancient halakha to fit the commercial context of the Islamic world in which he lived, a world in which partnership in business was much more common than in Talmudic times. This update, like the one in the Laws of Gifts for the Poor discussed above, is repeated by the later codifier, Jacob b. Asher (Ṭur Oraḥ Ḥayyim 366). He understood Maimonides' intention to update the halakha and made it even more explicit: "If a householder is a *commercial partner with his neighbors* [*shutaf ʿim shekhenav bi-sḥora*], *even if with one person in wine and another in oil*, he does not need to create a separate *ʿeruv*, *even if they had not formed the partnership for the sake of an ʿeruv*, provided it is all in one vessel."[9]

## 3.4 Commerce and Work on the Intermediate Days of the Festival (*Ḥol Ha-moʿed*)

An excellent example of how Maimonides builds on Gaonic and Andalusian precedents in an economic matter is to be had by considering the question of work on the intermediate days of a festival (Passover and Sukkot). This issue occupied the attention of the rabbis of the Talmudic period. The Mishna

(Mo'ed Qaṭan 2:4; Mo'ed Qaṭan 13a in the Talmud) restricts labor on those days to certain types of religious or subsistence economic activity: "It is not permissible to buy houses, slaves, or cattle except for what is needed for the festival, or where the seller has nothing to eat."

Characteristically, as this and other statements show, the discussion in the Talmud assumes agricultural work (Mo'ed Qaṭan 12a–b). Further exemplifying subsistence economic activity, it permits a lender to write a contract of debt if a needy person who lacks food asks for a loan, and it allows copying the scriptural text for phylacteries and other ritual objects and selling them if need be for one's own livelihood (Mo'ed Qaṭan 18b–19a). An early post-Talmudic compilation comparing Palestinian and Babylonian customs reports that Palestinian Jews did not work on the intermediate days of the festival (*ḥol ha-mo'ed*), whereas those in Babylonia did.[10]

### *3.4.1 Gaonic Background*

In the increasingly urban setting of early Islamic Iraq, as the Geonim report, most Jews no longer owned land. Archaeology confirms that this was a period of overpopulation in the agricultural lands around the capital of Baghdad and of land flight to the cities.[11] R. Naṭronai b. Hilai, Gaon of Sura (ca. 857/58–865/66), presumably reflecting the Babylonian custom just mentioned, extended the permission to work on the intermediate days of the festival to include poor craftsmen who had no choice but to work on those days, even if they had to work in a public place in order to be spotted by potential customers (the question posed to him concerned tailors and sandal makers).[12] Naṭronai also permitted people to engage in trade (*seḥora*) on the intermediate days of the festival if transacted in the privacy of their houses, since business entails only talking, and he permitted doing business openly, if necessary, to avoid a lost business opportunity. Naṭronai cites a precedent in the same tractate of the Talmud (Mo'ed Qaṭan 10b) that allows work on the intermediate days to prevent produce (dates) from going bad, deemed analogous to making a business deal that, if postponed, would entail economic loss—the Talmudic concept of "lost business opportunity," *praqmaṭia ovedet* (from Greek *pragmateia*, "business dealings") or *davar ha-aved*.[13]

Elsewhere, Naṭronai takes cognizance of the expansion of long-distance trade in the Islamic world. He considers a situation where a caravan departs only twice a year and one of them is scheduled to leave on the intermediate days of the festival. The Gaon expands the Talmudic dispensation about copying religious texts and adds that one may write and send a letter with the caravan to accompany merchandise or to convey instructions to a business associate located in a distant city, in order to avoid financial loss or to protect the well-being of his own family.[14] This allowance has all the earmarks of a concession to Jewish merchants. As the Geniza letters abundantly show, long-distance traders relied heavily upon letters reporting the activities of business associates, the progress of consignments of merchandise, and market fluctuations, and they regularly sent written instructions to partners or agents, instructing them about buying and selling and other matters vital to maximizing profits.[15] One of the constant refrains in the letters of Geniza merchants is the complaint that letters have not arrived, causing anxiety. This is true of Muslim business letters as well.[16]

### *3.4.2 Andalusian Background*

Merchant labor on the intermediate days of the festival occupies center stage in a fascinating question submitted to the Spanish legist R. Joseph ibn Migash (d. 1141), head of the yeshiva of Lucena, Spain, and teacher of Maimonides' father. The questioner writes that he had "warned some people not to buy and sell on the [intermediate days of the] festival." The violators complied by adhering to an even stricter standard, as prescribed by Ibn Migash in his teaching, by refraining from opening their shops or working even to avoid "lost business opportunity" or to meet the basic need for food. "Later," the questioner writes, "some people arrived from Córdoba and 'tore down this fence'[17] by permitting buying and selling openly in the marketplaces. When I expressed my astonishment, they deferred in this matter to your excellency, may God exalt you. As a result, God's name is being profaned in the presence of the Gentiles."[18]

Ibn Migash praises the questioner for encouraging his own townsmen to go beyond the call of religious duty by suspending their economic activities on the intermediate days of the festival. At the same time, he rules that the outsiders from Córdoba should be permitted to trade if it means avoiding lost business opportunity or hunger. He also categorically denies that he had taught that trade on those days was permissible, even in the absence of the extenuating circumstances spelled out in the Talmud.

### *3.4.3 Maimonides' Position on Work on the Intermediate Days*

Like Naṭronai Gaon and like Ibn Migash, Maimonides addresses the issue of doing business on the intermediate days of the festival in his own responsa. He praises a rabbinic authority in Palestine for proclaiming a *ḥerem* (excommunication) against anyone working on the intermediate days of the festival (in Palestine, we recall, it was customary to avoid work on all days of the festival, including the intermediate ones). But in the next breath, he qualifies, following the Babylonian Gaon Naṭronai: "If it is a case of a business deal to avoid lost business opportunity, people should engage in business transactions" (*yis'u ve-yittenu*).[19]

Maimonides codified this opinion in the Code. In *Hilkhot shevitat yom ṭov* (Laws of Repose on a Festival) 7:22, a halakha informed by his own merchant perspective on daily life, he ruled: "One should not engage in trade [*seḥora*] on the intermediate days of the festival, whether selling or buying. But if it is something that, if postponed, would entail lost business opportunity [*davar ha-aved*] regarding something that is not always available after the festival, for instance, when ships or caravans have just arrived or are about to depart and people are selling cheap or buying dear—in such cases, a person is permitted to buy or sell (on the intermediate days). One may not, however, buy houses or slaves or cattle except if needed for the festival."

Maimonides' intimate knowledge of the realities of long-distance trade stands out boldly in his comments about ships and caravans and how their arrival or departure could affect market prices, an elaboration that goes beyond Naṭronai Gaon's dispensation for writing letters to business associates. But Maimonides does not, like Naṭronai, restrict business to discussions in the privacy of one's home. Rather, he resorts to a ruling in the rival Palestinian Talmud that allows doing actual business with a caravan that is arriving and then departing on the intermediate days of a festival to avoid lost business opportunity.[20]

Notably, too, Maimonides extends Naṭronai's ruling on caravans to include ships. This is not surprising. Maimonides lived in Fustat, a city intimately linked to commerce in the Mediterranean through the port of Alexandria and with India through the port of Aden and the Indian Ocean. He knew as well as anyone that the arrival and departure of ships was one of the determining factors in marketplace activity, and conceded that merchants needed to be on the spot to take advantage of their movements into and out of the harbor if they were not to forfeit business opportunities.[21]

Two halakhot later, Maimonides sanctions work on the intermediate days of a festival in a different context (*Hilkhot shevitat yom ṭov* 7:24): "Whatever is forbidden to do on the intermediate days of the festival one may not instruct a Gentile [*goy*] to do. If he has nothing to eat, he may do whatever is forbidden to do on the intermediate days of the festival to provide enough for his livelihood. *Likewise, he may engage in commerce* [*'oseh seḥora*] *to provide enough for his livelihood.* It is permissible for a wealthy man to hire a poor man who has nothing to eat to do work that is otherwise forbidden on those days, so he may earn wages with which to provide for his livelihood. Likewise, one may buy things that are not needed for the intermediate days of the festival if the seller is in need and has no food to eat."

The supposed Talmudic source for the first statement is: "Whatever he may do, he may instruct a Gentile to do, and whatever he may not do, he may not instruct a Gentile to do" (Mo'ed Qaṭan 12a). The concern with the alleviation of poverty, also present in the Talmudic discourse, had particular immediacy in Maimonides' Egypt. As I have discussed elsewhere, the Geniza attests to the presence of a large population of poor in the Jewish community of Fustat, local poor as well as transient indigents or needy people seeking to settle down in that charitable community.[22] Each week, hundreds of hungry people, locals and foreigners, received a dole of loaves of bread and sometimes wheat as well.[23] The poor received subsidies to help defray the poll tax levied on every healthy, non-Muslim adult male. Geniza letters reveal that Maimonides was personally involved in charity in the community, particularly on behalf of redemption of captives (usually foreigners), the most costly item in the community's charity budget.[24]

The statement in 7:24 about protecting the hireling or the store owner from dearth addresses the plight of the "working poor" in Maimonides' Egypt, who earned meager, subsistence wages and could not afford to sacrifice income for an entire week twice a year (*ḥol ha-mo'ed* plus the festival days that precede and follow). Both weeklong Jewish festivals fell within the Mediterranean sailing season, which ran from April through October: the week of Passover in early spring and the week of Sukkot at the dawn of the fall/winter season.[25] Noteworthy is the clear allusion to Maimonides' own "ladder of charity" near the end of the Laws of Gifts for the Poor (10:7), which puts employment of a poor person, entering into partnership with him, giving him a loan, or making an outright gift at the top of the list of commendable methods of charitable giving ("workfare" rather than "welfare," to invoke anachronistically a political policy of some conservative opponents of government subsidies to the unemployed poor in American politics).

Most significant in terms of Jewish commercial life is the phrase sanctioning commerce: "*Likewise,* he may engage in commerce [*seḥora*] to provide enough for his livelihood." By using the word "likewise" (*ve-khen*), Maimonides separates this clause from the sentences before and after it that address the needs of the poor and signifies that he is adding something new. Seemingly, according to the codifier, the permission to engage in trade exceeds the Talmudic rationale—the concern that people might starve.

The Geniza merchants, we must remember, were not indigent. For them, the threshold of basic livelihood was higher than the subsistence level assumed by the Talmud in its discussion of work during the festival interlude. The Geniza merchants' livelihood depended upon doing business continually, with minimal interruption, constantly offsetting losses or potential losses with gains, always keeping their capital moving. Ships delivered and exported goods, and, for merchants, the inability to engage in trade during the full week of each of the two Jewish festivals could cost them dearly, especially because, as Maimonides himself states two halakhot earlier (*Hilkhot shevitat yom ṭov* 7:22), prices for buying or selling could be at their optimum when ships or caravans arrived. The halakha in question (7:24) follows naturally, therefore, from the earlier one, which explicitly allows transacting business with merchants traveling by ship or by caravan on the intermediate days of the festival and, by implication, in the marketplace itself, not just in the privacy of their homes, as stipulated more conservatively by R. Naṭronai Gaon. Refraining from work on the intermediate days of the festival could truly entail lost business opportunity—*praqmaṭia ovedet.*

Seemingly, Maimonides does not limit merchants' activities to corresponding with business associates, as stipulated by Naṭronai Gaon. In his merchant guise, Maimonides knew that traders needed to have direct and immediate access to markets to take advantage of business opportunities and favorable prices that might not be available if they had to wait until after the conclusion of the festival week, especially if caravans or ships were arriving or departing. This reality, more typical of the commercial Islamicate economy than of the agrarian world of the Talmud, called for greater halakhic flexibility. In his rulings on work on the intermediate days of the festival, both in the opinion he addressed to the rabbinic authority in Palestine and in his Code, Maimonides appears to have had in mind the reluctance of Jewish merchants like those of his native Córdoba to take time off from their business affairs for so many consecutive days twice a year. The responsum of Ibn Migash, which Maimonides is likely to have known, describes explicitly the habit of those merchants to engage in buying and selling on the intermediate days. Ibn Migash responds that they should not be barred from doing so if it meant avoiding financial loss. What Maimonides appears to have done in the Code, and to have gone further in this respect than Naṭronai Gaon, is to stretch the definition of *praqmaṭia ovedet* to accommodate contemporary merchant habits.

Writing three and a half centuries later, R. Joseph Caro seems to have understood Maimonides this way. In his Beit Yosef, he writes (Oraḥ Ḥayyim 539:4): "It seems from what [Maimonides] says that it is only permissible when he has nothing to eat. But it is possible that he also permits [a merchant to work] when he has limited assets and wishes to profit by selling, so he will have a surplus of money, for this, too, is tantamount to 'enough for his livelihood.'" Not just "enough for his livelihood" but "a surplus of money." Caro understood, as did Maimonides, that earning a livelihood through trade required always keeping ahead of the game, never letting one's cash reserves run low, never allowing one's liquid assets to lie fallow. We seem, therefore, to be witness to another instance in which Maimonides, well versed in the ways of commerce and business in general, adjusted the halakha to conform to the entrepreneurial spirit of the post-Talmudic Islamicate economy.

## 3.5 Commerce and the Sabbath

Exemplifying Maimonides' extension of a rabbinic law written in an agrarian context to fit the world of the Geniza merchants is his treatment of the question of certain types of work that must be avoided on the Sabbath. The Mishna, tractate Shabbat 23:3, states: "One may not hire laborers on the Sabbath, nor may one tell another person to hire laborers for him. One may not walk to the Sabbath limits [*teḥum*, the maximum distance allowed for a walk from home on the Sabbath] to await nightfall to hire laborers [i.e., to be nearer the place, beyond the limits, where one hires laborers] or to bring in produce, but one may do so to watch [one's own field, located beyond the limit, immediately upon nightfall], and then he may bring [home] produce with him. Abba Saul stated the general rule: 'Anything that I am permitted to instruct be done, I am permitted to await nightfall for it'" (i.e., at the Sabbath limits).

Like the Mishna, the Gemara (Shabbat 150a) situates this ruling in an agricultural context, exemplifying the principle with examples—hiring laborers and transporting produce—that indicate a society invested in farming.

Maimonides' approach differs markedly. In Laws of the Sabbath 24:1, he updates the Mishnaic and Talmudic texts to conform more closely to a world in which long-distance trade was widespread.

> Some acts are forbidden on the Sabbath even though they neither resemble nor lead to prohibited work. Why, then, were they forbidden? Because Scripture says, "If thou turn away thy foot because of the Sabbath, from pursuing thy business on My holy day. . . . And thou shall honor it, not doing thy wonted ways, nor pursuing thy business, nor speaking thereof (Isa. 58:13)." Therefore, one may not walk with one's goods on the Sabbath or even speak about them, for instance, to speak with one's partner [*shutaf*] about what to sell on the morrow, or what to buy, or how to construct a certain house; or what merchandise [*seḥora*] to take to such-and-such a place. These things and all others like it are forbidden, as it is written, "nor pursuing thy business nor speaking thereof," which means that speaking [about business] is forbidden, though thinking [about it] is permitted.

The type of economy assumed by this Maimonidean halakha is not the local and regional agrarian economy of the Talmud but the more wide-ranging commercial economy of the Islamic world. The Mishna speaks about walking the distance to the Sabbath limits in order to wait there to hire agricultural laborers after nightfall, when the Sabbath ended, or to carry produce from there back home. By contrast, Maimonides specifies travel for business ("walk with one's goods"), a significant nod to the long-distance trade pursued by Jewish (and Muslim) merchants. Then there is his all-important reference to partnership, which, in his time, represented a prominent (though not the primary) method of doing business, especially long-distance trade across the Mediterranean and India routes. This will be discussed in greater detail in Chapters 4 and 5.

Patently reflecting the agricultural society of the Talmudic era, the Mishna forbids instructing a person to "hire laborers for him." Characteristic of the Geniza world, Maimonides exemplifies the kinds of verbal exchanges forbidden on the Sabbath with discussions that business partners would be likely to have. Such conversations might include plans for marketing after the Sabbath ended or the geographical scope of the partnership or agency relationship—"what merchandise to take to such-and-such a place"—which was especially important in long-distance commercial ventures, where one person was often stationary and the other did the work. Business collaboration through agency relations (see Chapter 5), unlike partnership, was typically initiated orally, without written contract and without other formalities required by Talmudic law in partnerships. Maimonides, who, we shall see, instituted a significant reform in agency law, takes cognizance of this widespread phenomenon in the halakha under discussion here.

Unlike the halakha in the Code permitting trade on the intermediate days of a festival (section 3.3 above), this one, regarding the Sabbath, is stricter, in line with the Talmud and the sanctity of the day of rest. We are witness to the codifier's eye on contemporary economic life and hear a clear warning against the permissive attitude of Jewish merchants, who might be tempted to engage in trade on the Sabbath, or at least plan commercial ventures on the day that was biblically devoted to rest.

## 3.6 Commerce and a Husband's Conjugal Duty

A dramatic example of Maimonides' method of updating the halakha for a trading society is a halakha found in chapter 14 of Laws of Marriage (*Hilkhot ishut*), discussing a husband's conjugal duty to his wife, a duty stipulated in the Torah (Exod. 21:10) and discussed in the Talmud.

The underlying rabbinic source, as recognized by the commentators, is the Mishna in Ketubbot 5:6, which establishes a relationship between a husband's profession and his obligatory conjugal obligation. "If a man vowed to have no intercourse with his wife, the School of Shammai says: [She may consent] for two weeks. And the School of Hillel says: For one week [only]. Disciples [of the Sages] may continue being absent for thirty days against the will [of their wives] while they occupy themselves in the study of the law; and laborers for one week. The conjugal duty of a husband enjoined in the Torah [Exod. 21:10] is: every day for *ṭayyalin*; twice a week for laborers; once a week for ass-drivers; once every thirty days for camel-drivers; and once every six months for mariners. So R. Eliezer."[26]

Unsurprisingly, the Mishna assumes a noncommercial context. Furthermore, the focus is on persons who work locally (laborers, usually agricultural), or who travel away from their locality temporarily for study (not for trade), or who work in the "transportation industry" (ass-driver, camel-driver, mariners), occupations that necessarily took them away from home for shorter or longer periods of time. Left undefined are the *ṭayyalin*.

Maimonides bases his halakha on this Mishna but with significant elaboration. He begins (14:1) by stating as a general rule that a husband's obligation varies with his physical powers and his occupation. This general statement, a classic example of the "topic sentences" with which Maimonides introduces many chapters in the Code, flows from particular stipulations in the Talmud about the health of a husband or about his occupation, whether he be a tailor, weaver, ass-driver, mariner, or Torah scholar, and the schedule he must keep to in order to fulfill his conjugal duty.

> The conjugal duty enjoined in the Torah depends on each man according to his physical ability and his occupation. In what way? Men who are healthy, leading a comfortable and pleasurable life, who have no occupation to sap their strength, but who rather eat and drink and dwell in their own houses: their conjugal duty is every night. Laborers, like tailors, weavers, and construction workers, etc.: if their work is in the town, their conjugal duty is twice a week, and if their work is in another town, once a week. Ass-drivers: once a week. Camel-drivers: once in six months. Mariners: once in six months. Disciples of scholars: their conjugal duty is once a week, because Torah study saps their strength, and it is the practice of disciples of scholars to have intercourse on Sabbath eve once a week.

The halakha that follows (14:2) elaborates on the first. Noteworthy is the fact that it begins by introducing someone who seems not to have been taken into consideration by the Talmud: the long-distance merchant of the Geniza world.

> A wife may restrain her husband from traveling for commerce [*seḥora*] unless it is to a nearby place, so that he does not neglect his conjugal duty toward her. Hence he may not travel except with her permission. Similarly, she may restrain him from exchanging one occupation involving a frequent conjugal schedule for one involving an infrequent schedule, as, for example, an ass-driver who seeks to

> become a camel-driver (the former's conjugal schedule being once a week and the latter's once a month) or a camel-driver who seeks to become a mariner (whose requirement is once in six months). Disciples of scholars [*talmidei ḥakhamim*] may travel away to study Torah without their wives' permission for as long as two or three years. Similarly, if a man leading a comfortable and pleasurable life becomes a disciple of scholars, his wife may not restrain him at all.

The key to understanding Maimonides' inclusion of the traveling merchant at the beginning of this halakha is the undefined *ṭayyalin* of the Mishna. The rabbis of the Babylonian Talmud had no clear idea what this term meant, except that it connoted people who, unlike the others, live at home and are free from laborious obligations. One rabbi proposed that *ṭayyalin* are "day students," who, by nature, study nearby or in the town and can spend every night at home and thus be available sexually to their wives nightly.

In his Commentary on the Mishna, completed a decade before the Code, Maimonides defines *ṭayyalin*, with contemporary realia in mind, as "those who live an easy and restful life and do not engage in trade or in doing a service" (*alladhīna lā yatjurūna wa-lā yakhdumūna*).[27] We shall later see (Chapter 5, section 5.12) that the verb *yakhdumūna* is not part of a hendiadys with *yatjurūna*; rather, the verb *yakhdumūna* captures with precision the most common method of commercial cooperation in the Geniza world, called, among other terms, *khidma*, "service," a form of agency characterized by reciprocal commercial services. For the present, we may infer from Maimonides' ruling in the Code—and assume that he himself inferred—that those who do travel for commercial purposes are governed by a different standard, due to the mobile nature of their profession. Maimonides' understanding of *ṭayyalin* allows him to implicitly employ the rabbinic hermeneutic device *ha-yoṣe' min ha-kelal ha-melammed 'al ha-kelal* ("the exception to the rule that proves the rule") to teach that, while "a wife may restrain her husband from traveling for commerce [*seḥora*] unless it is to a nearby place," he *may* travel afar if she gives her permission. This wifely permission represented a necessary relaxation of the law in an economy that required merchants to travel great distances to faraway places and for long stretches of time.

Clearly, however, Jewish wives regularly gave their permission.[28] In a clause in a betrothal contract, a bride-to-be promises her groom that, once married, she will allow him to travel whenever he wishes.[29] The Geniza and the responsa of Maimonides copiously show that Jewish traders traveled as far as Spain and India and might be away from home and their wives for years at a time. Special arrangements often had to be made, such as allocating money for the wife's maintenance before departure. Alternatively, a husband might give his wife a conditional divorce document (*geṭ 'al tenai* or *geṭ zeman*), to go into effect after a stipulated period of time should he fail to return.[30] With this in hand, she could claim her divorce and be free to remarry.[31]

Real-life examples from the Geniza reveal how husbands and wives dealt with the hardships of long-distance separation. A legal document from the Geniza stipulates that a husband who intended to travel abroad agree to allocate twenty dirhems per month, namely, five per week, for his wife, plus some wheat. The stipend was to be used to pay his annual poll tax as well as for rent and other household expenses.[32] In another case, a woman complains that her husband traveled frequently without leaving her sufficient food. She took an oath refusing to cohabit with him any longer.[33] Another legal document (dated Tammuz 1356 Sel./1045 C.E.)[34] reports that a wife and her husband agreed that he could travel until a specific date. He left behind a *geṭ*, which, if he tarried, she could activate and become divorced.[35] Restrictions regarding husbands' travel were often written into prenuptial agreements, betrothal deeds, and marriage contracts.[36]

Sometimes an absentee husband settled down in a new place and asked his wife to join him there, or wished to take a second wife in his new location. Such cases gave rise to legal queries, as illustrated by a question posed to Maimonides, in which he ruled, in accordance with the Talmudic halakha (Shabbat 110a; cf. Mishneh Torah, *Hilkhot ishut* 13:17), that a wife could be compelled to relocate provided it entailed moving to a place that was similar to where she lived.[37]

The case that Maimonides addressed in that responsum, as well as his ruling in Laws of Marriage 14:2, is anticipated in a responsum of R. Isaac Alfasi. It relates the story of a Jewish storekeeper in Jaén who left his hometown for another city in eastern Spain. There he remained for ten years and took a second wife, leaving his first wife an *'aguna* (lit., "anchored" to her marriage). When the first wife demanded that he be fined "the 200 *qāsimī* dinars customary in Spain since the early days" for taking a second wife, he offered instead either to move his first wife to his new location or to split his time between wife number one in Jaén and wife number two in his new place of residence.

Alfasi's ruling displays keen knowledge of how economic realities affected marriage. Since the storekeeper had been a stationary breadwinner in Jaén and therefore unaccustomed to traveling, the Spanish halakhist ruled that he ought not to have gone to another city for business without his wife's permission, citing the very Mishna in Ketubbot that underlies Maimonides' abovementioned halakha. And since the errant husband had taken even further liberty by marrying again (without his wife's permission), he was obligated to pay the hefty fine.[38] Differing from what may be a North African /Andalusian deterrent to husbands taking a second wife without their first wife's consent, a ketubba clause in vogue in Maimonides' Egypt when he arrived there permitted a wife on her own initiative to compel her husband to divorce her if she did not approve of his taking a second wife or a concubine.[39]

In Maimonides' time, when travel for business to India was common and husbands often needed to be away for years at a time, wives certainly assented to long periods of separation, a concession to the family breadwinner's need to travel great distances in pursuit of livelihood. They did not normally insist on the letter of the law regarding their husbands' conjugal obligation, or demand a conditional divorce in advance. Maimonides' halakhic rationale about traveling for commerce—"he may not travel *except with her permission*"—echoes this reality.

## 3.7 Commerce and the Impotent Husband

Rabbinic law allows a woman whose husband is impotent and cannot make her pregnant to demand a divorce after ten years have passed. The basic law in the Talmud (Yevamot 64a) qualifies this, however: if one of them becomes sick or both of them are imprisoned during this period, that time is not counted in the ten years. In other words, the ten years must comprise a period when the couple are actually living together.

Amplifying the halakha, Maimonides makes room for the specific case of the traveling merchant (*Hilkhot ishut* 15:11): "If within those ten years he had *gone away for commerce* [*halakh bi-sḥora*] or was ill, or she was ill, or both were imprisoned, this time is not included in the ten years."

For the instance of commercial travel, Maimonides had some support from the Palestinian Talmud (Yevamot 6:6, Venice edition 7c; also Tosefta Yevamot 8:6), where, to illness and imprisonment, travel to *medinat ha-yam* is added. As noted earlier, this term in rabbinic literature seems originally to have meant the coastal district of Palestine. But it was taken by post-Talmudic Jews to mean a land "across the sea," outside the borders of the Land of

Israel, synonymous with the phrase *ḥuṣ la-areṣ*.[40] Living in the post-Talmudic Islamic world, Maimonides understands *medinat ha-yam* to mean travel abroad for the specific purpose of "commerce" (*halakh bi-sḥora*). As he does with other halakhot, he wants to make absolutely certain that the concessions for the impotent husband are extended to traveling merchants, a cadre of people represented abundantly in the Geniza documents and in his own responsa.[41]

* * *

The glosses pertaining to commerce in Maimonides' Code discussed in this chapter illustrate the codifier's effort to adjust rabbinic law to conform with the complex trading economy of the Islamic world. While most of these updates do not involve substantive changes in the halakha, they show that Maimonides intended his Code to serve a practical purpose for merchants and especially for judges faced with litigations arising from long-distance commercial ventures. In this, he went beyond his predecessor in Spain, R. Isaac Alfasi, whose abridgment of the Talmud, by dint of its structure and language, hews closer to the classical text, even though in his responsa, he frequently addresses immediate mercantile issues.[42] While Maimonides had precedents for some of the adjustments discussed in this chapter, and while it is possible that one of the Geonim, in some responsum or mini-code that has not survived (or surfaced in the Geniza), had interpolated references to "commerce" that were absent in the Talmud, it is nonetheless significant for appraising Maimonides' contribution that it was he who made the updated law part of the Jewish legal canon.

## Chapter 4

# Partnership

### 4.1 Partnership: *Shutafut/Sharika/Khulṭa*; *'Isqa*; *Commenda* (*Qirāḍ/Muqāraḍa/Muḍāraba*)

Long-distance trade in the highly mobile, monetized economy of the Islamicate world required partners and agents. Forms of partnership and agency relations, old and new, came to play a more important role in Jewish economic life.[1] In this chapter, I deal with partnerships, Jewish and Islamic. In Chapter 5, I take up the institution of commercial agency.

The old Talmudic institution of joint partnership (Hebrew, *shutafut*; Arabic, *sharika* or *khulṭa* ["mixing," i.e., of capital]) was readily available to Jewish merchants. Talmudic partnership is a formal institution, relying on a written contract between the parties, spelling out the nature and terms of their joint business venture, and requiring *qinyan*, the symbolic act confirming agreement, comparable to the handclasp, the *ṣafqa* accompanying the contract (*'aqd*) concluding a deal in an Islamic court.[2] Typically, a partnership entailed the purchase or sale of a commodity or commodities, using money or goods invested jointly by the partners, all of whom shared both losses and gains. As we saw in the previous chapter, Maimonides updated some halakhot regarding partnership to conform with business practices in the Islamicate marketplace.

Another form of commercial collaboration dating from Talmudic antiquity, called *'isqa* in Aramaic (Hebrew, *'eseq*), resembles a "silent partnership." The invested funds or goods originate with one of the partners only while the other contributes the work. The investment could be misconstrued as a loan, in which the return to the stationary investor looked suspiciously like repayment of principal plus interest, which is forbidden between Jews by biblical law. To avoid the appearance of usury, the rabbis of the Talmud construed this as a partnership with half the investor's money being considered a deposit and the other half a free loan (Bava Meṣi'a 104b).[3] Of the proceeds from the active party's business deals, half the profit was considered a product of the loan and accruing to him after repaying the loan amount, and the other half as profit on the investor's deposit and for the latter's benefit, after deducting an amount for the active partner's services. The active partner was held responsible for loss only to the portion of the investor's deposit.[4]

Talmudic rules governing business cooperation were compatible with the geographically limited Jewish commerce of the Talmudic period; but in the expanded economy of the Islamic world, with its extensive long-distance trade, Talmudic halakha imposed certain limitations on mercantile arrangements.[5] Muslim merchant practice, on the other hand, offered options for commercial collaboration that permitted greater flexibility. Differing from the traditional Jewish joint partnership while sharing some features with the *'isqa* was a form of commercial cooperation popular among Muslim merchants called *qirāḍ* (also *muqāraḍa* or *muḍāraba*). This partnership resembled and bore the advantages of the later, Latin *commenda* and was likely its model.[6] Operating as a kind of mutual loan, one partner "lent" money or goods to the other, who "lent" his work (though he might also invest some capital), returning to the investor an agreed-upon portion of the profit and keeping the rest for himself. Differing from the Talmudic *'isqa*, however, in the Islamic *qirāḍ*, the active merchant bore no responsibility whatsoever for financial losses to the stationary partner's invested capital.[7]

The Islamic *commenda* offered distinct advantages in an economy in which investment and long-distance trade comprised such essential elements, and it was accepted at an early stage into Islamic law.[8] It encouraged impecunious adventurers to take part in the enterprise, since they took very little personal financial risk, while they could anticipate benefiting from a portion of the profit. And it ensured investors ready access to business collaborators who were willing to do the hard work that they themselves did not wish to, or could not, do—work that usually entailed extensive travel and separation from family for long stretches of time.[9] The risk that the active *commenda* partner took, apart from the usual physical dangers, was limited to the loss of his time and effort and the portion of the profits he had anticipated receiving.

Because of its advantages in long-distance trade, including exemption of the active party from responsibility for loss, the Islamic *commenda* constituted the most common type of collaboration between Jewish and Muslim merchants.[10] Even among themselves, Jews chose to employ the Islamic form of *commenda* somewhat more often than the Talmudic *'isqa*.[11] In such cases, halakhic authorities were constrained, grudgingly, to recognize the reality as well as the fact that Jewish merchants often had recourse to Islamic courts to register such contracts and adjudicate disputes.[12] To be constituted in the Jewish court, a *muḍāraba* contract had to assign some responsibility for loss to the active partner.[13] In his role as a Jewish *muftī*, Maimonides responded to queries involving *commenda* contracts, which, if they exempted the active party from responsibility for losses, signified what the halakha calls the "dust of usury" (*avaq ribbit*), a rabbinic concept broadening the usury prohibition in the Bible. For that reason, Maimonides insisted that Jewish traveling merchants be accorded a greater share of the potential profits than the percentage stipulated for the stationary partner in an Islamic *commenda*.[14]

Vexingly for the researcher and doubtless for contemporaries as well, the same word, *qirāḍ*, was used for both the Islamic *commenda* and the Jewish *'isqa* because of the similarity between the two institutions. Because of the ambiguity, however, sources—Maimonides' responsa, especially—distinguish the two, calling the former *qirāḍ al-goyim*, "the *qirāḍ* of the Gentiles" (meaning Muslims); and the other, *qirāḍ be-torat 'isqa*, "*qirāḍ* according to the Jewish law of *'isqa*."[15]

## 4.2 Partnership Law in the Code

In what follows, I discuss several aspects of partnership and partnership law that Maimonides modified or updated in the Mishneh Torah in order to accommodate the custom of the merchants. Section 4.2.1 deals with a common practice of Geniza merchants to cope with risk by multiplying partnerships. The next section (4.2.2) discusses traveling partners. Section 4.2.3 takes up the question of partnership with a Muslim. The final section (4.2.4) addresses an aspect of partnership in agricultural produce that relied on knowledge of local merchant custom.

### *4.2.1 Diversifying Partnerships to Cope with Risk*

Long-distance trade, whether on land or by sea, brought profit but was also fraught with risks and danger.[16] Reports of brigandage on the caravan routes, of storms, shipwrecks, and, occasionally, piracy at sea, even wartime depredations, pepper the correspondence of Geniza merchants and crop up frequently in responsa dealing with losses incurred as a consequence of such calamities.[17] Maimonides was all too aware of the precariousness of mercantile life. In an oft-cited Geniza letter, his merchant brother, David, describes his own danger-filled journey across the desert from the Nile port of Qūṣ to the Red Sea port of ʿAydhāb en route to India. He met his death in a shipwreck in the Indian Ocean, possibly on that very journey. The tragedy plunged Maimonides into a depression that lasted a year. His letter (not from the Geniza) describing his melancholy mentions that he lost a lot of his own money because of that tragedy.[18]

Beyond physical perils, much of the uncertainty in long-distance trade stemmed from the unpredictability of markets. Fluctuating prices and the availability or unavailability of commodities loomed large in merchant planning, as their letters abundantly attest. Goods or coins could be lost to pirates at sea or to brigands on land. In the absence of the insurance that late medieval European merchants developed and that we have in modern society, how did Geniza merchants cope with risk?

Risk associated with transporting money could be diminished by keeping deposits in distant entrepôts with a "banker" and by using a *suftaja* to remit funds.[19] We have seen (in Chapter 2) that the Babylonian Geonim sanctioned this custom of the merchants. Uncertainties in the marketplace could be reduced by depositing goods with a "representative of the merchants," *wakīl al-tujjār* (Hebrew, *peqid ha-soḥarim*).[20] This individual, whose functions are familiar to us, thanks to the Geniza, helped limit the risks involved in business by serving as a proxy agent representing merchants in their legal claims against debtors. He also provided storage in his warehouse when other options for safekeeping of goods were lacking. He might even sell goods on behalf of the owner(s) in their absence, taking advantage of a good price in the marketplace.

Risk could also be diminished through diversification by forming separate partnerships with different people, an arrangement that was permitted in Islamic Ḥanafī law, even without the permission of the primary partner.[21] As numerous Geniza letters illustrate, a person sharing in a commercial venture with an investing partner, traveling with his money or goods and transacting business along the way, might do the same with another party.[22] By concatenating partnerships, merchants counteracted some of the financial risk involved in long-distance trade. If one partnership resulted in a poor showing of profit, another might be more successful, compensating for the loss. Diversification served a purpose, too, when one commodity being shipped was lost or damaged. Another might be delivered in good shape.

Maimonides addresses multiple partnerships in the Code in Agents and Partners 5:2, drawing on the Talmud but also incorporating material that does not appear to derive from that source. The halakha begins with a general statement: "If one of the partners deviates and sells on credit or goes on a voyage or goes to any other place or trades with other merchandise or does any similar thing, then he alone must pay for all the loss that ensues as a result of his disobedience, while if there is a profit, the partners, because he deviated, shall share it equally, in accordance with what they have stipulated in regard to profit." This summary of principle is then explained through concrete examples drawn from the Talmud:

> Therefore, if one gives money to another to be used in partnership to buy with it wheat for trading purposes, and the other goes and buys barley, or he gives him money to buy barley and the other buys wheat, then if there is a loss it is the loss of the latter who deviated, while if there is profit, they share it equally. Likewise, if he goes and forms a partnership with a third party, using money from the [first] partnership, if there is a loss it is his loss, and if there is a profit, they share it equally. However, if he forms a partnership with another person using his own money, if there is a loss it is his loss, and if there is a profit, the profit is also his. If they made some stipulation [in this matter], the stipulation determines all.

The ostensible source for this halakha, as recognized by the commentator Joseph Caro in his Kesef Mishneh, is the discussion in the Babylonian Talmud Bava Qamma 102a–b. The Talmud relates to the first part only: "If one gives money to his agent [*sheluḥo*] to purchase wheat, and he purchases barley," or vice versa, it considers how this deviation from instructions would affect his share of any profits. Like Rashi and Tosafot, Maimonides understood the Talmud to be referring to a partnership, in which profits are shared, so he changed the wording accordingly: "If one gives money to another to be used *in partnership*" (*be-torat shutafut*). This was important because "agency" in the Talmudic period was not a commercial institution; it became so only after the Islamic commercial revolution. (I discuss this form of commercial agency in Chapter 5.)

The part of halakha 5:2 about forming a partnership with a third party is absent in the Talmudic source in Bava Qamma. Maimonides introduces it with the term "likewise," an expression, as we have noted, that he often employs when adding something new that is analogous. The commentator Kesef Mishneh (Joseph Caro) wondered why Maimonides added it at all, since it was self-evident: if all the money was tied up in the first partnership, the active partner should have nothing to invest in another business deal. If, on the other hand, he possessed money of his own, either the loan portion of the first partnership or other moneys, it was obvious that he would be responsible for both gain and loss resulting from any partnership that he formed with a third party.

A simple solution presents itself if we assume that Maimonides added the statement about partnership with a third party (because such multiplication of partnerships, a measure to limit risks in long-distance trade, was entirely common among merchants in his day but not in the time of the Talmud) and that he wished to incorporate it into the halakha. Forming an additional partnership with another person using money from the initial partnership is discussed in Islamic law and disallowed in one type of Islamic partnership, called *'inān*.[23]

When such an arrangement was made by Jewish traders, it could give rise to legal questions. A case in point concerning a partnership between two merchants came before R. Isaac Alfasi. The active partner had used a portion of the money invested by the stationary partner to establish a partnership with a third party. When a dispute arose, the original partner wanted to impose an oath on the third party. Alfasi permitted this over the objections of that merchant because some of the money used for the second partnership had come from the first partner's original investment. His traveling partner was therefore in the position of his agent, making the original investor a partner with the third party as well.[24]

### *4.2.2 Traveling Partners*

Lack of familiarity with the commercial realia of Maimonides' world led to misunderstanding of many halakhot in the Code. Agents and Partners 5:4 represents a case in point. "If one of the partners says, 'Let us transport the merchandise to such-and-such place, where its price is high, and sell it there,' even if he assumes responsibility for any accident or loss, the other one is permitted to restrain him from doing so. He says to him, 'I do not want to give you my money and then have to chase after you to bring you to court in order to extract it from you.' This applies to every similar case."

This halakha is passed over in silence by the standard commentators. A similar case in the Talmud regarding traveling merchants is ignored because it does not concern partnership.[25] Apparently, the authorities could find no prior rabbinic underpinning for the ruling. What, indeed, lies behind Maimonides' very specific instructions regarding this aspect of commercial cooperation? The answer, I submit, lies in the economic realities of the Islamic world as documented in the Geniza and elsewhere.

Goitein notes that investors in the Geniza period were often quite specific about the itinerary to be followed by their partners.[26] A Geniza document about a partnership among three men relates how the traveling party, who had invested a much smaller sum than the two others, agreed to travel "to the region of Aleppo and Antioch, *not to any other [place]*."[27] A responsum (not from the Geniza) attributable to R. Isaac Alfasi regards a partnership in which the stationary, investing partner stipulated "that [the active partner] shall not go any place other than the place he is about to travel to."[28] In business partnerships for long-distance trade where one person was stationary, serving as the "silent" financial backer, he was naturally anxious to follow the progress of the merchant to whom he had entrusted money or goods. Through correspondence, he would keep in touch, eagerly awaiting news of the active partner's successes or failures. The business correspondence and legal documents in the Geniza brim over with this type of information.[29]

### *4.2.3 Partnership with a Muslim*

As a matter of general principle, forming a partnership with a non-Jew is prohibited by the Talmud—and in the Mishneh Torah, for that matter—if the non-Jew is a pagan idolater.[30] Three potential problems about Jewish business relations with Gentiles in general concerned the rabbis. Since non-Jews are permitted to work on the Sabbath, the rabbis were worried that a non-Jewish partner, acting as agent for the Jew for half the work he did that day, would put the Jew in the position of violating the commandment to rest on the Sabbath. Second, the rabbis were concerned about the possibility that an idolater engaged in business (such as partnership) with a Jew might take an oath and would naturally do so in the name of his god(s) or, being happy with the outcome of a business deal with a Jew, would go to his temple to thank his god(s).[31] The Jew would then be violating a biblical prohibition that "the names of other gods shall not be heard on your lips" (Exod. 23:13), which the rabbis took to mean that "the name of a pagan god shall not be uttered because of you." Third, the Jewish partner would transgress the commandment "You shall not place a stumbling block before the blind" (Lev. 19:14). Idolaters worshiping their gods in their pagan temples were "blind" to the fact that they were obligated to observe certain basic "natural" laws, the "Seven laws of the sons of Noah," among which was the commandment to worship one God alone.

In the Talmudic tractate on idolatrous worship ('Avoda Zara), the rabbis sought to regulate business relations between Jews and pagans so as to prevent the Jew from violating the above-mentioned injunctions. Unsurprisingly, when the Talmud considers and allows an interfaith partnership, it assumes the enterprise to be agricultural. "If a Jew and an idolater ['*oved kokhavim*, 'star worshiper'] received a field in partnership (as sharecroppers), the Jew may not say to the idolater, 'Take your portion [of the proceeds earned] on the Sabbath, and I will [do the same] on a weekday.' If they had stipulated this at the outset, it is permissible; but if they are settling accounts, it is forbidden" ('Avoda Zara 22a).[32]

Manuscripts of the Talmud and the early printed editions (Pisaro 1509–1517 and Venice 1520–1523), which were, in turn, based on manuscripts, have the word *goy*, usually translated "Gentile," in place of "idolater."[33] *Goy* is applied in the Bible to the idolatrous non-Israelite nations, though, in its core meaning of "people," it sometimes refers to the Israelite people themselves (Gen. 35:11; Deut. 4:7). In Talmudic antiquity, certainly in the time of the Mishna, before the triumph of Christianity, the typical *goy* was an idolater.

In medieval Europe, Christians suspected that Jews used the expression *goyim* pejoratively to malign them, a problem that became acute when Christians began to become familiar with the Talmud in the twelfth century. Since it became dangerous for Jews to allow the word *goy*, with its assumed derogatory connotation, to appear in the pages of the Talmud, the expression "star worshiper," an appellation unequivocally reserved for idolaters, was substituted for the term *goy* by Christian censors or by the Jews themselves.

European Jews in the early and high Middle Ages lived mostly in small communities, dispersed far and wide, and depended heavily on doing business with their Christian neighbors. A theoretical belief that Christianity was a latter-day form of polytheism because of the belief in the Trinity, along with the concern that a Jew in partnership with a Christian would violate one or more of the three prohibitions mentioned above, complicated Jewish economic life. Thus Rashi and the twelfth- and thirteenth-century commentators on Rashi and the Talmud, the Tosafists, found ways to differentiate between the Christians of their time and the pagans of old. The concern over Gentile oath-taking was therefore voided, and business with Christians was sanctioned.[34] The concern about Jews benefiting from profits earned by a non-Jewish partner's labor on the Sabbath remained, however.

In the Islamic world, Jews were mostly concentrated in urban areas, where they engaged in commerce, banking, small artisanal industries, and retailing, as well as medicine and government service. Partnerships, whether among Jews or with non-Jews, principally Muslims, marked the economic order to a much greater extent than in the Talmudic period. A ninth-century Iraqi Gaon's repetition of the Talmudic rule prohibiting Jews from forming partnerships with Gentiles fell on deaf ears.[35] Jewish merchants entered into partnerships with Muslim merchants, doubtless in greater numbers than the occasional mention of this in Geniza documents and responsa.[36] Islamic law condones partnership with *dhimmī*s, provided the Muslim serves as the active partner, in order to forestall transactions involving items, such as pork and wine, that are forbidden in Islam, or to avoid usury. In practice, however, as Jewish sources show, Muslim merchants, showing a large measure of trust in their Jewish counterparts, freely assumed the role of stationary partner while the Jewish partner traveled and did business.[37] Interfaith partnerships in trade and in crafts, an offshoot of the parity of non-Muslims and Muslims in commercial exchange, were normal and frequent and offered Jews and Muslims ample opportunity to form bonds of friendship and trust, an essential requirement in medieval merchant relations, a point to which we shall return in Chapter 5.[38]

In his halakhic writings, Maimonides maintained that Muslims were proper monotheists, hence not subject to restrictions that the Talmud placed on interaction with idolaters.[39] Thus, the issue of a Muslim partner pronouncing a pagan oath was a nonissue. The other problem that concerned the Talmudic sages—work done by a non-Jewish partner on the Sabbath—*did* matter, for the very same reason operating for all non-Jews, regardless of religion: a Jew is not supposed to benefit from work done by a Gentile partner on the Jewish day of rest.

The Geonim, in their day, received many queries—some of them discovered among the Geniza fragments—about partnerships with Muslims and had to address the halakhic questions that such arrangements raised. The issue in these legal opinions is, as expected, not the validity of the partnership per se but, typically, the question of profits from work done by the Muslim on the Sabbath.[40] Characteristic of the transitional nature of Jewish economic life from agriculture to commerce in early Islamic Iraq, a responsum of R. Naṭronai b. Hilai (Gaon from 857/858 to 865/866) concerns "a Jew and a Gentile [here, *goy* = Muslim] who acquired a field in partnership."[41] Another Gaonic responsum, regarding a partnership in plowing, asks whether, when the Gentile drives the animal to pull the plow on the Sabbath, his Jewish partner violates the commandment to let one's animals rest on that day.[42] Another questioner asked about the halakhic consequences when a Gentile irrigates a field held in partnership with a Jew on the Sabbath.[43] Notwithstanding Jews' extensive involvement in trade during the Gaonic period, often in partnership with Muslims, agriculture and interdenominational partnerships in agriculture did not completely cease in the fertile land between the Tigris and Euphrates Rivers in southern Iraq, where most of Babylonian Jewry lived.[44]

Maimonides received a question about an interfaith partnership between Jews and Muslims who operated a craft business together (the questioner wasn't sure if it was glassmaking or goldsmithery). Asked what to do about the earnings produced on the Sabbath, he ruled concisely that the profit earned on the Sabbath accrued to the Muslim alone, the earnings of Friday or any other weekday belonged to the Jewish partner alone, and the two should divide the profits of the rest of the week equally between them.[45]

In the Code, which was intended as a new and permanent canon of Jewish law, Maimonides worked the everyday reality of interreligious partnerships into the language of the halakha. Departing from the text of the Talmud in 'Avoda Zara quoted above, however, and taking into account the transformed economy of the Islamic world, he codified an updated version of the ancient ruling, switching the emphasis from an agrarian to a commercial context and shifting its location in the Code from the Laws of Idolatry to the Laws of the Sabbath.

> Regarding a person who forms a partnership with a Gentile [*goy* = Muslim] *in a handcraft, or in commerce or in a store* [*bi-mlakha o bi-sḥora o ba-ḥanut*], if they stipulated at the outset that the income of the Sabbath will be the Gentile's alone, be it a little or a lot, and the income of a different day in place of the Sabbath will be the Jew's alone, it is permissible. But if they did not stipulate this at the outset, then, when they come to divide [things] up, the Gentile takes the income of all the Sabbaths for himself and the rest they divide between them. He does not add anything for [the

Jew] for the Sabbath unless they stipulated [such] at the outset. If they received a field in partnership as sharecroppers, the law is the same. (Laws of the Sabbath 6:17)

In the next halakha (6:18), Maimonides echoes the opinion of the Geonim but adds a nuance of his own at the beginning. "If they did not stipulate [at the outset] and came to divide up the profit and the income of the Sabbath was not known, *it is my opinion that the Gentile should take one-seventh [of the week's proceeds] for himself and the rest should be divided [between them]*. If a person gives money to a Gentile [*goy*] as a *commenda* to do business with it, even though the Gentile transacts business on the Sabbath, [the Jewish partner] shares the profit with him equally. Thus ruled all the Geonim."

Several things are to be remarked on here. First, Maimonides places the ruling among the Laws of the Sabbath, not where someone familiar with the Talmud would expect to find it in the Code—namely, among the Laws of Idolatry. He did so, I surmise, because the essential issue in partnership with a member of the dominant Gentile group in his Islamic milieu was work done on the Sabbath, not the idolatrous nature of the partner's religion. Since Maimonides himself ruled that Muslims were steadfast monotheists, the Laws of Sabbath constituted for him a more logical place for the halakha.

Second, Maimonides does not shrink from using the word *goy*, found in many printed versions of the Code.[46] In the Muslim-Jewish world, *goy* was non-pejorative. It was the word standardly applied by Jews to Muslims (Christians were called *naṣrānī*, the normal medieval Arabic term, or *'arel*, a Hebrew word meaning "uncircumcised").[47] Conversely and appropriately, when repeating elsewhere the above-mentioned Talmudic halakha prohibiting partnership with an idolater (Agents and Partners 5:10), Maimonides eschews the word *goy*; rather, he writes, "it is forbidden to form a partnership with an idolater" (*'oved kokhavim u-mazalot*, "worshiper of stars and constellations").

Third, Maimonides, who was well aware of the diversified, urban occupational profile of the Jews of his time, gives primacy to handcrafts, commerce, and retailing. These Jewish walks of life, common in the Islamicate marketplace, are missing from the Talmudic urtext, which reflects the dominant agrarian lifestyle of the Jews of the Talmudic period. In addition to the vast amount of data on commerce in the Geniza, the documents attest abundantly to the widespread Jewish involvement in crafts, as many as 265 different types.[48] The agricultural partnership envisioned by the Talmud was sharecropping, hence the language "received a field in partnership," whereas the most common partnerships in Maimonides' time, apart from partnerships in long-distance trade, were small-scale craft partnerships, what Goitein calls "industrial partnerships."[49]

Fourth, Maimonides introduces as his own opinion a method for dividing the income of the partnership when the proceeds of the Sabbath are unknown. He stipulates that one-seventh of the week's total earnings should go to the Muslim, and the income for the other six days should be divided equally between the partners. We may imagine that he sought in this novel way to avoid weekly haggling between the Jew and his Muslim partner—a logical and equitable solution, aimed at avoiding conflict that could end up in litigation in an Islamic court, which had exclusive jurisdiction in mixed litigations between Muslims and non-Muslims.

Finally, conscientious codifier of ancient Jewish law that he was, Maimonides does not ignore the agrarian context of the Talmud entirely. For one thing, Jews in the Geniza world were not completely detached from the soil.[50] In Maimonides' agriculturally rich Andalusian homeland, in particular, Jews still farmed in the eleventh and twelfth centuries. The responsa of R. Isaac Alfasi of Lucena, Spain (d. 1103), and of his student R. Joseph ibn Migash (d. 1141) bear ample witness to this.[51] Moreover, since Maimonides intended the Code as a permanent (and new) canon of Jewish law, one that was to remain in effect even in the messianic age, he had to include all possibilities, including agricultural partnerships. Nonetheless, characteristic of his method of updating to conform to the post-Talmudic life, he shifted the word "field" in the Talmud to the end, almost as an afterthought, subordinating the original, agrarian premise to other, more prominent aspects of the urban economy in his own day—with the pithy sentence: "If they received a field in partnership [as sharecroppers], the law is the same."

In contrast, Alfasi, whose *Halakhot* sticks closely to the language and running text of the Talmud and who deals with Jewish agricultural activity in Spain in his responsa, retains the Talmud's unitary reference to partnership in a field.[52] This makes Maimonides' departure from the language of the Talmud here all the more striking.

The commentators on the Code, who discuss the halakhic aspects of 6:18 extensively, say nothing about the transposition of the law of partnership with a non-Jew from one context to another, namely, from the Laws of Idolatry to the Laws of the Sabbath.[53] Nor do they show concern about the addition of the words "handcraft," "commerce," and "store" featured at the beginning, or the relegation of the Talmud's original language about partnership in a field to the end. There was Gaonic precedent for expanding the range of partnerships to encompass urban professions, and Maimonides' formulation fit the medieval urban Jewish economy with which the commentators themselves were familiar. Joseph Caro, author of the sixteenth-century Shulḥan 'Arukh, the code of Jewish law that is normative for traditional Jews to this day, and who lived in Safed, a city located on the flourishing trade route to and from Ottoman Damascus, adopted Maimonides' addition, "commerce or store," along with additional examples of nonagricultural partnerships omitted by Maimonides. Notably, though, out of faithfulness to the Talmud, Caro restored the word "field" to its pride of place at the head of the list.[54]

### *4.2.4 Partnership in Agricultural Produce and the "Aging" Process*

Another example of how Maimonides updates the halakha to take into consideration contemporary economic realities and local custom concerns partnership in agricultural produce. In chapter 5 of the Laws of Agents and Partners (5:5), following a series of rulings on partnership practices, Maimonides rules: "If one of the partners wishes to age [*le-yashen*] the produce for the recognized [i.e., customary] period of time [*'ad zeman ha-yadua'*], the other cannot restrain him from doing so. However, if there is no [recognized] time for that particular produce, the other may restrain him from doing so."

Caro, author of Kesef Mishneh, found what he believed to be a source for this halakha in the Babylonian Talmud, tractate Giṭṭin, a passage concerning the times of the year when produce or wine should be sold.[55] A Tosefta passage (Bava Meṣi'a 4:18) that parallels the Mishna in Giṭṭin, in turn paralleled by a passage in the Palestinian Talmud, is even more to the point because it deals explicitly with a partnership. "If someone gives money to another to buy produce on a profit-sharing basis and one of them wishes to age it [i.e., to delay the time of sale beyond the time they agreed for it to be sold], the other may restrain him."[56] Yet Maimonides' first sentence *permits* a partner, under certain circumstances, to subject the produce to aging before selling.

R. Abraham b. David of Posquières found this Maimonidean halakha unintelligible. Radbaz, the chief rabbi of Cairo in the early sixteenth century and a merchant himself, understood the realities of trade in agricultural commodities, as did Maimonides. In his commentary on the Laws of Agents and

Partners in the Code, he explains why the other partner may restrain him. "Aged" produce, he says, is worth more than fresh produce, but if the merchant-partner exceeds the time for "aging" it, the produce becomes less and less valuable (*neḥesarim ve-holekhim*), and something bad can happen to it (*me'uttadim le-miqreh*).[57]

I believe, in fact, that Maimonides was adapting a ruling found in the classical halakhic sources to fit a specific reality of commerce during his own time, a reality of which Radbaz, living in Egypt centuries later was evidently aware. The context I am referring to is the marketing in the Geniza period of agricultural products, particularly fruits. As part of long-distance trade, many fruits were imported to Egypt—presumably, to satisfy the tastes of the many immigrants to that country from Palestine, Syria, and Iran. Since imported fruits—Goitein gives the examples of apricots, peaches, and plums—were perishable, Goitein observes, "they must have been transported in a dried or half-dried state and were then sold in the street of the *naqliyyīn* or *nuqliyyīn*, the Street of the Sellers of Dried Fruit."[58] Jewish merchants, especially those involved in long-distance trade, had therefore to age—that is, dry—the fruits first. Naturally, they needed to know exactly how much time was needed to complete the aging/drying process before sale. If too much time elapsed from the time the fruit was left to dry out, or too little time was devoted to the process, this could result in a spoiled product, worth less in the marketplace than fruits dried to specification and sold within a reasonable amount of time.

Showing thorough familiarity with the ways of the marketplace, Maimonides, with his merchant know-how, seems to be regulating the practice of drying ("aging") produce by long-distance traders and specifically the import of dried fruits to Egypt. If one partner buys fruit that needs to be dried for long-distance transport, he needs leeway to accomplish this. If there is a prescribed (i.e., customary) amount of time for aging the fruit, the other partner may not interfere; if he is disappointed with the price that the fruits fetch in the marketplace, he cannot hold his partner liable. This could happen, for instance, if there were a glut on the market at the time of sale. If, however, the time for aging is uncertain, the first partner has the right to restrain the other from taking a chance with their joint investment.

This relatively straightforward explanation of the halakha reflects Maimonides' intimate knowledge of procedures for marketing produce, as described in the Geniza documents. His ruling does not exist in this specific form in the classical rabbinic sources. The codifier appears to have adapted the Tosefta passage (with its parallel in the Talmuds) to suit the purpose.

Radbaz, as I have shown in connection with the system of charity collection,[59] understood this passage in the light of the realia of Egypt and the Mediterranean trade, which, as a merchant, he knew firsthand, albeit from a later period. Unlike the Posquières rabbi, he knew exactly what Maimonides had in mind.

# Chapter 5

# Commercial Agency (*Ṣuḥba*)

## 5.1 Laws of Agents and Partners

Working with a corpus of legal material—the Talmud—that had been written centuries earlier, when commerce played a relatively minor role in Jewish life and when few Jews, if any, engaged in long-distance trade, Maimonides gleaned what he could from the rabbinic sources and assembled material on commercial cooperation in Laws of Agents and Partners (*Hilkhot sheluḥin ve-shutafin*), part of the Book of Acquisition (*Sefer ha-qinyan*).[1] The juxtaposition of agency and partnership is surprising in light of the fact that the Talmud does not consider agency an aspect of commercial enterprise (see below, section 2). Maimonides treats agency and partnership together because Jewish merchants in the Geniza world employed both institutions in long-distance trade and because the institutions possessed several similar properties. Maimonides deals with agency first and partnership last, I assume, because, as the Geniza documents illustrate, agency relations took precedence in the choices merchants made when entering into business collaboration.

The present chapter explains in detail the central and dominant role that agency relations (Judaeo-Arabic, *ṣuḥba*) played in Jewish commerce in Maimonides' time and earlier. This sets the stage for an account in the following chapter of how Maimonides, preceded by Saadya Gaon (d. 942), addressed a gap between Talmudic partnership law and contemporary mercantile practice of agency. Drawing an analogy between partnership and agency, Maimonides amended the halakha to enable Jewish courts to enforce informal, unwritten agency contracts, providing Jewish merchants with an equivalent alternative to the Islamic judicial system.

## 5.2 Agency in Jewish Law

Agency (*sheliḥut*) as a legal concept is formally recognized in Jewish law—in contrast, for instance, to Roman law.[2] It is expressed by a Talmudic maxim, "a man's agent is like himself" (*sheluḥo shel adam kemoto*).[3] Talmudic agency could take many forms, but in all cases, the agent is delegated to perform a single, one-time task. The classic cases come from family law. A groom unable to be present at his wedding can appoint an agent to deliver the marriage contract and thereby effect marriage with his intended bride from afar. The agent pronounces the formula "Behold, you are consecrated to So-and-So by means of this money or this contract," two of the accepted means of concluding a marriage. A husband can also appoint an agent to deliver a divorce document (*geṭ*) to his wife, or she can designate an agent to accept it on her behalf. Maimonides covers these cases in the Code in the Laws of Marriage (*Hilkhot ishut*) and the Laws of Divorce (*Hilkhot gerushin*), respectively.[4] A Jewish court, furthermore, can appoint someone to perform a task on its behalf (*sheliaḥ beit din*). Another common form of agency in the Talmud occurs when a person grants someone his power of attorney to act as his proxy legal agent to collect a debt or a deposit, the only form of agency in the Talmud that requires a writ of appointment and *qinyan*. This type of agency assumed heightened importance in the Islamic period and underwent modification to suit the transformation in Jewish economic life.[5] It is discussed below, in Chapter 7.

Importantly, in contrast to a partner, the Talmud does not hold an agent, who receives no payment for his services, liable for nonperformance of his delegated task and, barring gross negligence, frees him from taking an oath attesting to the honest execution of his specific mission.[6] Unlike a partner, he cannot be compelled to take an oath attesting to the honest discharge of his duties. This leniency of Talmudic agency law proved to be an obstacle to enforcing commercial agency dealings, a "custom of the merchants" that Jews learned in the Muslim marketplace and that dominated Jewish long-distance trade in the Islamic world.

## 5.3 Agency in Islamic Law

Agency (Arabic, *wakāla*) is a recognized legal institution in Islam as well.[7] But, unlike the Talmud, which conceives of agency as a one-time assignment,

Islamic law envisages a wide range of agency relations that were necessary in the complex economy of the Islamic world. Discussing the various economic functions that *wakīls* performed and that could lead to dispute between an agent and his principal, the Andalusian jurist and philosopher Ibn Rushd (d. 1198), known in Europe by his Latinized name, Averroës, cites problems arising from business affairs: "loss of the property remaining with the agent, or [disputes] about its return to the principal, or about the price at which he has sold or purchased when he was ordered to sell at a fixed price, or it could be about the commodity [*mathmūn*] itself, or it could be about the identification of the person whom he had instructed to make payment, or it could be due to a claim from a tort."[8] None of these could be adjudicated according to the Talmudic law of agency.

Udovitch describes a variation of *wakāla* called *ibḍā'* or *biḍā'a*, which he designates "quasi-agency." It entailed a type of unremunerated custodianship with its own rules and expectations. A theoretical statement in al-Sarakhsī's (d. ca. 1096) compendium of Ḥanafi law, regarding the actions that an agent (*muḍārab*) in a *commenda* may take with the investor's property, gives the following description (in Udovitch's translation): "And [the agent] may entrust it to the care of another party [*lahu an yubḍi'ahu*], because doing this is part of the custom of the merchants [*li'an al-ibḍā' min 'ādat al-tujjār*], and the agent will have need for it in order to achieve profit. For trade is of two kinds: local, in one's own town, and long-distant, in another town. And the agent cannot personally supervise both of these by himself. And were he not permitted to give the capital to the care of others [*al-ibḍā'*], and to have the power of appointing agents [*al-tawkīl*], and the right to leave it as a deposit [*al-īdā'*], then he would have to miss out on one of the two types because of the preoccupation with the other type."[9]

Udovitch equates *ibḍā'*, a "custom of the Muslim merchants," with a form of agency practiced by Geniza merchants and which I call *ṣuḥba*-agency.

## 5.4 *Ṣuḥba*-Agency

Differing from both the Talmudic joint partnership (*shutafut*) and the Talmudic *'isqa* discussed in the previous chapter, both of which presume written contracts, witnesses, and the symbolic act of acquisition (*qinyan*), and differing, too, from the Islamic *commenda*, merchant letters in the Geniza reveal a form of commercial collaboration, unknown in the pre-Islamic Jewish world, that was even more common than partnerships. Described by Goitein as "informal 'cooperation'" or "formal friendship" (Arabic, *ṣuḥba*);[10] likened by Udovitch to the Islamic *ibḍāʿ/biḍāʿa*;[11] taken in another direction by economist Avner Greif;[12] and, most recently, treated in minute detail by Mediterranean economic historian Jessica Goldberg,[13] in this "custom of the merchants," one party entrusted goods or money to another on the basis of trust, and the recipient, acting as agent rather than partner, traded with these on the owner's behalf, without receiving remuneration, without sharing in the profit, and without responsibility for unavoidable loss. The services provided by the agent were at some later date reciprocated by the owner. The close similarity between this institution and the Islamic *ibḍāʿ* supports the claim, based on Goitein's intuitive insight and on Udovitch's study of Islamic commercial law, that the Geniza documents can serve as a source for merchant practice in general in the Islamic Mediterranean and in the Indian Ocean.[14]

In the form of commercial agency practiced by the Geniza merchants, which I call *ṣuḥba*-agency (the terms "companionship," *ṣuḥba*, and "friendship," *ṣadāqa*, as well as the noun *aṣḥābunā*, "our associates/companions," were used),[15] the agent counted on the fact that his "friend" would return similar uncompensated services.[16] A *ṣuḥba* between merchants could last a very long time, kept alive by alternating favors. In this regard, it resembles the institution of gift and counter-gift identified with the work of French anthropologist Marcel Mauss and his scholarly successors.[17] Importantly, *ṣuḥba*-agency was normally arranged face-to-face or even by letter, without a written contract and without *qinyan*. It relied upon the reciprocal expectations and the trust that normally assured the reliability and honesty of business "friends." According to the law of the Talmud, however, as a form of agency, the institution lacked the legal enforceability that other, more conventional, contractual partnership arrangements offered.

## 5.5 The Debate About the Maghribī Traders

This last point brings us to the lively debate generated by the work of economist Avner Greif, thanks to whom the Geniza has become a household word in economists' and economic historians' discourse for over two decades. Greif is rare among economists in combining historical evidence with conventional econometric tools. Aware of the sparse evidence in the Geniza of court decisions resolving merchant disputes in the *beit din* or of Jewish judicial means for enforcing agency relations, Greif applied game theory to the Geniza evidence. His results led him to posit the existence of a closed, commercial consortium, or "coalition," of Jewish merchants (following Goitein, since many, though not all, of them were from North Africa, Greif called them the "Maghribī merchants"). These merchants, Greif maintained, enforced agency contracts through "private-order" sanctions, relying on a multilateral reputation mechanism that prevented agents from cheating or otherwise controverting the principal's wishes. Members of the in-group reported instances of malfeasance to the rest of the consortium, bypassing legal instruments and the mediation of the Jewish courts. This system assured agents' compliance with the instructions of the investor, for, were they to act contrary to his instructions, they would face being blacklisted and forfeiting access to the services of all other merchants in the coalition. In Greif's view, this system arose because "the legal system failed to provide a framework within which agency relations could be organized. The court was usually unable to verify agents' claims and actions or to track down an agent who had emigrated. . . . Even if an agent could be located, litigation was expensive and time-consuming."[18] We shall return to Greif's claim about the failure of the legal system later on.

Greif's model has appealed to many economic historians because, among other things, he proposes a theory that explicates the difference in economic growth between the Islamic world and the European West ("The Rise of the West" in the later Middle Ages). He theorizes that the constraining, "collectivist" mentality of Middle Eastern merchants, exemplified by the Geniza Maghribī traders, with their closed coalition, discouraged ventures with anonymous investors or agents, limiting economic growth. By contrast, the more liberal, "individualist" way of thinking of late medieval Genoese merchants, which allowed them to use anonymous agents, facilitated pooling of resources more broadly, nurturing economic expansion.

Greif's critics have challenged his model of the closed coalition and its reputation mechanism in contract enforcement. Some argue that formal contracts and the instrumentality of the courts were more prevalent than he assumed or than the evidence indicates. Many object to his ascription of the binary contrast between European and Middle Eastern economic development to the individualist-collectivist dichotomy.[19] Jessica Goldberg (see below) takes the middle ground, positing a mixed regime of informal (reputation-based) and formal business methods, the latter expressed in recourse to courts, Jewish or Muslim, or to other state institutions. Though controversial, Greif's work is extremely important because, among other things, it underscores the importance of "informal" agency, as contrasted with formal partnership, in the Islamic Mediterranean trade during the Geniza period, because it emphasizes the role of the "merchants' law" in the day-to-day commercial activity of the Jewish traders—supporting Udovitch's claim about the existence of a "'law merchant' of the medieval Islamic world"—and because his model has pressed others to look more closely at the historical evidence.[20]

## 5.6 *Ṣuḥba*-Agency and the Problem of Contract Enforcement

Goitein's and Udovitch's impression that "informal" commercial agency was far more common than formal partnership has now been confirmed statistically by Goldberg. Using sophisticated social science software to perform "content analysis," she tracked twice as many (67 percent) "friendship" arrangements as the combined total of formal partnerships (24 percent) and transactions using junior associates or slave-agents (7 percent).[21] She contends, however—differing in this respect from Goitein and Udovitch—that this seemingly "informal" practice, which she calls "reciprocal agency" or "mutual service agency," was not quite so informal, since it assumed an enforceable, underlying, even though unwritten, agency contract that protected the rights of the principal over the property given to an agent to transact with. While the social matrix of such relationships was informal, insofar as commercial favors were arranged with *ṣuḥba* associates without drawing up contracts, if an agent was suspected of mismanagement, the dispute could still be litigated in a Jewish or Muslim court. Merchants would anticipate this possibility *ex ante* by making use of the Islamic law of agency as implemented by state officials and by ensuring that their agency-related activities were witnessed by other merchants, should need for litigation arise in the future.[22]

Yet, despite the presence of thousands of legal documents in the Geniza, we have very little indication of how commercial agency disputes (as opposed to conflicts over partnerships) were resolved in the Jewish legal system—the very anomaly that caught Greif's eye and led him to locate contract enforcement in the Maghribī merchant consortium, with its private-order, reputation mechanism.

But the paucity of evidence in the form of court decisions in agency disputes should not be surprising. By its very nature, and in contrast to partnerships, *ṣuḥba*-agency entailed unwritten, informal agreements and did not require a witnessed contract or the symbolic act of *qinyan*. Thus, in the case of a dispute, the parties could not easily provide evidence in court regarding their collaborative arrangement, unless a third party was available and able to give testimony—either someone who happened to have been present at the moment the agency relationship was initiated or someone who had observed the agent's activities. Moreover, as noted previously, Talmudic law absolves an agent from responsibility for loss if he fails in the performance of his mission. Unlike a partner, he cannot be obligated to take an oath in court avowing his trustworthiness in handling the agency assignment. This limited the potential for resolution of an agency-related dispute in the Jewish court. In short, Talmudic law was ill-suited for enforcing *ṣuḥba*-agency relations on halakhic grounds, but not because judicial procedures were particularly expensive or necessarily drawn out.

We also have to consider that, precisely because Talmudic law lacked jurisdiction over mercantile agency, many, if not most, quarrels over agency relations were settled through some sort of out-of-court settlement or compromise—either formal arbitration or informal, mutual agreement. Of course, many disputes would have been litigated in Islamic courts, where there was no hesitancy to impose an oath on an agent, even a *dhimmī*.[23] As we shall see in the next chapter, Maimonides, who well understood that Jewish merchant-agents regularly applied to Islamic courts to settle quarrels, instituted a reform of the halakha to enforce commercial agency agreements in a Jewish court by making *ṣuḥba*-agents subject to the same exculpatory oath as a partner.

## 5.7 Informality in Partnerships

Apart from commercial agency, perhaps under its influence, informalism infiltrated partnerships as well. Goitein noticed that the Geniza contains a scarcity of contracts for partnership in long-distance trade (as opposed to contracts for craft partnerships),[24] either joint active partnerships (*shutafut*) or the "silent partnership," *ʿisqa* variety.[25] Gideon Libson refers to this lacuna when he states that "practices of the Geonim in facilitating trade by foregoing [*sic*] talmudic formalities in matters of acquisition (*kinyan*) are well understood in the context of Muslim commercial law and practice of the time."[26]

Ackerman-Lieberman and Goldberg, independently, showed that the word *muʿāmala*, usually translated as "mutual business dealings," sometimes refers to a partnership arranged informally, as when the parties lived at a great distance from each other and could not appear together in a *beit din* to draw up a contract, perform *qinyan*, and symbolically lift up a purse containing their respective cash investments.[27]

## 5.8 Formalism and Informalism in Islam

At this juncture, it is important to state that the binary opposition in scholarship about merchant practice between formalism and informalism has much to do with a larger discussion in Islamic scholarship contrasting formal, corporate institutions in the West with their apparent absence in the less formal Islamic East, at least during the classical period. This conversation is represented, for instance, in research describing the special character of the Islamic city.[28] In merchant practice of the Geniza world, both means of cooperation, partnership *and* agency, formalism *and* informalism, were present, though the evidence of the Geniza business correspondence shows that the informal dominated over the formal. It also shows that the formal (partnership) and the informal (*ṣuḥba*-agency) operated side by side between the same merchants, sometimes at one and the same time, to such an extent that this often led to confusion.[29] It is important to state, too, that what may seem informal to us, especially when contrasted with more familiar, formal structures in the West, was doubtless understood by the actual actors as having its own kind of formality (note Goitein's term "formal friendship").

The implications of these findings for the existence or absence of formal business arrangements in the Judaeo-Arabic world should not be overstated, however. In Islam itself, formal, written, contracts were in theory considered nonessential. Oral testimony fulfilled the function of records on papyrus or paper. On the other hand, this testimony itself was governed by formal rules and required the presence of impeccably trustworthy witnesses, called *ʿudūl*, to observe the proceedings and notarize documents. Furthermore, as a kind of aide-mémoire, written and signed contracts adhering to conventions described in Arabic formulary manuals were regularly employed. These Islamic manuals originated in Iraq during the Gaonic period and had their counterpart among the Geonim.[30]

What seems informal, therefore—in both Judaism and Islam—existed within a system that knew and practiced formal canons of evidence. The relatively small number of partnership contracts for long-distance trade in the Geniza should probably be seen in the light of Islam's downgrading (in theory, at least) of the requirement for written contracts as well as a sign of the predominance among the Jews of unwritten, reciprocal agency contracts in long-distance trade. Both these modes of commercial collaboration—formal partnership *and* informal reciprocal *ṣuḥba*-agency—are copiously represented in merchant letters, with the latter outnumbering the former by a significant proportion.

What exists in the Geniza of partnership documents (as distinguished from letters between partners) indicates that many merchants followed formal, halakhic procedures in that domain, codifying and later on dissolving their partnership agreements in written instruments in accordance with the laws of the Talmud, and adjudicating disputes before Jewish judges.[31] Partnership contracts for long-distance trade, though rare in the Geniza, are included in the formularies of the Geonim.[32] References to partnership contracts and legal proceedings are found in the Gaonic responsa as well and, in smaller numbers, in the much less plentiful corpus of responsa of Maimonides and those of Isaac Alfasi and Joseph ibn Migash.[33]

Equally important, in all forms of business cooperation, with or without written instruments, whether formal partnership or informal *ṣuḥba*-agency, much that was discussed and agreed upon at the outset had to be modified later on. Market fluctuations, commercial requests, and other considerations, such as danger on the seas or on the caravan routes, constantly changed, and this necessitated changes in the agreed-upon plan. Partners and *ṣuḥba* associates alike regularly wrote letters containing new instructions to those on the road. These letters substituted for face-to-face speech.[34] That, I submit, forms the background to R. Naṭronai Gaon's responsum, discussed in Chapter 3, permitting merchants to write letters to business associates if a caravan was about to depart on the intermediate days of a festival, so they could send instructions to business associates intended to ward off financial loss and preserve the well-being of their families.

## 5.9 Hayya Gaon's Responsum to the Merchant in Gabes, 1015

A responsum of R. Hayya b. Sherira Gaon (d. 1038), the most influential Babylonian rabbinic scholar of the Geniza period, formally sanctions instructions sent by mail from one merchant to another.[35] In 1015, he received a question from the city of Gabes in southern Tunisia concerning a dispute between two merchants, a father-in-law and a son-in-law, referred to respectively as Reuben and Simeon (in Jewish responsa, the children and wives of biblical forefathers are used as pseudonyms). Reuben had sent Simeon some merchandise to sell—seemingly acting as an agent.[36] When, after much time had passed, Reuben requested his money and earnings, Simeon reminded him that he had earlier written with instructions to give the proceeds to Simeon's own father, apparently another of Reuben's business associates. Reuben denied having so written. Simeon could not find the letter in question but had his late father's financial records, which showed a sum of money on Reuben's account.

Hayya Gaon responded that instructions sent by letter were equivalent to instructions delivered orally. "Since Reuben and Simeon transacted business via letters from one to the other, and it was their custom that, when Reuben wrote to Simeon to give something [to someone], Simeon would follow his written instructions. . . . Their letters are considered the same as oral instructions." This ruling, confirming the efficacy of letters in substituting for a formal, written contract, is extremely significant. The leniency was followed in agency relations, where a contract was not written, and when forming partnerships at a great distance. The Gaon ruled, further, that Simeon could substantiate his claim of innocence of any wrongdoing by taking an oath. This reference to an exculpatory oath of probity for what seems to be an agent is surprising, given what has been said above about the Talmudic exemption of agents from taking such an oath. We shall return to this peculiarity and its significance later on.

## 5.10 The Vocabulary of Reciprocity

The ubiquitous use of agency based on trust and the expectation of reciprocal business favors—Goitein's "formal friendship," Udovitch's "quasi-agency," Greif's "agency relations," Goldberg's "mutual service agency," or the term I use, *ṣuḥba*-agency—gave birth to a specialized vocabulary that permeates the Geniza business correspondence. Apart from the word *ṣuḥba* itself, Goitein calls attention to three other terms associated with merchant-agency that denote this form of collaboration: *risāla*, "consignment," "shipment" (which also occurs as a participle, *marsūl*, "consignee");[37] *khāṣṣa*, "personal account";

and—more rarely—*biḍāʿa*, "goods," recalling the *ibḍā/biḍāʿa* of Islamic commercial law.[38]

Other words and phrases that have hitherto gone largely unremarked also belong to this vocabulary of reciprocity. One of them is *ḥāja*. Its dictionary meaning is "a need" or "a request."[39] The word is extremely common in Geniza letters. A keyword search through the more than 4,300 historical documents currently in the Princeton Geniza Project's browser[40] (summer 2016) retrieves more than 250 occurrences of the word. The locution occurs regularly and formulaically at the end of business letters as an offer of reciprocity, in variants of the expression: *in takūn* (sometimes *yakūn*) *laka ḥāja fa-tusharrifnī bihā* (or *bi-qaḍā'ihā*), literally, "if you should have a request, honor me with [the task of] fulfilling it."

A synonym for *ḥāja* is *khidma*, "service"; we find, for instance, *in kāna li'l-mawlā khidma yusharrifhu bihā*, "if my master should have a service [to be performed], honor me with it."[41] Sometimes, *khidma* occurs synonymously alongside *ḥāja*.[42] The "institution" of reciprocal service agency is summed up succinctly in the words of one merchant-agent writing to his counterpart: "He who gives service gets service [in return]" (*man khadama khudima*).[43] Importantly, merchants maintained a clear distinction between mutual service agency and partnership. A merchant writes to a colleague offering him options: "If you don't prefer [a regular partnership arrangement], I'll serve you [*akhdumuka*, a verbal form of the noun *khidma*] in this *barqalū* [a midsize bale]: I'll sell and buy and send you [the purchased goods]."[44]

*Ṣuḥba*-agency could, though probably only on rare occasions, extend beyond the dyadic level. When a Jewish merchant writes, "if [the *ḥaver* Abū Zikrī, namely, Judah b. Saadya, later the first "Nagid" of Egypt] or you, my lord, or a friend [*ṣadīq*] have a request [*ḥāja*] to honor me with, I shall be very happy to fulfill it," he is offering to do a favor, not only for his correspondent-friend but also for a "friend" [*ṣadīq*] of his friend.[45]

Other examples of the vocabulary of reciprocity abound in the Geniza. A merchant writing from the Yemenite port of Aden asks his addressee in Fustat: "Please do not withhold from me your letter [in which you charge me] with any service [*khidma*] or requests [*ḥājāt*]."[46] A merchant scolds his correspondent: "I never ask anything from you, whereas my master and his brother are always making requests" (*min ahl al-ḥawā'ij*).[47] Particularly telling is the following in a merchant's letter: "If my master considers me fit to honor me with fulfilling a request [*ḥāja*] or doing a service [*khidma*] for him, I shall carry it out."[48] Here, as elsewhere, the merchant describes the popular reciprocal business arrangement where one trader performs a "service" for another.

The following passage from an unpublished Geniza letter employs the term *khidma* in a way that clearly describes a *ṣuḥba*-agent reporting to his counterpart about services he had promised to perform on the latter's behalf. "Regarding the sword, by God, my master, I was unable to procure it. By God, I am sorry about that, because I have been given the honor to serve you [*atasharruf bi-khidmatihi*]. If it befalls me to buy it, I shall send it to Your Excellency. By God, should you ever have a[nother] service [*khidma*] to honor me with, do honor me with carrying it out."[49]

The clear distinction that Geniza merchants made between formal modes of business collaboration and the more popular, informal brand of *ṣuḥba*-agency speaks loudly in a truncated phrase in a fragmentary letter mentioning litigation over a transaction "through a written contract [*sheṭar*], not through a request [*ḥāja*]."[50] Compared with the Talmudic partnerships, the *ṣuḥba* system was an entirely new way of doing business, fashioned in the Islamicate marketplace by the custom of the merchants, perhaps carried over from the pre-Islamic trade of Arabia, and shared by Jewish and Muslim traders alike.

## 5.11 The Typicality of Jewish Merchant Practice: Mutual Service Agency in Muslim Merchant Letters

That the Geniza documents can be read as evidence of merchant custom in general has been an axiom of scholarship for three generations of historians, beginning with Goitein.[51] Udovitch put the "Goitein hypothesis" on solid footing with his findings that Geniza merchant behavior in the eleventh century echoes descriptions of commercial collaboration in early Islamic (Ḥanafī) law. What has always been lacking, however, is evidence of typicality from medieval Muslim commercial documents themselves.[52]

The key to this evidence—the "smoking gun," if you will—is the "vocabulary of reciprocity." Hitherto unnoticed, this vocabulary, which permeates Jewish business correspondence in the Geniza, commonly crops up in letters of Muslims about business affairs existing among the Arabic documents on papyrus or paper.[53] The vocabulary of reciprocity appears in these letters even earlier than the Geniza period. In a ninth-century letter addressed to a Muslim textile merchant in the Fayyūm district of Upper Egypt, the writer states: "Do not fail to write me a letter informing me of your affairs and your circumstances and all your requests [*jamī'i ḥawā'ijika*], for in [fulfilling] them, there is blessing, God willing."[54] In a letter from the tenth century, a Muslim asks a friend to purchase an item and, at the end of the letter, exactly where such expressions occur in Geniza correspondence, writes, offering reciprocity: "Do not deprive me of your letters, including news of your affairs [*akhbāraka*] and circumstances [*aḥwālaka*] *and any request* [*ḥāja*] *that may befall you, so that I may speedily fulfill it, with God's help, to your satisfaction.*"[55] This sentence paraphrases nearly verbatim a statement at the end of a Geniza letter of a Jewish merchant, which Goitein translates in his discussion of formal friendship: "Do not withhold from me your letters with reports about your well-being and your requirements [*ḥawā'ij*], so that I may deal with them, as is my duty."[56] Similarly, in another Muslim missive, the writer formulates his offer of a reciprocal favor in words that mimic the language of Jewish Geniza merchants: "Honor me with all your requests" (*watusharrifnī bi-jamī'i ḥawā'ijika*).[57] The vocabulary of reciprocity was not limited to letters of Muslim merchants found among the papyri and paper documents preserved in the hot and dry climate of the Egyptian Fayyūm. We find it in letters of Muslim traders operating out of the Red Sea port of Quṣayr al-Qadīm in the thirteenth century.[58]

These examples prove—for the first time, with unassailable evidence from *Islamic* documentary sources—that reciprocal commercial agency was, indeed, part of the general "custom of the merchants." Practiced by Muslims and Jews alike, it amounted to a veritable commercial lingua franca and gave concrete expression to the thorough embeddedness of the Jews in the medieval Islamicate economy. In the case of the Jews, it represented the dominant form of commercial collaboration. As I have noted in a previous publication, the *ṣuḥba* system had a *longue durée* in Islamicate marketplace practice; it was in use as late as the twentieth century in Morocco and elsewhere.[59] The early Arabic papyri featuring the vocabulary of reciprocity attest to the universal, commonplace, and diachronic nature of this practice and suggest that reciprocal agency stemmed from the custom of the merchants in the pre-Islamic trade of Arabia.[60]

### *5.11.1* Ṣuḥba*-Agency with Muslims*

The properties of mutual trust and reciprocal service embodied in the "vocabulary of reciprocity" shared by Jewish and Muslim merchants enabled adherents of each faith to form agency relations with members of the other.

Roxani Margariti has pointed to the use of *ṣuḥba/aṣḥāb* terminology with reference to non-Jews in letters of Jewish merchants on the India route, and these non-Jewish merchants must necessarily have included Muslims.[61] The Geniza preserves ample evidence of Jews using Muslim *wakīls*.[62] Abraham, the son of Maimonides (d. 1237), was once queried about a town that held its market on the Jewish Sabbath. The questioner wanted to know if it was permissible halakhically to appoint a Muslim as his agent (he calls him *wakīl*) to buy and sell on his behalf in that town on that day. Abraham ruled favorably, provided that the Jew did not state explicitly to the Muslim that he should do so on that day.[63]

### *5.11.2 Agency Disputes and the Islamic Court*

Islamic law reserves exclusive jurisdiction for itself in mixed litigations.[64] Disputes between Jewish and Muslim *ṣuḥba* associates naturally had to be adjudicated before a Muslim judge, presumably on the basis of the Islamic law of *ibdāʿ*. Since this form of agency had no basis in Talmudic commercial law, Jewish traders, even among themselves, would have had to turn to the Islamic courts, which were generally receptive to intra-*dhimmī* litigation, in agency-related matters.[65] As we shall see in the next chapter, Jewish jurists—Saadya Gaon and Maimonides, in particular—sought ways to assimilate *ṣuḥba*-agency into the Talmudic scheme so that Jewish merchants would not continually challenge Jewish communal autonomy by exploiting their access to the Islamic legal system.

## 5.12 Ambiguity in Commercial Collaboration

Despite the clear functional and linguistic distinction that Geniza merchants made between partnership—whether it be joint active partnership (*shutafut/khulṭa/sharika*), *ʿisqa*, or the Islamic *commenda* (*qirāḍ*)—and *ṣuḥba*-agency, these forms of business collaboration regularly operated side by side at one and the same time, and this often led to ambiguity, especially when one or another of the parties lacked clarity about the terms of collaboration. When, for example, a merchant writes to his business associate regarding a commodity sent by the latter: "We did not know if it was for your personal account [*li-khāṣṣatika*], or for the partnership [*li'l-khulṭa*], because there was no [accompanying] letter from you," he was expressing an ambiguity that many

Geniza traders faced.[66] A series of accounts from the mid-eleventh century, in which a merchant summarizes various commercial transactions with different people, some designated as *khāṣṣa* and others as *khulṭa*, is emblematic of the complexities of merchant practice that could lead to ambiguity, confusion, and even judicial strife.[67]

### *5.12.1 A Tale of Two Merchants*

A fascinating case from the Geniza that began in 1075 and that I have discussed elsewhere illustrates how the terminology of reciprocal agency could lead to ambiguity and, in its wake, to arbitration or litigation.[68] It concerns a business venture between two merchants, the prominent Fustat merchant of Maghribī origin, Judah b. Moses ibn Sighmār, and his long-time *ṣuḥba* colleague, Abraham al-Raḥbī. The object of their business deal was a large piece of ambergris belonging to Judah, half of which he sold to al-Raḥbī, while retaining ownership of the other half. Al-Raḥbī set out for Syria to sell the entire undivided but jointly owned chunk of ambergris, the whole evidently being more valuable than the sum of its parts (and probably impossible physically to divide, anyway). The terms of their agreement appear to have been ambiguous—or, at least, confusing. While Judah claimed that it was a partnership, he also asked al-Raḥbī to "do a service for me with the part of it that is on my own personal account" (*yakhdumunī bi-mā yakhuṣṣunī*), employing the technical vocabulary of reciprocal agency. In 1085, after ten years of trying unsuccessfully to get what he considered to be his due from his elusive, itinerant business associate, Judah went into action. While sojourning in Alexandria, he heard that al-Raḥbī was in Fustat. He decided to challenge him through a proxy legal agent in the capital, the well-respected *parnas*, or charity administrator, Eli b. Yaḥyā. Eli was to try first to obtain a settlement out of court (*bi-lā moshav*, "without a session [of the court]"; *moshav* is Hebrew for the Arabic *majlis*); if that failed, he was to sue al-Raḥbī in the Jewish court under the laws of partnership, imposing an oath called *al-yamīn 'alā adā' al-amāna*, "the oath on fulfillment of the trust." As an agent, al-Raḥbī would have been immune from prosecution and from an oath, since *ṣuḥba*-agency (unlike partnership) did not fall under Talmudic law. We don't know whether and how this dispute was resolved.

Out-of-court settlements were not uncommon. There is evidence, for instance, in the responsa for North Africa, Judah ibn Sighmār's original home, of Jewish merchant sessions where disputes were arbitrated; presumably, the settlement was then brought before the Jewish judge for ratification.[69] Geniza court records of disputes between partners reveal that, on occasion (and doubtless more often than the documents indicate), rather than prolonging the litigation and waiting for a decision of the court, "honest and upright elders" (*ziqnei yosher ve-kosher*) stepped in to act as arbitrators.[70] It is likely that the same was done out of court when two parties came into conflict over agency arrangements, which, by nature, would not have left a paper trail. If al-Raḥbī refused to arbitrate (thinking, for instance, that, as an agent, his behavior could not be challenged in court), Eli was to summon him to the *beit din* for a formal hearing and judicial decision (*dīn*), after being required as a "partner" to swear "the oath on fulfillment of the trust." What exactly this oath was will be discussed in Chapter 6. The ambiguity surrounding their business relationship—was it a partnership or an agency association?—is precisely the type of uncertainty that, as I shall argue below (Chapter 6, section 6.3), led Maimonides to amend the halakha so as to subject a commercial agent to the same oath of probity that the Mishna prescribed for a partner.

Maimonides was fully aware of the central role that the *ṣuḥba* system, with its emphasis on *khidma*, "service," played in Jewish mercantile life. He declared its distinction from partnership in the very title and organization of his Laws of Agents and Partners. As we have seen, too, he explicitly mentions *khidma* as a type of commercial cooperation in his Mishna Commentary, in connection with the halakha regarding a wife's conjugal rights (Chapter 2, section 2.5 above). The *ṭayyalin*, who have a daily conjugal obligation, are, Maimonides says, "those who live an easy and restful life and do not engage in commerce or in doing a service" (*alladhīna lā yatjurūna wa-lā yakhdumūna*). Here the word *yakhdumūna* patently refers to the specific type of agency, based on reciprocal service (*khidma*), and differing from partnership (subsumed under the term *yatjurūna*).

## 5.13 Informality and Ambiguity in Commercial Cooperation: Three Cases from Maimonides' Responsa

Maimonides came face-to-face with the problem of informality and ambiguity in his role as jurisconsult. We may imagine that these cases and others like them are among the reasons that prompted him to seek a halakhic solution in his Code to the lacuna in Talmudic halakha regarding enforcement of commercial agency. This recalls Hallaq's theory that legal change in Islam originated with *fatwās* issued by *muftīs*, and, in turn, transformed by "author-jurists" into changes in normative law. In Maimonides' case, *mufti* and "author-jurist" were combined in one and the same person.

### *5.13.1 An Illustrative Case That Came Before Him Concerns a Dispute over a "Consignment" (*Risāla*)*

*Risāla*, it will be recalled, is one of the terms used to describe *ṣuḥba*-agency. The *risāla*, in this case, entailed a consignment of merchandise that a trader had entrusted to his brother in Egypt before leaving for India. After a nine-year absence, on the point of death in India, the owner directed in his will that the money he had with him be delivered to his brother back home. He then died. Back in Egypt, the India trader's brother wished to use proceeds from the sale of the *risāla* to reimburse himself for the nine years of poll-tax payments that he had made on behalf of his absent sibling. But, characteristic of such informal arrangements, no contract had been written that might have stipulated the disposition of these goods should the traveling merchant never return. Maimonides ruled that the surviving brother might reimburse himself for the poll-tax payments but not from the *risāla*, which, in that economic universe, belonged privately to his India trader brother and hence to the latter's heirs after his death. Maimonides decided that the brother must limit himself to any other money of his brother's that the latter had sent from India.[71]

### *5.13.2 Another Case, Also Involving an India Trader and the Nature of a Business Collaboration, Describes a Dispute That Arose When Reports Reached Home That the Merchant Had Died in a Shipwreck*

The stationary partner who had given the merchant money as a *qirāḍ* investment claimed recompense from the dead man's children, who were his heirs. They rejected the partner's demand that they bring proof that their father had died. Rather, they insisted that the claimant himself prove that their father was still alive—simply late in returning home—and, if their father still possessed some of the stationary partner's goods, he should make a claim in court. The whole case hinged on the nature of the partnership, which was ambiguous. If it had been a Talmudic *'isqa*, the traveling merchant would have borne some responsibility for losses; if it had been an Islamic *qirād* (*commenda*), he would have been relieved of liability, and all the money would have gone to his heirs.

Maimonides' responsum shows his awareness of the ambiguity. "The orphans are not obligated to prove anything. If the investor proves that [the father of the orphans] is dead and he possesses a *qirāḍ* contract attested by Jewish witnesses [meaning that it was a Talmudic *'isqa*, not an Islamic *commenda*] and also proves that the deceased possessed goods [at his death], [the case] should be decided according to the terms of the contract. But as long as he cannot prove that the man has died, he has no claim whatsoever."[72]

### *5.13.3 Ambiguity Leading to Litigation Between Two Merchants Who Disagreed About the Terms of Their Business Collaboration Underlies a Fascinating Pair of Responsa Submitted to Maimonides*

The queries, which reached Maimonides' desk consecutively, are a bit difficult to follow at first sight. They use the conventional pseudonyms, Reuben and Simeon, but, confusingly, the names are reversed in each version. To avoid misunderstanding, in what follows I shall refer to the stationary merchant as A and the traveling merchant as B.[73]

We learn first that A gave B one and one-third *qinṭārs*, about 133 *raṭls*, amounting to about the same number of our modern pounds, of Indian indigo, a common commodity dealt in by the Geniza traders. He was to sell the indigo in Sicily. According to the first query, "A [the stationary merchant] said to the other [B, the traveling merchant]: 'Take this with you.' But at the time, they were not exact about the matter, nor did either impose any stipulations on the other. B's assumption was that he was fulfilling a request [*ḥāja*] for A without having a share in the profit, but he did not say this explicitly."[74]

B employs the "vocabulary of reciprocity," describing his understanding of the deal as typical *ṣuḥba*-agency. In this kind of arrangement, as we have seen, one party fulfilled a *ḥāja* or a *khidma* on behalf of the other, without remuneration and without responsibility in case of loss, but in expectation of benefiting from a reciprocal favor from the other merchant sometime in the future.

As described vividly in the first version of the story, the ship on which the active merchant (B) sailed was attacked en route by pirates. The unfortunate trader was captured, and the pirates seized the goods that he was transporting—goods that were his own as well as goods belonging to others. Some of the merchandise, he says, was held as *qirāḍ*. Owing to the ambiguity of that term, it could have been either a Talmudic *ʿisqa*, in which the active merchant shared in both profit and loss, or an Islamic *commenda*, in which the traveler bore no responsibility for loss.

After redeeming himself from captivity, luckless B returned home, and for sixteen years, none of the people who had entrusted him with merchandise made any claims against him, "knowing what had befallen him." But he eventually had a falling out with A over some unstated matter, and the latter sued him for the value of the indigo, claiming that B had purchased it from him for 42 dinars (on credit)[75] and still owed him the money as an outstanding debt.

The traveling merchant defended himself with the following testimony, quoted verbatim in the second question submitted to Maimonides: "Some sixteen years ago, I had occasion to travel to Sicily. A had 1 1/3 *qinṭārs* of indigo that had cost him 37 1/3 dinars. He gave them to me without indicating the stipulations (*setam*), and I was not sure whether he intended it to be a *commenda* (*qirāḍ*) or a 'consignment' (*risāla*), and, if a *commenda*, whether it was according to Islamic law [*ḥukm al-goyim*] or Jewish law [*ḥukm al-yahūd*]. But I am certain that I did not take it as a personal debt" (*fī l-dhimma*).[76]

The core of the problem lay in the ambiguity at the time the arrangement was made, since neither party had stated his intention explicitly. Sixteen years after the fact, one of them claimed that he had sold the indigo to the traveler on credit and that he still owed him the money; sixteen years after the fact, the traveling merchant stated that he had been given the indigo to carry out a "request" (*ʿalā annahu yaqḍī fīhi al-ḥāja*) for the owner, meaning that he was doing a business favor on agency and hence had no responsibility for the loss.

Maimonides begins his first responsum by invoking an epistemic concept in Islamic jurisprudence and substantive law. "These obscure matters conducted without verbal explicitness nonetheless bear circumstantial indications [*qarāʾin*] and insinuations [*talwīḥāt*] that make explicit clarification unnecessary, but the halakha [*al-fiqh*] cannot determine precisely what those indications are. It is a matter between the person and his Creator."[77]

*Qarīna* (plural, *qarāʾin*), a term from Islamic jurisprudence, means a circumstantial or contextual indication that clarifies an ambiguous legal statement.[78] Maimonides employs this term from Islamic law to explain how business collaboration of the "informal" variety regularly practiced by Jewish merchants could, or at least ought to, be clarified by the parties. Since in this case, however, A and B could not agree on the intended terms of their commercial arrangement, Maimonides goes on to explain that the dispute can be resolved only by oaths. The traveling merchant should swear that the arrangement had been based not on purchase of the indigo and not on profit/loss basis but on agency (*risāla*), and that he assumed that his counterpart had intended the same thing. Or he could shift the burden of proof (the oath) onto the stationary investor by having him swear that he had sold him the indigo and was still owed the money. Since these business arrangements depended on the custom of the merchants, Maimonides makes the point that there was nothing in Jewish halakha (which he calls by the Arabic name for jurisprudence, *fiqh*) that could decide the matter. Since people were wary of swearing oaths, lest they, even if inadvertently, perjure themselves before God, Maimonides hoped that the oath would bring out the truth. Unfortunately, we do not know how the dispute was resolved.

This pair of responsa and the episode that they dramatically depict highlight the limits of informality. No system, not the least a commercial system in which investments, profits, and losses, often amounting to large sums, are at stake, can function successfully with ambiguity. This ambiguity is normally overcome with a written contract. As their business correspondence abundantly shows, however, the Geniza merchants more often than not collaborated without written contracts. They decided the terms orally, sometimes amplified or modified in letters, and, especially in the case of *ṣuḥba*-agency, they relied upon trust and anticipated reciprocity. Normally, however, they knew, and mutually acknowledged, the parameters of the arrangement, even if through informal assumptions, statements, or gestures, as Maimonides explains. When this failed to define the terms of business association to the satisfaction of all parties, Jewish law had rather limited ability to resolve the disagreement. In such a case, the parties might end up in litigation before the Muslim *qāḍī*. Maimonides, who, as we shall see (in Chapter 9), frowned upon this solution, codified an ingenious halakhic reform to forestall Jewish resort to Islamic courts in commercial agency disputes, which, as he knew firsthand from cases like the ones that we have just discussed, often resulted from ambiguity or misunderstanding. This halakhic reform is the subject of Chapter 6.

# Chapter 6

# *Ṣuḥba*-Agency in the Code

## 6.1 Monitoring Commercial Agents' Honesty: Contract Enforcement and the Halakha

With his merchant background and his experience as a jurisconsult, Maimonides was fully aware of the ambiguities that complicated relations between merchants when they were unsure, or disagreed about, whether their commercial collaboration consisted of a partnership or a *ṣuḥba*, and if the former, what type of partnership. He was, further, cognizant of the fact that the interdenominational custom of the merchants tended to collapse differences between Muslims and Jews in the marketplace, breaking down barriers and encouraging Jewish merchants to rely on the Islamic judicial system in order to ensure that agents acted honestly, or to adjudicate disagreements. Finally, mindful of the fact that the Talmud lacked a means of enforcing *ṣuḥba* arrangements, he took a bold step in the Code to accommodate *ṣuḥba*-agency within the framework of the halakha. His intention, I contend, was to provide Jewish traders with an equivalent alternative to the Islamic judicial system and thereby to stem the tide of what, in his eyes, represented a defection from Jewish law and from the authority of the autonomous Jewish community.

Maimonides was not the first Jewish legist to seek a halakhic solution to this lacuna in the Talmud; he was preceded in this by Saadya Gaon in the tenth century and perhaps by Hayya Gaon in the eleventh. But it was Maimonides who took the bold step of creating a new halakhic category of commercial agency law to accommodate the non-Talmudic merchant custom.

## 6.2 *Ṣuḥba*-Agency in the Code

The very first halakha in Laws of Agents and Partners (1:1) categorically defines and codifies commercial agency, describing it in terms that perfectly fit the real-life practice of *ṣuḥba*-agents, as depicted in the Geniza. The passage represents a substantial elaboration of the Talmudic sources identified by the commentators, which stem from marriage and divorce law. "If one says to his agent [*sheluḥo*], 'Go out and sell a piece of land for me, or movables,' or 'Buy these for me,' then the latter is empowered to buy and sell and to perform his agency mission [*sheliḥuto*], and all his actions pertaining thereto are valid."

Lest anyone think, as many Jews doubtless did, that this form of agency required formal acts stipulated in the Talmud for partnerships, such as writing a contract, or the symbolic act of acquisition (*qinyan*), or witnessing the transaction, Maimonides goes on in the same halakha to explain: "He who appoints an agent [*shaliaḥ*] does not need to ratify the appointment by a *qinyan*, nor does he need witnesses thereto. Oral agreement [*ba-amira*] alone is sufficient; witnesses are necessary only as evidence in case one of them makes a denial, as is the rule in all pleas."[1]

Oral agreement without the formal halakhic, judicial procedures required in other transactions was already in vogue among Jews during the Gaonic period. Libson attributes these exceptions to Talmudic procedure to a desire on the part of the Geonim to foster "the stability and regularity of commercial life, at the same time creating uniformity in the world of international trade."[2] To this we may add that oral, face-to-face communication in that society, both Jewish and Islamic, was, at least as a theoretical postulate, more highly valued than written agreement, despite the increased availability of paper in the period that coincides with the vast hoard of letters and other written material from the classical Geniza period.[3]

Given the absence of written contract in *ṣuḥba*-agency and the lack of a halakhic provision for judicial enforcement, and given the coexistence of agency and partnership as modes of commercial cooperation in the merchant community, Maimonides turned his attention to the Mishnaic "oath of partners" (*shevuʿat ha-shutafin*). This oath was used to confirm honesty and trustworthiness in a case concerning monetary matters where there was a possibility, however slight, of malfeasance or cheating by one of the partners. The underlying halakha (Mishna Shevuʿot 7:8) lists five people who, as summarized by Maimonides in Agents and Partners 9:1 on the basis of rabbinic sources, "must take an oath enjoined by rabbinic law, even if the claim is based only on a possibility that he stole from the other person in his business dealings or was not careful with the accounts they had between them." The five are: (1) partners (*shutafin*), (2) sharecroppers (*arisin*), (3) guardians (*apoṭropin*) (people appointed by the court to care for orphans), (4) a wife who transacts business in the house, and (5) a person called, enigmatically, "the son of the house" (*ben ha-bayit*).

What these five have in common is explained with lucidity by Maimonides: "These are prone to reason that whatever they take from the property of the owner is rightfully due them, inasmuch as they carry out the business and do the work. The Sages have provided therefore that they should be required to submit to an oath, even if the claim against them is based only on a possibility, in order that they perform all their work properly and in good faith" (*be-ṣedeq ve-emuna*).[4]

Who, however, is the enigmatic "son of the house" of the Mishna? The Talmud, in a baraita in the Gemara (Shevu'ot 48b), explains that he is "not someone who frequents the home of the householder [lit., 'walks in and out'] but rather someone who hires and dismisses laborers or buys and sells produce for him"—what we might call a farmer's foreman.

Oaths, as stated previously, whether prescribed in the Torah or extended by the rabbis of the Mishna to other cases such as the "partners' oath," were considered extremely grave because of the widely held belief that perjury, which the all-seeing God would, of course, uncover, would bring divine retribution upon the individual and even upon the entire community. The Geonim stipulated that the oath of partners was to be administered with solemnity while holding a scroll of the Torah. If the person swore that he had not acted dishonestly, his testimony was accepted.[5] If he refused to swear, those present would draw the necessary conclusion.

As explained earlier, the rabbis of the Talmud were reluctant to impose an oath on agents; an oath implied a measure of mistrust that could easily deter people from assuming agency assignments. The merchant-agent 'Ayyāsh b. Ṣadaqa, writing in the mid-eleventh century, complains to his counterpart, the prominent merchant Nahray b. Nissim, with whom he had a *ṣuḥba*, about "the oath which you have had me take."[6] With the proliferation of *ṣuḥba*-agency in the Geniza period, however, occasions for suspecting business agents of misconduct multiplied. A means was needed to assure agent compliance, what economists call "contract enforcement." Maimonides found those means by making an agent susceptible to the same exculpatory oath as a partner.

He did this through a bit of ingenious exegesis, drawing an analogy between the "son of the house" of the Mishna, as understood by the Gemara, and the commercial agent. He begins in Agents and Partners 9:4, adopting the Talmud's agrarian-based definition of "son of the house," repeating its language verbatim. This person, like a true partner or a sharecropper, is required to pronounce an oath while holding a holy object (*bi-nqiṭat ḥefeṣ*), if suspected of dishonesty. In the very next halakha (9:5), however, Maimonides, using analogy, introduces a new law, extending the "oath of partners" to include commercial agents. "If a man consigns something to another on agency [*meshalleaḥ*, from *shaliaḥ*, 'agent'] to sell, or if he consigns him money on agency [*shalaḥ*] to buy him produce or merchandise [*seḥora*], *even if he does not pay him for this* [*work*] *and he has no share in the profits or any benefit from this agency mission* [*sheliḥut*], *inasmuch as the latter does business with the money of the other person, he is like a 'son of the house.'* Therefore, he can require him to take an oath, based on an uncertain claim [*mi-safeq*] that he has not robbed him while bringing him the merchandise he bought or part of it,[7] or the money for which he has sold [the merchandise] on his behalf."

Here, using analogical reasoning and inference ("*like* a 'son of the house'"), Maimonides expands the list of those subject to the partner's oath of innocence to include the commercial agent. Apart from the analogical marker "like," a subtle change of language signals this move. Whereas in halakha 9:4, as in the Talmud, Maimonides understands "son of the house" to be an agricultural employee who "buys or sells produce" (*perot*), halakha 9:5 describes an agent who receives "*money to buy for him merchandise* [*seḥora*] *or produce.*" He adds the word *seḥora*, which, elsewhere in the Mishneh Torah, he adopts when updating a rabbinic ruling written for an agricultural society (see above, Chapter 3).[8] Moreover, the agent (*shaliaḥ*) performs his assignment without compensation: "even if [the owner of the property] does not pay him for this [work] and [the agent] has no share in the profits or any benefit from this agency mission" (*sheliḥut*). In short, by analogizing between the "son of the house" and a commercial agent, Maimonides makes the latter subject to the same oath as the five Mishnaic candidates for the oath of partners. Like a partner or a sharecropper or any of the others, the *shaliaḥ*, if suspected of malfeasance, inaccurate reporting of accounts, or cheating—even if the suspicion is slight—can be required by the principal to swear to his honesty. The oath must affirm, Maimonides writes, "that he has not robbed [the principal] while bringing him the merchandise he bought or part of it, or the money for which he has sold [the merchandise] on his behalf."

I submit that Maimonides' depiction of the agent in halakha 9:5 constitutes a precise description of the unremunerated *ṣuḥba*-agent of the Geniza documents, who played such a vital role in long-distance commerce in the world in which the great jurist lived and whose legal problems he regularly met up with as a jurisconsult. Creatively employing analogy, he holds the uncompensated business agent liable to be subjected to the same oath of probity as the "son of the house" in the Mishna.[9] This use of analogy, it should be said, differs from the rabbinic technique of analogy based on the occurrence of similar lexical items in holy scripture, the *gezera shava* of biblical hermeneutics. It lies closer to the Islamic logical method of *qiyās*, "analogy," defined as "a new judicial source [that] responds to the need to find solutions not foreseen in the texts and to define rules applicable to new situations" and "a means of establishing a judicial ruling not provided for in the texts."[10]

By nesting this custom of the merchants smack in the middle of a string of Talmudic halakhot dealing with partnership and similar forms of business relations requiring an oath to establish credibility, Maimonides assimilated it to an older rabbinic concept. He, in effect, incorporated a custom of the Muslim and Jewish merchants into a larger Talmudic scheme, bringing the agent-"friend" into the halakhic fold. In a world in which formal and informal business arrangements existed side by side, often between the same merchants simultaneously, and in which, by consequence, the boundaries between partnership and agency were often blurred, this made perfect sense. It constitutes, therefore, yet another case where custom in the wider society served as a source of Jewish law.[11]

I have already alluded several times to a motive for Maimonides' novel halakha. The oath, which had to be taken in a Jewish court, afforded a comparable and equivalent alternative to resolving disputes in an Islamic tribunal, where there was no reluctance to impose oaths on agents, even on non-Muslims.[12] Furthermore, the oath-threat added a Jewish legal deterrent to the restraining force imposed by the prospect of forfeiting future business favors by tarnishing one's reputation. In other words, we may say that Maimonides recognized and sought to solve the problem of "contract enforcement" inherent in a system that relied more on informal arrangements than on formal written contracts.

We have to consider the possibility that Maimonides engaged in *ṣuḥba*-agency in his own merchant life—with his brother, David. But, if so, he must consistently have played the role of stationary investor, with his brother acting as agent, running the family business of importing precious gems from

India. Maimonides' reciprocity would have been caring for his brother's family in Fustat, when the latter was away. This arrangement would explain how Maimonides could have made a living and still had time for his scholarship. His resort to the practice of medicine in the royal court in Cairo and at home in Fustat probably followed on the demise of the brothers' business consortium, when David died in a shipwreck around 1170. The work as professional physician taxed him greatly, as we know from a famous letter, but, to our good fortune, it did not prevent him from completing his Mishneh Torah and his Guide for the Perplexed.

## 6.3 A Gaonic Antecedent: Saadya Gaon's Halakhic Solution

Another possible way to have incorporated *ṣuḥba*-agency into the halakha would have been to resort to the Talmudic law of bailments. In fact, more than two centuries before Maimonides, Saadya Gaon chose precisely this route, subsuming *ṣuḥba*-agency under the halakha of the compensated bailee (*shomer sakhar*) by understanding the reciprocal agency services as a form of compensation. According to Talmudic halakha, the *shomer sakhar* can be required to take a judicial oath (*shevu'at ha-piqqadon*, "the oath of bailment") in court to acquit himself of responsibility for damage to or loss of the bailment put in his charge. In his Book of Bailment (*Kitāb al-wadī'a*), partially recovered from the Geniza by Robert Brody, Saadya writes: "The second example [of remunerated bailee, *shomer sakhar*] is when the depositor gives him a release from performing a task on his behalf *or when he promises him that he will perform a task for him* [in the future]."[13] This incidentally proves that Jews engaged in *ṣuḥba*-agency relations two hundred years before Maimonides, prior to the documentation in the Geniza—and, we may assume, even earlier.

Maimonides himself was not adverse to applying the law of bailments when it was relevant. We read, for instance, about a man who transported a *risāla* of pepper to be delivered to the owner's family in Alexandria. Instead, he sold the pepper and held on to the money. Confronted by the owner, he admitted violating his wishes and agreed to return the value of the pepper, which had since dropped in price, or to buy pepper at the deflated price. The court assented, but Maimonides reversed its decision and demanded full restitution, since the man had "stolen from a bailment" put into his trust.[14] What distinguishes this case from *ṣuḥba*-agency, however, is that the owner of the pepper had not intended that the man would serve as an agent, transacting business with the pepper, but simply as a bailee responsible for delivering the bailment—the shipment of pepper—intact to his family.[15]

The Jewish laws of bailment did not adequately serve the complexity of mutual service *ṣuḥba*-agency. Product of the largely sedentary and agrarian society of the Bible (Exod. 22:6–14) and elaborated in largely agrarian Palestine (especially Mishna Shevu'ot, chapter 8), the laws of bailment envisioned safekeeping of another person's money, goods, or animals. *Ṣuḥba*-agents did much more than hold property for safekeeping or receive items to deliver intact to a designated recipient. Rather, they were given goods or cash to buy and sell in accordance with the principal's verbal instructions, or to transact business "as they saw fit," an instruction found in many Geniza letters about agency.[16] Commercial agents traveled great distances, buying and selling, starting with the owner's property, striving to make a profit for the principal and to avoid loss. This far exceeded the mandate of the Talmud's bailee, who was simply asked to temporarily safeguard an item entrusted to his care.

Much more so than the owner of a bailment, Jewish merchants were rightfully concerned that unscrupulous *ṣuḥba*-agents, operating far from the immediate vicinity of the owner of the property, might act opportunistically, departing from the principal's instructions. The agent might travel to destinations not agreed upon or stray from the types of transactions that he was supposed to pursue on the owner's behalf. He might sell or purchase on credit without the owner's permission. A *ṣuḥba*-agent might even falsify accounts in ways that could prove difficult to trace or to challenge without a judicial means of enforcement.

Maimonides, who regularly rendered judicial opinions on commercial matters and understood the custom of the Jewish merchants very well, rejected Saadya's solution to the problem of agency enforcement via the laws of bailment.[17] On the other hand, both his solution, analogizing between the "son of the house" of the Mishna and the commercial agent, and the solution proposed by Saadya Gaon more than two centuries earlier, illustrate, perhaps better than any other example we have adduced in this study so far, how exogenous factors affected evolving Jewish law during the Islamic period. As we shall see below, Maimonides' own solution was taken by some later commentators to be a radical departure from the received legal tradition.[18]

## 6.4 The Oath on Fulfillment of the Trust: *Al-yamīn ʿalā adāʾ al-amāna*

There is other evidence, besides Saadya's halakhic solution, of evolving efforts before Maimonides' time to enforce agency obligations within the framework of Jewish law and the Jewish courts. One hint of this process is Hayya Gaon's responsum of 1015 to Gabes, Tunisia, discussed in Chapter 5, section 5.9, in which the Gaon prescribed an oath for a merchant, apparently acting as an agent, to back up his claim.

What was the oath to which Hayya was referring? Other Geniza documents establishing or dissolving partnerships mention an Arabic oath, *al-yamīn ʿalā adāʾ al-amāna*, "the oath on fulfillment of the trust." Merchants would agree to "fulfill the trust" when carrying out the terms of their partnership. Upon rendering accounts at the termination of a venture, one partner would release the other from all future claims, including the demand that he swear that he had fulfilled the trust (*amāna*) that underlay their collaboration.[19]

*Amāna* in Islamic law, Udovitch explains, "is a property attaching to a number of different contractual relationships, such as partnership, *commenda*, deposit, etcetera."[20] Jews in the tenth century were familiar with the concept. The Karaite Bible exegete Yefet b. Eli (latter half of the tenth century) understood its application in Islamic commercial law. Commenting on Hos. 2:22: "And I will espouse you with faithfulness [Hebrew, *emuna*, cognate of Arabic *amāna*], then you shall be devoted to the Lord," Yefet explains: "*Emuna* is one of the commandments set aside unto itself, intending thereby fulfillment of trust [*adāʾ al-amāna*] *and the employment of trust in purchase and sale and partnership* [*sharika*] *and testimony in rulings and so forth*."[21] The property of *amāna* described by Yefet is alluded to in the Code in Maimonides' rule that partners and, by analogous association, commercial agents, must carry out their duties "properly and in good faith" (*be-ṣedeq ve-emuna*).

In 1085, the "oath on fulfillment of the trust," described as a partner's oath, crops up in the legal action by Judah ibn Sighmār against Abraham al-Raḥbī.[22] A decade later, it figures in the lawsuit pitting the representative of the merchants in Fustat, Yequṭiel b. Moses, against his *agent*, the India trader Joseph al-Lebdī, a case first brought to light by Goitein.[23] This trial, which extended from November 1097 to the summer of 1098, left what Goldberg has aptly called "the longest paper trail in the Geniza."[24] Characteristic of the informal nature of agency relations, no written contract was offered into evidence during the proceedings. In a bid to settle at least some aspects of the dispute that brought them to the *beit din*, al-Lebdī and Yequṭiel were both asked at one of the court sessions to take an oath "on fulfillment of the trust" (*'alā adā' al-amāna*)—al-Lebdī in connection with his agency assignment and Yequṭiel in connection with property of al-Lebdī that he was sequestering in his warehouse. The oath, which was to be administered to the subjects while holding a Torah scroll, as stipulated by the Geonim, was postponed pending the arrival of further information from Aden.[25] In another, unrelated, legal matter concerning al-Lebdī as agent, the court again directed him to take "the oath on fulfillment of the trust" (*al-yamīn 'alā adā' al-amāna*).[26]

Goitein suggested identifying the Arabic oath in the Lebdī lawsuit with the Talmudic "bailee's oath" (*shevu'at ha-piqqadon*), evidently assuming, like Saadya, that this was the only halakhic oath that could possibly have been imposed in this instance.[27] Mordechai Friedman, editor of Goitein's posthumous book on the India trade, disagrees, citing a Geniza document in which a merchant forming a partnership vows to act honestly "regarding the obligation to act properly and to fulfill the trust [*luzūm al-ṣidq wa-adā' al-amāna*] in all my endeavors."[28] Friedman also mentions a fragment of a legal responsum (not from the India Book corpus) addressed to a merchant, apparently a contemporary of al-Lebdī, instructing him to take an oath "on fulfillment of the trust" (*'alā adā' al-amāna*). The rabbinic respondent explains that it is "similar to an oath prescribed by the Torah; there is no difference between them. Namely, one takes an oath while holding a Torah scroll, and thereby he satisfies the law in full."[29] Apparently, the recipient of this responsum was unfamiliar with the oath and its form, suggesting that the oath for a business agent was not (yet) an accepted feature of halakha in practice.

Friedman notes, further, that an oath with the name *'alā adā' al-amāna* is not found in any published treatise on Jewish law.[30] He proposes—correctly, in my view—that it be identified with the "oath of partners" of the Mishna (Shevu'ot 7:8), the *shevu'at ha-shutafin* discussed above. He points to an unpublished fragment of an unidentified Judaeo-Arabic legal monograph containing instructions for a guardian of orphans, one of those listed alongside the partner, the sharecropper, the woman doing business from her home, and the "son of the house" in the Mishna. The guardian in the unpublished manuscript page must "swear that he fulfilled the trust [*'alā annahu addā al-amāna*] in his duties." Friedman speculates, reasonably, that the fragment comes from one of the very partially preserved Gaonic legal monographs on judicial procedure."[31] He also suggests that the oath, given its Arabic title, "reflects Muslim usage."

In fact, the expression *adā' al-amāna* comes straight from the Qur'ān. "If you are on a journey and cannot find a scribe, then a security deposit should be handed over. But if you trust one another, let the trustee fulfill his trust, and let him fear God, his Lord [*falyu'addi l-ladhī 'tumina amānatahu walyattaqi l-lāha rabbahu*]. . . . And do not conceal testimony. Whoever conceals it is a sinner at heart. God is aware of what you do" (Sura 2:283). The verse is, further, echoed in Islamic legal terminology used to describe a type of partnership (*mufāwaḍa*) that was sanctioned by the Ḥanafī school of Islamic law. The phrase in the exact form, *adā' al-amāna*, appears in the "Book of Partnership" in the legal compendium *Kitāb al-aṣl*, by al-Shaybānī (d. 804 or 805), a resident of Iraq, where the yeshivot were situated, and one of the Ḥanafī school's founding fathers. "Fulfillment of the trust" and "fear of God" figure as necessary qualities for forming a partnership, according to Ṭaḥāwī (d. 933), in a formulary for creating a partnership.[32] *Adā' al-amāna* is also remarked upon by the eleventh-century Ḥanafī jurist al-Sarakhsī, in his mammoth commentary on Shaybānī's work. From Shaybānī's "Book of Partnership," Udovitch quotes a formula for such a partnership contract that is suggested by the author (note the echoes of Sura 2:283): "This is a document stating the agreement upon which X the son of Y and A the son of B entered into a partnership. They entered the partnership in a God-fearing manner and with *adā' al-amāna*," on which Sarakhsī comments: "This contract is a contract of *amāna*, the aim of which is the attainment of profits, and this is attained by the fear of God and fulfillment of the trust" (*adā' al-amāna*).[33] Wael Hallaq writes: "[A]ll jurists agree that, because fiduciary duty (*amāna*) is integral to any contractual partnership, partners do not bear liability for each other's property except when they commit negligence (*taqṣīr*) or cause damage through a fault of their own (*ta'addī*). Furthermore, the presumption of fiduciary duty does not require of partners more than *an oath (yamīn) with regard to the declaration of profits they made and the losses they incurred in conducting the business of the partnership*."[34]

Sources from the Geniza and elsewhere indicate that the Qur'ān-based concept of *al-yamīn 'alā adā' al-amāna* was taken over into Jewish judicial procedure and identified with the "oath of partners" imposed on the five individuals listed in Mishna Shevu'ot 7:8.[35] The oath referred to the quality of *amāna*, or "trust," that attached to different modes of business collaboration and for which a partner might be asked to swear in court that he had acted honestly, reporting losses and gains truthfully. The records of the Lebdī lawsuit and possibly Hayya Gaon's responsum of 1015 regarding the merchant of Gabes suggest that, in certain instances, the oath could be imposed on a commercial agent as well. In this regard, Friedman refers to another unpublished document mentioning a trader—seemingly acting as an agent, not a partner—who transported merchandise for a friend and who took an oath "that he sold them and fulfilled the trust concerning them" (*annahu abā'ahā wa-addā lahu al-amāna fīhā*).[36]

This kind of Jewish adoption of an Islamic term and concept had precedents. Gideon Libson has argued, for example, on the basis of comparison between Islamic and Jewish law as it evolved during the early Islamic period, that aspects of Islamic judicial procedure were adopted by Jewish jurists (the Geonim) to meet the needs of the new commercial economy. In support of this hypothesis, he discusses the example of the "oath of destitution" (*yamīn al-'adam*), an Islamic instrument used in assessing an impoverished debtor's assets, a legal procedure that has no basis in the Talmud.[37]

### *6.4.1 Migrating Terms, Migrating Law*

How did the oath *adā' al-amāna* "migrate" from Islam into Judaism? It is likely that this occurred through the same process that Libson has suggested for other Islamic customs: "One of the main channels of contact through which Islamic law could influence Jewish law, whether directly or indirectly, was through Jews having recourse to the Islamic courts." Libson argues, further, that Jewish legal authorities (the Geonim) "sought halakhic dispensations in line with the laws of the host society, enabling the Jewish courts to offer legal solutions similar to those obtainable under Islamic law."[38]

We may think of this as yet another example of cross-fertilization, or diffusion—what legal historians, following the coinage of Alan Watson, call a "legal transplant." In this case, the transplant, from Islamic judicial procedure into Jewish law, was facilitated by "migrating words and concepts."[39] It is not certain when the courts began to impose this oath on agents. The admittedly meager evidence of Hayya Gaon's responsum of 1015; the complaint around 1060 by 'Ayyāsh b. Ṣadaqa about "the oath" that his *ṣuḥba* associate, Nahray b. Nissim, had forced him to take; the "oath on fulfillment of the trust" that figured in the "tale of two merchants" (1085); and the appearance of the oath in the Lebdī lawsuit suggest that it was already available to the courts in the eleventh century, perhaps as early as the beginning of the century but at the latest, by the end.[40] If it nonetheless crops up so seldom in the Geniza or in responsa with regard to agency relations, this simply reflects the fact that commercial law as structured in the Talmud did not contemplate an institution with its properties and, most likely, that Jewish merchants settled their agency disputes out of court or resorted to Muslim courts to resolve quarrels.

On this understanding, Maimonides' ruling in Agents and Partners 9:5, subjecting the unremunerated *ṣuḥba*-agent to the same probative judicial procedure imposed on a partner, represents an effort to make normative the new and dominant form of commercial collaboration in the Islamic world within the structure of Talmudic legislation on partnership. It was meant to shore up the enforceability of unwritten agency contracts through the instrumentality of the Jewish courts, to place agency and partnership on a similar footing as regards court procedure, and to offer Jewish merchants and commercial agents a Jewish equivalent alternative to settling disputes in an Islamic court. Like a partner, the *ṣuḥba*-agent would hold a Torah scroll in the synagogue and swear to the fulfillment of his fiduciary duty, in Maimonides' words, "that he has not robbed [the principal] while bringing him the merchandise he bought or part of it, or the money for which he has sold [the merchandise] on his behalf."

## 6.5 Reactions to Maimonides' Ruling

None of the commentators on the Code could find a precise Talmudic source for Maimonides' ruling on an agent's liability for this oath; indeed, there is none. Seeking to provide an underpinning for the seemingly innovative halakhic rule, the fourteenth-century commentator Migdal 'Oz claims to have found a source for the ruling in a Gaonic responsum,[41] as does the commentator R. David ibn Abi Zimra (Radbaz), chief rabbi in Cairo during the first half of the sixteenth century, though he seems simply to be parroting Migdal 'Oz.[42] The responsum in question, however, as far as I have been able to determine, is not extant, unless Migdal 'Oz had in mind Hayya Gaon's responsum to Gabes of 1015.

There is some tentative basis for this assumption. A statement in Hayya Gaon's legal monograph on oaths, *Kitāb mukhtaṣar fī fiqh wujūb al-aymān* (known in Hebrew as *Mishpeṭei shevu'ot*), may contain an allusion to this. Explaining the Mishna of the partner's oath (Shevu'ot 7:8), Hayya defines "son of the house" in a commercial rather than an agricultural context, exemplifying him as follows: "He transacts business with the *money or goods* [*an yakūna mutaṣarrifan bi-māl aw bi-matāʿ*], as the rabbis said: 'the son of the house' spoken of is not someone who frequents the home of the householder but rather someone who buys and sells produce for him or hires and dismisses laborers."[43] R. Hayya also (purposefully?) reverses the order of the Talmudic definition of *ben ha-bayit*, placing "buys or sells produce" before "hires and dismisses laborers." Even if Hayya Gaon's responsum acted as a precedent for Maimonides, it took Maimonides to make the leap and create a whole new category in commercial halakha, analogous to, but differing from, partnership, namely, *ṣuḥba*-agency.

Halakha 9:5 in Laws of Agents and Partners met with stringent objection from R. Solomon ibn Adret (Rashba) (Barcelona, d. 1310), who firmly rejected Maimonides' analogy between the "son of the house" and an agent. If the Mishna had meant to teach such a novel ruling (*revuta'*), it would have used the word "agent" (*shaliaḥ*), Rashba opined. Concerned that the oath requirement would discourage people from serving as unpaid agents, Rashba adopted Rashi's definition. Rashi (R. Solomon b. Isaac, d. 1105) of Troyes, France, gives an explanation that is consistent with the agrarian world of the Talmud and also of the northern European Jewish society in which he lived. *Ben ha-bayit*, Rashi glosses, is a member of the family, "one of the brothers who takes care of the assets after their father's death."[44] For the same reason as Rashba, Radbaz felt that Maimonides' ruling was "somewhat problematic." He proposed to resolve the difficulty by asserting that the agent had the option of stipulating in advance that he be exempt from having to swear an oath.[45] Clearly, however, both he and Rashba considered Maimonides' ruling to represent an unsupportable departure from the law of the Talmud.[46] So did Joseph Caro in the sixteenth century. In his commentary on the Code (Kesef Mishneh), as well as in his Beit Yosef, he cites Rashba's objections approvingly and omits Maimonides' ruling from his own code, the Shulḥan 'Arukh, altogether.[47]

These responses underscore the problematic nature of *ṣuḥba*-agency for a legal system based on a less developed economy, the agrarian economy of the Talmud. From a theoretical standpoint, therefore, the instance at hand represents a clear-cut case of the divergence between law and society described by Alan Watson with respect to Roman and English law. At the same time, in keeping with Watson's speculation about the role of codification in reconciling differences between law and society, Maimonides the codifier updated the law with an amendment meant to absorb *ṣuḥba*-agency into the mainstream of halakha, using his best interpretative skills.

Rather than a radical innovation in Talmudic law, as the above-mentioned later commentators seem to have taken it, I suggest that Maimonides was codifying a procedure that had, over time, migrated from Islamic to Jewish legal procedure in the form of the "oath on fulfillment of the trust." He sought to "Judaize" this "legal transplant" from Islam, to give it legitimacy within the halakha, and to use it to enable Jewish courts to enforce informal (unwritten) contracts on reciprocal agency, the system that, as Goitein, Udovitch, Greif, and Goldberg have all described, was employed ubiquitously by the Geniza merchants.

Maimonides' ingenious extension of the "oath of partners" to include commercial agents, though taken by later authorities to be an unacceptable halakhic innovation, presumably represented, in his view, an alternative and more appropriate solution to the problem of contract enforcement than that of Saadya. Especially in view of the porous boundary between partnership and *ṣuḥba*-agency, a unified oath applying to partners and commercial agents alike would, in Maimonides' judgment, go a long way toward dealing with the ambiguity that often forced business collaborators into litigation and—all too frequently—via recourse to the Islamic court.

Though it failed to strike permanent roots in Jewish law, Maimonides' reform of the halakha of agency represents an exemplary case in which he deployed codification to close a gap—indeed, a wide gap—between Talmudic law and the society in which he lived.

### *6.5.1 Back to Greif*

Gaonic and Maimonidean efforts to find a place for *ṣuḥba*-agency within the framework of the halakha tend to support Avner Greif's opinion, quoted above in Chapter 5, that "the legal system failed to provide a framework within which agency relations could be organized." But his reasons—that "the court was usually unable to verify agents' claims and actions or to track down an agent who had emigrated" and that "[e]ven if an agent could be located, litigation was expensive and time-consuming"—overlook the more fundamental problem. *Ṣuḥba*-agency was simply unknown to Jews before the Islamicate commercial revolution. Pre-Islamic, Talmudic law had no mechanism to deal with this type of business collaboration, to enforce agents' "fulfillment of the trust" (*amāna*) and their honesty. But the solution that Greif offers—his economic model of a private-order closed consortium of Maghribī merchants—is unnecessary. Jewish *ṣuḥba* merchants might settle their differences out of court, through arbitration, as was proposed in the first instance by the merchant Judah ibn Sighmār in his claim against Abraham al-Raḥbī.[48] They might bring their dispute before the Jewish court if, in the absence of a written contract, they could summon witnesses to testify. They also had the option, which evidence suggests that they regularly exercised, to seek resolution of wrangles over agency relations in an Islamic court. There—even with the associated "court costs" (which the Geonim condoned as long as the costs were not bribes)—commercial agency (*ibḍā'*), the Islamic counterpart of *ṣuḥba*-agency, constituted a recognized, legal form of commercial collaboration, and there, a defendant's oath was considered sufficient to establish his innocence in a dispute between non-Muslims and even between a Jew and a Muslim.[49] These reasons, among others, would seem sufficient to explain the near-total absence in the Geniza of Jewish court documents containing legal judgments,[50] which is what led Greif, using econometrics, to propose his ingenious hypothesis and solution in the first place. If Jewish merchants relied on reputation and trust to assure agent dependability, as they most assuredly did, we should understand this as a response to the shortcoming of Talmudic commercial law that caused Jewish traders to resort to Islamic courts or to resolve disagreements through arbitration, a shortcoming that Maimonides attempted to rectify by extending the "oath of partners" to the *ṣuḥba*-agent.

## Chapter 7

# Proxy Legal Agency

### 7.1 The Rabbinic Power of Attorney—Proxy Legal Agency

As we have seen in the previous chapters, Maimonides updated, altered, or even, in the case of *ṣuḥba*-agency, innovated halakhot in order to accommodate the new commercial order. Nonetheless, where he felt it was appropriate or necessary to adhere to the Talmudic norm in the face of an economic "reform" by his rabbinic predecessors, he did not hesitate to oppose them. A clear example is his reversal of the Gaonic *taqqana* easing the operation of Talmudic proxy legal agency, an important tool of merchants in the Islamic world. As we shall see, he had good reasons for deferring to the ancient text.

This form of agency was embodied, as today, in a power of attorney, a document (Hebrew, *harsha'a*; Aramaic, *orakhta*) authorizing someone to act legally in the name of the principal, who, for one reason or another, was unable to represent himself in person. In the Talmudic period, a power of attorney would be assigned to an agent to carry out claims against a party holding an item belonging to the principal. The proxy agent acquired temporary ownership of the property, which he could then claim as a stand-in for the owner. By virtue of the power of attorney, he acted with the owner's complete authority, his every act considered as if it were being performed by the principal himself. A legal procedure was instituted whereby money on deposit—though not intangibles such as loans—could be conveyed as an adjunct of a land transfer (*aggav qarqa'*) as small as four cubits.[1] Debt collection was excluded because rabbinic law stipulates that one cannot sell or transfer property that is given with the expectation that it will be expended (*le-hoṣa'a nittena*); hence it lacks a physical existence (*ein adam maqneh davar she-lo ba' la-'olam*).

In the predominantly agrarian community of Talmudic Babylonia, this method worked well. In the dynamic, geographically widespread arena of Jewish business activity in the Islamic world, however, with money and other property needing to be collected at great distances, proxy legal agency needed greater flexibility. At the same time, fewer and fewer Jews owned agricultural property, at least in Gaonic Babylonia. That is why the Geonim in the ninth century ruled that a widow and her deceased husband's creditors could collect the debt due them from her husband's liquid assets ("movables"), as well as from his real estate.[2]

Since the Talmudic power of attorney, which assumed landownership—at least four cubits—no longer adequately served the needs of Babylonian Jewish society, the early Geonim instituted a further reform of the halakha to avoid situations in which people might incur financial loss if they could not lay claim through proxy agents to property that was in the hands of others. This legal change is called a *taqqana* in Maimonides' Code and in other Andalusian sources. It extended the Talmudic procedure for power of attorney (Arabic, *wakāla*) to claims involving cash, including debts. To accommodate the landless creditor, the Geonim allowed him to use the symbolic "four cubits of land owned by every Jew in the Land of Israel" for the adjunct land transfer.[3] In this way, Gideon Libson notes, "[t]he geonim . . . gave Jewish law a flexibility equal to that of Islamic legal practice, which permitted considerable leeway in the recovery of debts and appointment of agents. Jews were thus able to emulate their Muslim neighbors in the laws governing commercial transactions involving money (*mu'āmalāt*), and the result was a uniform practice."[4]

Maimonides knew this Gaonic innovation very well. By his own time, it was in regular and constant use throughout the Mediterranean and on the India route, for movable commodities, including money on deposit, which the Talmud allowed, as well as for debts, which it did not. The Geniza documents, plentiful from the beginning of the eleventh century, bear ample witness to this.

Maimonides was not wholly at peace with the Gaonic deviation from the law of the Talmud.[5] He insisted that the agency arrangement be based on actual, not fictitious, landed property, as the Talmud prescribes, and he frowned upon collection of debts by proxy altogether—again, in keeping with the Talmudic restriction. In this case, therefore, Maimonides appears to be a legal conservative, out of pace with society and its economic needs, confirming Alan Watson's main thesis about the inertia of private law. As we shall see, however, things are not so simple.

The Code states (Laws of Agents and Partners 3:7; the subdivisions of this long halakha are my own):

> [a] If one has money deposited with another and he wishes to authorize a proxy agent [*le-harshot shaliaḥ*] to obtain it for him, then ratification by a *qinyan* is of no avail here because current coin cannot be acquired by symbolic barter. What, then, does he do? He gives the agent a piece of land of the smallest dimensions, and he transfers title to the money by dint of land, in order that he may obtain the money with this power of attorney. He then goes and takes the man to court in order to get the money.
>
> [b] If one has a loan with another, he cannot write a power of attorney for it, even if the debt is supported by a deed, because a loan is given with the expectation that it will be expended and one cannot transfer title to a thing that lacks a physical existence. He therefore has no other way by which to transfer title to his loan unless it was done in the presence of all three parties, which is a law without a [legal] reason, as we have already explained, or by transferring the deed of the indebtedness itself by writing it and handing it over, because he thus transfers the lien that is in the deed. Such is the rule as it seems to me from the Gemara.

In passage [a], Maimonides summarizes the Talmudic principle. Property can be transferred through a power of attorney if it is linked to transfer of ownership of even a tiny plot of land. In the second passage [b], the codifier repeats the Talmudic rule that proxy transfer does not apply to loans because it is expected that a loan will be expended and, lacking a physical existence, it cannot be transferred.

Next (passage [c]), Maimonides cites the Gaonic innovation, giving their rationale about the adverse impact that the inability to collect loans from borrowers located in a remote place would have on the economy. But he dismisses their ruling as "tenuous and weak."

> [c] The Geonim, however, have ordained [*tiqqenu*] that we do permit a power of attorney even for a loan, lest everyone take the other's money and go to another country. They have further ordained that if one designates a power of attorney to obtain the

> money that he has with another or to sue the other for a loan, and he has no land [by dint of which to transfer ownership of this debt to the agent], he can transfer to him four cubits of land from his share in the Land of Israel, and transfer title to the money to [the proxy agent] by dint of that land. These enactments are tenuous and weak, for who can say he has a share in the Land of Israel? Even if he is entitled to such a share, it is not in his possession.

## 7.2 Why Did Maimonides Dismiss the Gaonic Reform?

Maimonides shows full awareness here of the economic reasons behind the Gaonic innovation, namely, the prevalence of long-distance commerce, with its heavy reliance on credit; and the decline of landownership in the Jewish community in Iraq in the early Islamic period. Why, then, does he frown upon using the legal fiction in a power of attorney that, in his own day, served such a vital function in Jewish trade?

One of the Ashkenazic glossators on the Mishneh Torah, R. Meir b. Yequṭiel ha-Kohen of Rothenburg (1260–1298), student of his namesake, R. Meir of Rothenburg, evidently unsettled by Maimonides' dismissal of the Gaonic fiction, sought a classical rabbinic text to back up the codifier's rejection. In his Haggahot Maimuniyot, printed in the margins of the standard edition of the Code, he purports to have found precedents in the Talmud for Maimonides' statement that the land "is not in his possession." But his justification of Maimonides' position begs the main question, for the cases in the Talmud that he adduces envision landownership that was real, as opposed to the fictional artifice of the Geonim. Unsurprisingly, in light of the economic realities of his own Christian milieu, Haggahot Maimuniyot says nothing about Jewish ownership of land in Ashkenaz, because it was quite rare, owing to the nature of feudal agricultural holdings, with its required Christian oath of fealty, or because ownership of urban property was difficult for Jews, if not impossible.

## 7.3 Land Ownership in Maimonides' Egypt and in al-Andalus

Another explanation for Maimonides' seemingly stubborn stance suggests itself—an explanation that, like the Gaonic innovation itself, is rooted in the economic circumstances of the Islamic world. In Egypt, Jewish ownership of land, particularly urban real estate, was quite common, as the Geniza documents abundantly attest.[6] Maimonides' responsa contain questions mentioning houses or parts of houses possessed by Jews, as well as stores, sometimes shared with Muslim business partners.[7] Jews frequently rented apartments in courtyard houses to or from other Jews and even rented to Muslims, though the latter activity was frowned upon because such cohabitation was often a cause of inconvenience and friction arising from the clash of Jewish and Islamic religious laws and customs—for instance, the stricter requirement in Islam of female veiling.[8] Sales of urban property are also documented in the responsa, as they are in the Geniza.[9]

Jews bequeathed and inherited apartments and donated entire houses to the community as pious trusts, *heqdesh* or *qodesh* in Hebrew, similar to *waqf* bequests in the Islamic community (the Jews used the Arabic word as well). Rents from these properties supported various communal needs, such as upkeep of the synagogue, salaries of communal officials and teachers of orphans, payments to Muslim officials, and direct charity.[10] In Maimonides' homeland, agriculturally rich al-Andalus, Jews still worked the land in the eleventh and twelfth centuries. In short, in Maimonides' world, actual Jewish ownership of real property often rendered the Gaonic artifice unnecessary.

## 7.4 The Geniza Evidence

What do we find "on the ground" among the Geniza documents? The Geniza contains an abundance of actual powers of attorney, which ended up "buried" there after the proxy agent had completed his designated mission.[11] These were issued for collection of claims of both tangible commodities and cash, the latter including proceeds from partnership enterprises—in actuality, debts owed by the active party to the stationary investor. But the vast majority of these documents follow the Gaonic accommodation, employing the fictional four cubits of land in the Land of Israel. Only a few (even if they are representative of a larger number than the ones preserved) refer to actual, owned property, in keeping with the Talmud and with the strictures expressed in Maimonides' Code. They utilize such phrases as "four cubits of my land," or "four cubits of land from my compound in Fustat, Egypt,"[12] or "four cubits in my courtyard."[13] The power of attorney of 1085 in which the merchant Judah b. Moses ibn Sighmār appointed the Fustat *parnas* Eli b. Yaḥyā as his proxy legal agent in his claim against his elusive partner (or agent) Abraham al-Raḥbī, uses the realistic, as opposed to the fictitious, formula.

By the eleventh century, however, as the vast majority of the Geniza powers of attorney shows, the Gaonic device was firmly implanted in legal procedure, despite the widespread ownership of urban real estate by Jews and, in places like al-Andalus, of agricultural land. The predominance of powers of attorney using the Gaonic artifice might be explained by the fact that many who actually owned property used the formula "four cubits of land from my share in the Land of Israel" either out of the habit of scribes, who relied on "published" formularies, written by or dependent upon the Geonim,[14] or to avoid the possibility that an unscrupulous agent might actually claim permanent ownership of their property if they stipulated real rather than "fictional" property, since the halakha required that the parcel of land be given to the agent as an outright gift.[15]

In returning to the law of the Talmud, in this case, Maimonides was likely also influenced by the fact that the Talmudic formula was still in vogue in his agriculturally rich, native al-Andalus. The wording of powers of attorney in formularies from Spain could have stood as a precedent for his ruling against the Gaonic device.[16] His seemingly stubborn rejection of the Gaonic procedure should be seen, therefore, not simply as reluctance to grant that every Jew possessed symbolic property in the Land of Israel—his stated rationale. It should be understood, too, as encouragement to fellow Jews to stick to Talmudic principle when traditional legal structures adequately served current social or economic conditions. In other words, his conservatism in this matter was not a product of "inertia," in Watson's words (a resistance to change), but a conscious attempt to make contemporary practice—Jewish property ownership—consistent with halakha, to bring law and society together where there was no conflict between them.

## 7.5 The Status of the Land of Israel and Jewish Land Ownership

It cannot be ruled out that Maimonides was also concerned about the change in the political status of the Land of Israel following the Crusader conquest in 1099. In his time, Palestine, where he and his family stayed for about a year after leaving Almohad Morocco and before settling permanently in Egypt,[17] was Christian territory; it would not be repatriated for Islam until Saladin's reconquest in 1187, a decade after Maimonides completed the Code. Unlike the Muslim rulers of Palestine, who allowed Jews to own property, the European invaders hailed from places where Jews normally were not able to do so. Under these circumstances, and despite the rabbinic principle that "land cannot be stolen,"[18] the universal claim of Jews to ownership of "four cubits of land" in Palestine must have seemed weak—even untenable—so that the Gaonic device could not, in any event, be utilized. This possibility seems to underlie Maimonides' insistence at the end: "Even if he is entitled to such a share, it is not in his possession."[19]

If, then, at first glance, the halakha of power of attorney in the Mishneh Torah shows Maimonides to be a conservative legist, steadfastly adhering to ancient law in the face of economic transformations, even to the point of reversing a "progressive" innovation of the Geonim—therewith confirming Watson's main thesis about legal inertia—this is only partially true. Maimonides was, in fact, quite attentive to economic realities: Jewish ownership of land in his Andalusian homeland and in his new home in Egypt, and perhaps also the political reality of Crusader occupation of Palestine. The Gaonic device, necessary in the early Islamic period in Iraq, when fewer and fewer Jews possessed land (for economic, not legal, reasons), was unnecessary for Jewish owners of landed property in Maimonides' Egypt and in his Spanish homeland. Social and economic circumstances in Egypt and Spain were different from early Islamic Iraq, and thus, in this specific case, the law of the Talmud could and should be upheld.

## 7.6 A Maimonidean Loophole

It is all the more surprising, therefore, that, at the end of this very long halakha, Maimonides seems to back off from his categorical rejection of the Gaonic innovation. He qualifies it as follows:

> [d] The Geonim themselves, who enacted this *taqqana*, declared that we do not say, "Let the law cut through the mountain" [a rabbinic metaphor meaning, roughly, that the law in question was "engraved in stone"] but that it was enacted only to intimidate the party who is sued; that if he consent to argue the case in court and to give the agent the money on the strength of the power of attorney, it will be discharged because an agent with this weak power of attorney is no worse than an agent who is appointed in

> the presence of witnesses. If, however, the man sued does not wish to argue the case with him in court, he may not be compelled to pay or to swear an oath until his counterparty himself appears. They also ruled that if one has made a loan to another, whether with a note of debt or with a *qinyan* before witnesses, then even if he denies it in court, a power of attorney can be issued against him because this constitutes denial of mortgaged property. But if it is a loan made orally that he denies, they did not enact that a power of attorney be issued for it.

After asserting earlier (section [c]) that "these enactments are tenuous and weak," why does Maimonides seem here to leave the door open? I submit that this, too, reflects contemporary realities: the ubiquitous reliance on credit as a means of investment; the frequent, long, and distant separation of investors from partners or from agents; and the recurrent need to resort to proxy legal agents to collect debts or reclaim merchandise.[20]

Maimonides was as aware as any other member of a merchant family of the essential role that credit played in investment. In one of his responsa, he answered a query about the practice of *ṣabr* (lit., "patience"), namely, deferred payment for a commodity at a higher price. This was a veiled form of interest that Muslims also employed.[21] Showing pragmatic attentiveness to merchant custom and to the need for credit that seemingly violated the biblically rooted halakha forbidding usurious transactions between Jews, Maimonides ruled that this *ṣabr* should be countenanced because "it is the custom common in business transactions between people, and without it, most types of livelihood would come to a standstill."[22] As we have seen (in Chapter 2), Maimonides ruled in the Code that a partner might sell on credit items for which it was customary to do so.

The great codifier's realistic pragmatism in the matter of proxy agency for collecting debts comes out in his response to a query about a creditor who wished to use a proxy agent to reclaim moneys owed him. Maimonides expressed his principled disapproval: "power of attorney is objectionable" (*madhmūm*). However, he goes on to say, an exception could be made in case of necessity (*ḍarūra*)—for instance, when the parties were in different cities, or when the claimant was ill. In the absence of such extenuating circumstances, however, a power of attorney to collect debts was forbidden.[23]

## 7.7 Realistic Flexibility

Here, then, we seem to have a reasonable explanation for the loophole in the law of proxy legal agent in the Code. Whether a trading arrangement operated as a true Talmudic *'isqa* or as an Islamic-type *qirād* (*commenda*); whether a merchant was owed money for items sold for deferred payment at an inflated price; or, as was common, a merchant enlisted the services of a *ṣuḥba*-agent to engage in long-distance trade on his behalf—claims requiring a power of attorney arose on a regular basis. These claims often concerned money owed (debts). It is not far-fetched to conclude that Maimonides built a loophole into the Code to allow the use of the power of attorney based on the Gaonic artifice, provided, as his language suggests, that it was used within limits, as a means of "intimidating" recalcitrant debtors to fulfill their obligations voluntarily.

Here, in a nutshell, lies the reality behind Maimonides' presentation of the law of legal agency in the Code. He objected in theory to the Gaonic fiction, especially where it was unnecessary—where people owned land and could and therefore should abide by the Talmudic procedure. But he knew from vast personal experience that, in practice (as the Geniza attests), Jews regularly used the device out of "necessity" in the mobile world of local and long-distance commerce. We are witness, therefore, to a jurist who, like many Islamic jurists during the formative period of Islamic law, employed a flexible and realistic approach, paying careful attention to the custom of the merchants in order to bring law and society into harmony.

# Chapter 8

# Sale and Contract

We have now seen from his method of codification that Maimonides was acutely attuned to the realities of the Islamicate marketplace: the extensive mobility of merchants; their modes of commercial cooperation, including the popular form of reciprocal commercial agency (*ṣuḥba*-agency); the interfaith business cooperation between Jews and Muslims; the use of credit as a means of investment; the urge on the part of merchants to work on the intermediate days of the festival; the wide use of proxy agency to collect debts or to deal with business associates; and, in general, the "custom of the merchants."

In this chapter, we examine Maimonides' approach to basic practices of buying and selling in order to illustrate further his halakhic response to the custom of the merchants. We begin with the institution of transfer of ownership. At the end, we bring an example of Maimonides' adjustment of a halakha responding to a technological innovation in the Islamic world that affected the writing of contracts: the use of paper in place of other writing surfaces.

## 8.1 Buying and Selling in the Interdenominational Marketplace

The very first section in the Book of Acquisition, the Laws of Sale (*Hilkhot mekhira* 1:1), opens with the following overarching statement about contract law: "Purchase of an object is not effected by verbal agreement [*eino niqneh bi-dvarim*], even if witnesses testify to that agreement. Thus, [if a person says,] 'I sell you this house,' 'I sell you this wine,' or 'I sell you this slave,' and the price is set, and the buyer agrees and says, 'I have bought,' and the seller says, 'I have sold'; and they both say to witnesses, 'Be witnesses for us that this one has sold and this one has bought'—the transaction is not valid, and it is as if there had never been an agreement between them. The same applies to the donor of a gift and its recipient."

The title sentence of this opening halakha is seemingly based on the Talmudic statement "whoever transacts business verbally [*ha-nose' ve-noten bi-dvarim*] does not effect transfer of ownership, but whoever retracts, the spirit of the Sages is displeased with him."[1] But Maimonides' formulation is more categorical. Also, by positioning it as the topic sentence of the Laws of Sale, he seems to be declaring a primary and ironclad rule. In buying and selling, informal, verbal agreement does not convey title under any circumstances, even if the agreement is affirmed by witnesses. Underscoring this, the next halakha (1:2) stipulates: "If the purchase is effected by one of the methods for effecting acquisition, the purchaser acquires title, and they do not need witnesses at all, and neither may retract." Maimonides makes explicit what these permissible methods are in the chapters that follow, which codify the modes of acquisition that are sanctioned by Jewish law.

In chapter 7 of the Laws of Sale (7:8) Maimonides takes up the matter of buying and selling through verbal agreement again.[2] "As for him who transacts business by mere verbal agreement [*bi-dvarim bilvad*], it is proper that he keep his word, even though he has not taken any money or made any marks of identification on the purchased article or left any pledge; and whoever retracts, whether the buyer or the seller, though he is not obliged to submit to the curse of 'He who punished,' is considered as one lacking in trustworthiness [*mi-mḥusarei emuna*], and the spirit of the Sages is displeased with him."

This halakha, drawn again from the Talmud, speaks to the moral obligation implicit in a verbal transaction, but it begs the question: Why does Maimonides feature—and so definitively reject—informal, verbal transactions at the very beginning of the Laws of Sale and insist on strict adherence to the three rabbinically acceptable forms of acquisition? Is he perhaps responding to a practice among merchants that he wishes to correct? Is this an instance where—like the instance of legal proxy—rather than accommodating merchant practice by updating the halakha, he insists on the Talmudic norm? And, if so, why?

Before addressing these questions, it is useful to review the formal acts required by the rabbinic sages to effect transfer of ownership, as summarized by Maimonides himself in the Laws of Sale. In his characteristically orderly manner, he collects together the many scattered Talmudic rules about this subject and classifies them logically. He begins with the three kinds of things that can be acquired: (1) immovables, (2) slaves, and (3) movables. These are introduced, though in a different order, at the beginning of the Thirteenth Gate of Hayya Gaon's Book on Buying and Selling, in a chapter headed: "The most weighty of all, the fundamental root of buying and selling, since it concerns acquisition of movable property, of slaves, and of immovables."[3]

Following the Talmud, Maimonides distinguishes between immovables, that is, real property (a house, a field), and movables, exemplified by such commodities as wine, oil, produce, and flax—the last, incidentally, the principal agricultural product, grown abundantly in Egypt, in which Jewish Geniza merchants traded heavily.[4] Slaves (and a legally analogous commodity, animals) are classified in between those two categories. For immovables, title is acquired, as prescribed in the Mishna (Qiddushin 1:5), in one of three ways: by payment of money (*kesef*), through the writing of a contract (*sheṭar*), or by performing a physical act that indicates taking possession (*ḥazaqa*), such as building a fence around the property.

Chapter 2 in the Laws of Sale takes up the acquisition of slaves and cattle, which is accomplished by the same three methods as land or a house. Regarding movable objects, chapter 3 explains the three methods that, according to the Talmud, may be employed to transfer title: lifting (*hagbaha*), pulling (*meshikha*), or handing the object to the purchaser (*mesira*).[5] Payment of money, writing a sales contract, or performing an act of possession does not alone transfer ownership of movable objects. In actual fact, in the Geniza world, written sales contracts were concluded only for real property, like houses, as well as for slaves (also for books).[6] This means that other methods must have prevailed among merchants when buying and selling merchandise.

I hypothesize that Maimonides' stringent insistence on adherence to the Talmudically ordained methods of acquisition stems from awareness of an Islamicate marketplace custom that Jewish merchants knew and probably imitated, or might have been tempted to imitate. In Islamic law—and this was hotly debated for several centuries—the dominant and preferred method for transferring title to an object is through verbal "offer and acceptance," *ījāb wa-qabūl*. Joseph Schacht defines *ījāb* ("offer") as "together with the acceptance (*ḳabūl*), one of the two essential formal elements which for the juridical analysis constitute a contract, which is construed as a bilateral transaction. Offer and acceptance can be expressed verbally (also in the form of compliance with an order, e.g., by the words 'sell me' and 'I sell you herewith'), or by the conclusive acts of the parties, e.g., the silent exchange of goods if that is the local custom, at least if the objects exchanged are of small value."[7]

This method is "informal" in the sense that it does not require a written bill of sale. "Given the Kur'ānic emphasis on mutual consent," writes Islamic legal scholar Frank E. Vogel, "Islamic law gives considerable attention to the means by which consent is manifested and agreement concluded. It does not choose the avenue of formality, beyond requiring that words be exchanged that convey, explicitly or implicitly, an unambiguous offer (*īdjāb*) and acceptance (*ḳabūl*). The Shāfi'ī school, which was dominant in medieval Egypt, went so far as to declare that only words adequately reflect a party's assent, and hence neither contracts in writing nor contracts by tacit exchange (*mu'āṭāt*) were valid."[8]

"Offer and acceptance," explains legal historian Aron Zysow, "are understood as performatives, that is constitutive, dispositive utterances (*inshā'*). For this reason, the law requires that both offer and acceptance be couched in the past tense, which is promissory (*'ida*). Analyzing offer and acceptance as performatives is directly related to the notion that the parties are creating immediate entitlements in each other. In the case of sale, the property in the goods ordinarily passes to the buyer as soon as the contract is formed—that is, upon the exchange of offer and acceptance. . . . Words became fully capable and, in some instances, uniquely capable of effecting a transfer of property."[9]

We are now in a position, I believe, to suggest a plausible explanation for Maimonides' disqualification at the beginning of the Laws of Sale of transfer of ownership by words alone and his strident insistence upon the formalism of rabbinic law. I submit that his categorical rejection of acquisition by the mere utterance of expressions like "I sell you this object," and "I have bought this object"—phrases echoing the typical performative verbal exchanges in Islamic "offer and acceptance"—represents a response to Jewish imitation of Islamic practice in buying and selling.[10]

An explanation for why Jewish traders might have preferred to follow the custom of Muslim merchants rather than the strict law of the Talmud in this matter is not far to seek. In the interdenominational marketplace, or at the busy loading and unloading docks in the harbor, where doing business with Muslims went on all the time, the peculiarly Jewish symbolic gestures—whether lifting, pulling, or handing over—confirming acquisition would have lacked legal force in an interdenominational transaction. On the other hand, Islamic law recognized the validity of offer and acceptance for non-Muslims as well as for Muslims.[11] When buying from and selling to Muslims, it would have been necessary for the Jewish merchant to follow the custom of the Muslim merchants of offer and acceptance. The Arabic legal documents published by Geoffrey Khan from the Cambridge Genizah collections, which include sales contracts between Muslims and Jews as well as between Jews, contain a clause confirming that "the buyer accepted all this from this seller with a valid acceptance" (*qabūlan ṣaḥīḥan*).[12] In some cases, the document states that the buyer "accepted this from [the seller] with a valid acceptance in negotiations that took place between them [*bi-mukhāṭaba jarat baynahumā*] concerning that," a formula that reflects the performative offer and acceptance between buyer and seller.[13] The much more abundant *sharīʿa* court records from Ottoman Jerusalem in the sixteenth century show that Jews regularly transferred title by offer and acceptance, even when they were transacting a sale with other Jews.[14]

We may imagine, therefore, that many Jewish merchants of the classical Geniza period were in the habit of conforming with the customary practice of the Islamicate marketplace even in transactions among themselves, outside the courtroom, using verbal offer and acceptance rather than one of the halakhically approved methods for transfer of title. Furthermore, in the informal, personalistic business environment in which Jewish merchants operated, where face-to-face agreement sufficed for initiating *ṣuḥba*-agency, verbal offer and acceptance in buying and selling would have seemed a natural mode of exchange. Maimonides' emphatic ruling, "[p]urchase of an object is not effected by verbal agreement, even if witnesses testify to that agreement," seems to respond to what—to him—was an unacceptable imitation of the custom of the Islamic merchants, which amounted to a departure from the Talmudic norm.

Goitein already sensed that the first sentence in Maimonides' Laws of Sale embodied a firm rejection of Islamic offer and acceptance, though he notes that the restrictions imposed upon verbal offer and acceptance become moot when Maimonides comes, in chapter 5:5, to the law of symbolic barter (*qinyan*), according to which all things, movable and immovable alike, are acquired by the parties grasping the opposite ends of a kerchief or some other small object, symbolically confirming the transfer of ownership.[15] But this method of symbolic exchange would not have been relevant in transacting business with Muslims and, for the reasons suggested above, may have fallen by the wayside even in intra-Jewish exchange. This is not the only place in the Code where Maimonides presents both the Talmudic halakha and a variation on the statement reflecting an aspect of real life on the ground.[16]

### *8.1.1 Qinyan Siṭumta*

Maimonides seems to strengthen his objection to verbal transactions in another ruling, later on in the Laws of Sale. In 7:6 and 7:7, he addresses the Talmudic procedure of *siṭumta*, described earlier in this book (Chapter 2), though he does not mention the Talmudic-Aramaic term.[17] The Babylonian Talmud recognizes the validity of acquisition of title to movables—exemplified by wine—through verbal agreement, if it is accompanied by an act called *siṭumta*, "seal," to assert ownership of the item, when that procedure conforms with local custom. As explained earlier, *siṭumta* constitutes the precedent for the rabbinic principle in mercantile exchange expressed by the maxim *minhag mevaṭṭel halakha*, "custom overrides the halakha," a maxim mentioned twice in the Palestinian Talmud and cited by Rashba as deriving from the practice of *siṭumta* described in the Babylonian Talmud. A buyer would mark the purchased merchandise with an identifying seal, called by the commentator Rashi *ḥotam she-roshmin*, "a seal that is marked," and *roshem*, "mark," by Maimonides. An unidentified Gaon states explicitly that the term has an Arabic equivalent, which he transcribes *roshem*, unmistakably alluding to the Arabic cognate *rasm* (plural, *rusūm*). Importantly, the Gaon specifies transactions in "wheat, barley, and wine" (not just the "wine" specified in the Talmud), three agricultural commodities that Geniza merchants bought and sold.[18]

Quoting the discussion of *siṭumta* in the Talmud, the Babylonian Gaon Hayya b. Sherira summarizes this practice in his Book on Buying and Selling (we have only the translated medieval Hebrew version):[19] "This is the mark [*rishum*] that a person makes on the item he purchased in order to indicate that he bought it. This matter is entirely determined by [local] custom. If it is the custom in that place that they convey ownership by marking alone, [the Jewish merchant] also takes possession by marking, even without pulling. If the custom of acquiring ownership by marking is not practiced and someone marks [an item], no one may force the other to honor the transaction, though if one of them retracts, he is subject to the curse 'He who punished.'"[20]

Maimonides rules along the same lines at the beginning of Laws of Sale 7:6, with a restatement of the Talmudic halakha of *siṭumta*, though characteristically, and unlike Hayya Gaon, he does not quote the Talmudic source: "If one sells something to another by mere verbal agreement [*bi-dvarim bilvad*] and the price is agreed upon and the buyer thereupon marks [*rasham roshem*] the purchased article in order that there be an identifying sign recognizable as his, even if the buyer has paid none of the money, then if either one of them retracts after it has been marked, he is subject to the curse 'He who punished.' However, if it is the local custom [*minhag ha-medina*] that such a mark [*roshem*] conveys perfect title, the purchased article is thereby acquired and the buyer is obligated to pay the purchase price."

In the following halakha (7:7), Maimonides adds an important qualifier that is absent in the Talmud: "It is clear that [the procedure of *siṭumta*] must be done in the presence of the seller or when the seller states 'mark your purchase,' indicating that he has resolved to transfer ownership, as we have explained concerning the symbolic acts of possession [*ḥazaqa*] and pulling [*meshikha*]."

This qualification is passed over in silence by all the standard commentators except one, Maggid Mishneh, who states: "This is self-evident [*pashuṭ*], for [*siṭumta*] is not preferable to other modes of acquisition."[21] Maggid Mishneh often employs the term *pashuṭ* when he cannot find an explicit source in the Talmudic or post-Talmudic corpus. Evidently, in this case, he sensed that Maimonides' ruling contained a novel element, which, however, he excused as being "self-evident."[22]

What really lies behind Maimonides' seemingly "self-evident" statement? From Geniza letters, we know that Jewish merchants shipping goods labeled their parcels to identify ownership, whether they had bought the items for themselves or purchased them on behalf of someone else for whom the package was destined. This labeling was part of the process of registering cargo at the loading dock when determining freight costs and also to assess customs duties, and it is mentioned in Islamic legal texts as well as in the letters of thirteenth-century Muslim traders found at Quṣayr al-Qadīm on the Red Sea coast.[23] A court record from the Geniza, one from among many, describes a bale of silk "with a tablet engraved with the name, in Arabic and in Hebrew, of [the drowned merchant] Joseph b. Samuel b. Sabāḥ, marked [Arabic, *rusima*, cognate of Hebrew *rasham*] on the outside."[24] A letter to the India trader Abraham ibn Yijū mentions a consignment of Berbera mats that "[w]e wrapped . . . in canvas and your name is written on it in Arabic and Hebrew."[25] In another letter to the same India trader, the writer itemizes expenditures, including, again, "Berbera mats that are in a package marked in Hebrew and Arabic."[26] Yet a third letter mentions "goods, namely, six *manns* of good . . . silk in a waterproof satchel. On top of the satchel is a canvas on which is written 'Abraham Yijū, sent by Joseph ben Abraham.'"[27] The merchant Nahray b. Nissim sends his agents and partners an accounting of cargo dispatched by sea to Sicily, containing items both for various partnerships (*khulṭa*) of his and for his "personal account" (*khāṣṣatī*), including one "for my personal account, in a small bale of indigo, labeled: belonging to Khallūf b. Mūsā" (*'alayhi li-Khallūf ibn Mūsā*).[28] The same Nahray inscribed the six-cornered star among other marks (he called it *'alāma*) on his own consignments.[29] Sometimes these labeling practices were quite misleading, resulting in uncertainty as to the actual owner of the parcel.[30]

Maimonides was surely aware that Jewish merchants signed or otherwise labeled merchandise that they bought. I submit that in Laws of Sale 7:7, he wished to emphasize that merely marking a parcel for purposes of identification, without a written sales contract or other Jewishly approved means of transfer of title, did not validate ownership, unless the labeling took place at the moment of purchase, in the presence of the seller, with the seller's permission, amounting to the conclusion of the sale. Put differently, Jewish merchants who concluded transactions verbally—"offer and acceptance," in Islamic parlance—could and should rely on the Talmudic method of *siṭumta* to certify their purchase by combining this act with the seller's verbal acknowledgment of the sale. Verbal offer and acceptance in the Islamic mode had to be accompanied by labeling at the moment of purchase, fulfilling the Talmudic *siṭumta*. Laws of Sale 7:6–7, therefore, reinforces the categorical opening sentence of the first chapter of the Laws of Sale: "Purchase of an object is not effected by verbal agreement."

Why, we may ask, does Maimonides maintain a strict (we might say "conservative") approach to the methods of sale, especially in light of what we have shown earlier—that he acknowledged and codified fundamental aspects of "informal" business cooperation and other customs of the merchants that pervaded Jewish commercial practice in his time? Do his objection to verbal transactions and his insistence that Jewish merchants mark their purchases at the moment of sale and "in the presence of the seller" constitute a case of law being out of step with society, confirming Alan Watson's main thesis, based on his study of Roman and English law?

The answer is, of course, yes. But Maimonides, we may imagine, had his reasons. One reason would be that he wished to uphold the Talmudic requirement that sales be ratified by a symbolic act, including, as in the case of *siṭumta*, acts consonant with local merchant practice. We may suppose, however, that his staunch opposition to informal transfer of title "by verbal agreement" alone—that is, by the Islamic customary procedure of offer and acceptance—flowed from a special concern. Informal reciprocal agency, as we have seen, could be assimilated to Jewish law and brought under the jurisdiction of Jewish law courts by incorporating *ṣuḥba*-agency into the halakha through the analogical extension of the Mishnaic oath of partners (the "son of the house") to a commercial agent suspected of malfeasance. But offer and acceptance, patently an Islamic procedure embedded in Islamic holy law, presented a different situation, especially if it was practiced to the exclusion of one of the Talmudic procedures. If we are reading through the prism of the Geniza evidence correctly, this seems to have been the case. It almost necessitated adjudication before a *qāḍī* when disputes arose—even disputes between Jews—and, as a general rule, Maimonides, like other Jewish legists, opposed Jewish recourse to Islamic courts. As we will discuss in Chapter 9, this concern weighed heavily in his codificatory decisions on commercial matters in the Code. Labeling bales at any other stage of the process of exchange was insufficient. Laws of Sale 7:6–7, therefore, reinforces the categorical opening sentence of the first chapter of the Laws of Sale: "Purchase of an object is not effected by verbal agreement."[31]

## 8.2 The Material Used for the Contract

Though, as the documentary remains in the Cairo Geniza suggest, Jewish businessmen, like their Muslim counterparts, often transacted their affairs without written contracts, Talmudic commercial law presumes their existence and prescribes rules for their execution. I discuss here one halakha in the Code that is of particular interest because it demonstrates Maimonides' attention to an aspect of material culture underlying commercial practice while, at the same time, echoing a rabbinically based preference for writing down the conditions of commercial cooperation.

The seventh halakha in the first chapter of the Laws of Sale (1:7) stipulates the material that may be used for writing a business contract. In the process of restating a Talmudic ruling, Maimonides seizes another opportunity to accommodate contemporary realia within the halakha. "How does one acquire title by deed? If [the transferor] has written on *neyar*, on *ḥeres*, or on an *'aleh*, 'My field is gifted to you,' or 'My field is sold to you,' the moment the deed reaches the hand [of the transferee] he acquires title, even if no witnesses are present, and even if the deed itself does not have any monetary value."

The Talmudic source for this halakha identified by the commentator Maggid Mishneh is a baraita in tractate Qiddushin (26a), which discusses whether real property can be acquired by deed. The Talmud there permits the use of two writing materials for contracts, namely, *neyar* and *ḥeres*. *Ḥeres* is a potsherd made from clay, which was used as a writing surface in antiquity.[32] *Neyar* in the Talmud derives from the Akkadian word for "papyrus" or "parchment."[33]

Jewish divorce documents needed to be especially durable because divorced wives needed to hold on to them to prove that they were free to remarry. Animal skin was the toughest material, and, typically, divorce documents preserved in the Geniza are written on such a writing surface. For writing divorce documents, the ancient Tosefta (Giṭṭin 2:3) permits certain types of leaves (*'alim*) as well—leaves of olive trees, leaves of gourd plants, and leaves of carob trees—because they are said to be durable (*bar qayyama*). Maimonides' halakha concerns business deeds, not divorce documents. Why, we may ask, does he add "leaf" to the two options stipulated in the Talmud for writing such documents?

In medieval Egypt and elsewhere in the Islamic world, thanks to a technological advance, paper became the cheapest and most common writing material, replacing papyrus (which, nonetheless, remained in use until the tenth century, when it ceased to be produced).[34] Paper, invented by the Chinese, was employed in the parts of Central Asia conquered by the Arabs in the eighth century. By the tenth century, it was in use across the Islamic Empire, as far away as Islamic Spain. It was called by a name of Persian origin, *kāghad* or *kāghid*.[35] Introduced into Egypt in the ninth century, by the tenth it was being manufactured locally in that country and widely used instead of papyrus.[36] The main raw material was linen, which was produced from the abundant flax grown in the country. Cordage (rope made of flax) was also employed.[37] The Cairo Geniza papers provide abundant material evidence for the history of the production, written uses, and trade in paper in the medieval Mediterranean.[38] Most legal documents in the Geniza, other than divorce decrees—for instance, records of court proceedings, bills of sale, release documents, and even marriage contracts—not to speak of everyday letters, are written on paper.[39]

The old rabbinic term *neyar*, meaning "papyrus," eventually assimilated the meaning of the Arabic word *waraq*, to designate paper.[40] In the halakha in question, Maimonides includes *neyar* in its new meaning, validating its use as one of the writing surfaces halakhically acceptable for business documents. At the same time, he did not wish to subvert the ancient halakha, which sanctions the use of papyrus, especially since papyrus was still available in Egypt. To maintain the Talmudic stipulation that papyrus and clay shards may be used for business deeds, and given the fact that the old Hebrew word for papyrus, *neyar*, was now used to designate paper (the word "paper" itself derives from the word "papyrus"), Maimonides needed a new word for papyrus. He found a solution by choosing the word *'aleh*, "leaf," already approved by the Tosefta for divorce documents. The word "leaf" was, of course, a fitting choice to represent the papyrus reed.

What we see, then, in this halakha, is another example of Maimonides' careful attention to merchant custom and his method of incorporating into Jewish law daily practice in the society in which he lived, even to the point of changing the halakha. He expanded the classical pair of writing materials used for contracts in the ancient world—papyrus and clay potsherds—to include the new and, in fact, most common writing material in his time—paper—thus "legalizing" this technological innovation in the medieval Islamic business world, an innovation that, by his time, had long been in common use among merchants in the Islamicate marketplace.

# Chapter 9

# Judicial Autonomy

## 9.1 Preserving the Autonomy of Jewish Courts and the Rule of Jewish Law

I have now shown—convincingly, I hope—that, like the Geonim before him, Maimonides strove to adapt the halakha to modes of business practice that were not envisioned in the agrarian-based Talmud. I have suggested that, like the Geonim, he wished to provide Jewish merchants with an alternative and comparable equivalent to the Islamic legal system.[1] He was aware of the powerful centrifugal forces drawing Jews—and not only merchants—to Islamic judicial venues, threatening Jewish judicial autonomy, the rule of halakha, and the source of authority for jurists like himself.

The problem of Jewish recourse to Gentile courts occupied rabbinic leadership as early as the Roman period, when the sages (Mishna Giṭṭin 1:5) regulated recourse to Gentile (Roman) courts (*arkha'ot shel goyim*, better rendered "registries")[2]—a sure sign of how prevalent this practice was. The rabbis sanctioned applying to Roman courts in pecuniary matters—for the purpose of registering deeds and contracts.[3] Divorce decrees and deeds of manumission of slaves, documents needing careful Jewish judicial oversight, were explicitly excluded from this allowance.

## 9.2 Islamic Policy

Islamic law and administrative policy formally recognized the religious and communal autonomy of the *dhimmī* communities. At the same time, jurists exhibited a variety of conflicting views regarding adjudication of *dhimmī*s in

Muslim courts. Statements like the following, by a twelfth-century jurist and contemporary of Maimonides, express a "pro-autonomy" policy: "We are commanded to leave them and what they believe alone," and "The protected people are bound by what is among them."[4] Mixed litigation—cases involving Muslims and non-Muslims—had to be brought before a *qāḍī*. Some Muslim jurists permitted *sharī'a* courts, at the *qāḍī*'s discretion, to hear cases involving disputes *between* non-Muslims. Others, going to the extreme, insisted on the primacy of Islamic jurisdiction in intra-*dhimmī* cases, asserting the territoriality of Islamic law and the hierarchical hegemony of Islam over the religious minorities. The principle is embodied in the maxim *ilzām ḥukm* (or *aḥkām*) *al-islām 'alayhim*, "subjugation to the authority [*ḥukm*] (or laws [*aḥkām*]) of Islam."[5] This statement effectively declared that, for non-Muslims as for Muslims, *sharī'a*, the holy law of Islam—like Jewish law, a repository of both civil and religious legislation—was the law of the land.[6]

The Qur'ān itself laid the foundations for the various views: "If they come to you [Muḥammad], either judge between them or decline to interfere. . . . If you judge, judge in equity between them" (Sura 5:42); and "Judge between them by that which Allah hath revealed, and follow not their desires, but beware of them lest they seduce you from some part of that which Allah hath revealed unto you. And if they turn away, then know that Allah's will is to smite them for some sin of theirs. Lo! many of mankind are evil-livers" (Sura 5:49).[7]

The formulary for the pact with non-Muslims in al-Shāfi'ī's *Kitāb al-umm* (ca. 800), whose school of law was dominant in Egypt,[8] tells us something about the status of non-Muslim merchants in Islamic courts. In monetary dealings between *dhimmī*s and Muslims, al-Shāfi'ī says, jurisdiction rests with the Islamic authorities. Regarding intra-*dhimmī* commercial affairs, however, "we shall not supervise transactions between you and your coreligionists or other unbelievers nor inquire into them, as long as you are content." But, it goes on to say, "if one of you or any other unbeliever applies to us for judgment, we shall adjudicate according to the law of Islam."[9] Commercial transactions and inheritance cases between *dhimmī*s are among those singled out by an eleventh-century Andalusian manual of Mālikī law as meeting the requirements for Muslim jurisdiction, commercial law being a field of legal equality for non-Muslims.[10]

Islamic contracts (in Judaeo-Arabic, *ḥujja bi-madhhab al-goyim*, or sometimes *kitāb 'arabī be-'eidei goyim*) are often mentioned in intra-Jewish litigation that came before the Jewish *beit din* or before a jurisconsult like

Maimonides.[11] Dozens of such documents ended up in the Geniza. Geoffrey Khan published sixty-three from the Cambridge University Genizah collections alone.[12] The documents record transactions between Jews and Muslims, between Jews and Christians, and even between Muslims, including Muslim marriage contracts and deeds from sale of property, the last probably having passed into Jewish hands at the time of some subsequent sale.[13] Almost half the documents are records of sale, lease, or endowments of property. As in the case of houses and other buildings in modern deeds, the physical boundaries and other architectural features of the property had to be registered with the authorities, should any challenge to the buyer's rights in the property arise in the future. The attestation and signatures of certified Muslim witnesses on these documents strengthened the legality of the transaction. The non-Muslim courts had little, if any, power to enforce these matters. Another reason for *dhimmīs* closing real-estate deals in the presence of what we may call, mutatis mutandis, the "civil" authorities is that the government collected a tax and a commission on the transaction.[14] By law, moreover, any transaction between a Muslim and a *dhimmī* or between *dhimmīs* of different religions *had* to be concluded in an Islamic court. Preference for Muslim jurisdiction and certified Muslim witnesses is evidenced by acknowledgments of debt between Jews as well.[15]

The documents published by Khan, alongside responsa and other evidence of Jews appearing before Muslim judges and possessing legal documents from Islamic courts, indicate a positive and confident attitude toward Islamic jurisdiction coming from the bottom up. Jews viewed Islamic tribunals as a place where they could normally expect to receive fair treatment. Looking at the matter from the top down, we may say that (following one of Goitein's keen insights) Muslim jurists considered the non-Muslim courts to be a kind of branch of central authority.[16] Christian Mueller makes a similar claim about the legal status of *dhimmīs* in the Islamic West.[17] Anver Emon argues, with complexity, that *sharīʿa* as "rule of law" facilitated pluralism in the Islamic state, whereby *dhimmīs*, simultaneously outsiders and insiders, were subject to Islamic rules of general welfare (*muʿāmalāt*), while being exempt from Islamic religious practice (*ʿibādāt*) and free to practice their, albeit inferior, religion without impingement and under the protection of the state.[18]

Jewish and Muslim judges often cooperated. A Jew might solicit the opinion of a Muslim jurist as to whether Islamic law permitted a certain action. Maimonides was once asked for a ruling in a case where two married sisters had asked Muslim jurists (*fuqahāʾ al-muslimīn*) about their entitlement in Islamic law to exercise the right of preemption to purchase property of an adjacent (Muslim) neighbor.[19] A Muslim judge might return a case to the Jewish court if he did not wish to rule in the matter.[20] When a dispute over a young wife's right to grant her husband ownership of part of her dowry was brought before a Muslim *qāḍī* and the judge was presented by the parties with contradictory claims about Jewish law, he decided to wait before deciding "until we read what the *ra'īs* [namely, Maimonides] writes about this."[21] The openness of the Islamic judiciary to non-Muslim participation, like the dispersal of what I have called "Dhimmi law" within the *sharī'a*,[22] should not be underestimated. No less than the interdenominational equality in the marketplace and the symbiosis between Jewish and Islamic cultures, it strengthened Jews' feeling of embeddedness in majority society and mitigated their inferior legal and social status. At the same time, the relatively free access to the Islamic legal system posed a serious challenge to Jewish autonomy and to the authority of the Jewish halakhic leadership, beginning with the Geonim.

## 9.3 Gaonic Accommodation

Given the Mishnaic dispensation regarding notarization of legal documents by Roman courts, and given Muslim openness to *dhimmī* presence in their courts, the Babylonian Geonim extended the Mishnaic license to include Islamic courts, provided that local Muslim judges and professional witnesses were known to be just and honest and that they forswore forged documents.[23] But Jewish traders did not stop at registering deeds and contracts in Islamic courts. They also took advantage of the option offered by Islamic authorities to seek redress there in business disputes. The evidence for this in the Geniza and in the responsa gives the strong impression that what we see represents but the proverbial tip of the iceberg; we only hear about this when there was a problem that brought merchants before the *beit din* and left a paper trail in the Geniza or in the rabbinical responsa. Islamic legal institutions, part of the state apparatus, offered a degree of enforcement that was far more effective than the coercive tools available to the Jewish judiciary. Moreover, as we have seen, much of Jewish business was conducted in accordance with merchant custom that had currency in the Islamicate marketplace and that had, as Udovitch has shown, been incorporated into Islamic law during its formative period.

The temptation to cross over to the Muslim judiciary must have been even greater in those places, especially small Jewish settlements, where Jewish courts were presided over by laymen—elders and other dignitaries in the community who often lacked thorough training in the profundities of Jewish law.[24] In the specific case of *ṣuḥba*-agency, Talmudic law was ill-equipped to enforce the informal, unwritten contract that underlay the arrangement, whereas Islamic law and courts recognized the institution in the form of *ibḍāʿ*. This is why Saadya Gaon in the tenth century sought a halakhic solution to the problem of enforcement by considering the *ṣuḥba*-agent a paid bailee and why Maimonides in the twelfth century applied his exegetical imagination to equating an agent with a partner.

Although crossing the permeable boundary between Jewish and Islamic courts chipped away at Jewish autonomy, rabbinic authorities were realists. Where economic loss was involved, such as a debt or an inheritance or a deposit needing to be collected from a fellow Jew, and one litigant spurned the Jewish authorities, a Gaon ruled (citing Talmudic sources) that a claim could and indeed should be made in an Islamic court.[25] Standard clauses in Jewish court releases exempting parties from any future challenge in Gentile courts (*dinei goyim* or *nimmusei goyim*)[26] prove how common boundary-crossing—"forum shopping," in the parlance of historians of law and society—in the legal arena must have been.

According to Islamic legal theory, *sharīʿa* courts did not recognize non-Muslim testimony in mixed litigations with Muslims, but Jews and Christians could testify against one another and even submit to a defendant's oath of innocence in a dispute with a Muslim.[27] According to some authorities, they were sometimes required by Islamic judicial procedure to take the oath in their respective houses of worship, swearing by their respective holy books.[28] Like third-party testimony in Judaism, oaths in Islam had evidentiary value.[29]

Rabbinic leadership disapproved strongly when members of the community repaired to Islamic tribunals simply because provisions of Islamic law were more favorable than the halakha. For example, in inheritance, Jewish law denies daughters a share in their father's estate if he has living sons. Islamic law awards females half the amount bequeathed to male siblings: a half-share was better than nothing.[30] Or, a Jewish wife might go over the heads of the Jewish *beit din* and appeal to a Muslim *qāḍī* to terminate her marriage, perhaps even threatening to convert to Islam in order to benefit from Islamic law's prohibition of marriage between a non-Muslim man and a

Muslim woman. Scholars have suggested that this was an underlying motivation for the early Gaonic *taqqana* (in 650 or 651) allowing a wife who could not bear to live with her husband to "rebel" (*moredet*) against him, forfeit the money coming to her from her husband in case of divorce, and obtain a divorce from the Jewish court immediately, rather than waiting until after the yearlong cooling-off period mandated by the Talmud.[31] Using the Islamic legal system for economic matters was one thing. Turning to the *qāḍī* in matters of marriage and personal status was another. These were religious matters requiring halakhic procedures and Jewish oversight, much more so than inherently secular business dealings.

A case from tenth-century Córdoba reported in al-Wansharīsī's compilation of Islamic responsa from the Islamic West vividly illustrates the complex interplay between *dhimmī* and Islamic jurisdiction in marital and personal status law.[32] A Jew embroiled in a dispute with his wife requested to have the case transferred to the Muslim court. He claimed that the Jewish judges were prejudiced against his father and that documents in the matter had originated from a previous Muslim judge and been signed by Muslim witnesses. Five Mālikī jurists queried in the case issued *fatwā*s. Their rulings ranged from requiring the Islamic court to hear the case; to allowing the Muslim judge, at his discretion, to do so only if both parties agreed; to referring it back to the Jewish court if the substance of the dispute fell under Jewish law, especially because the wife possessed no documents witnessed by Muslims; to requiring the Muslim judge to take the case if he ascertained, through investigation, that the Jewish judges were indeed prejudiced against the plaintiff's father. These *fatwā*s illustrate the complex interplay between *dhimmī* and Islamic jurisdiction even within the same Islamic school of law, as well as the regularity with which Muslim judges and jurists confronted the phenomenon of *dhimmī* recourse to Islamic tribunals.[33]

## 9.4 Syriac Christians and the Islamic Courts

The penchant for turning to Islamic courts affected Christian *dhimmī*s as well, much to the disapproval of the ecclesiastical leadership, who, like the rabbis, took this as a challenge to their authority. This subject has been studied thoroughly in a comparative vein by Uriel Simonsohn.[34] More was at stake, however, for the Syriac bishops than for the Geonim. The bishops presided over a rigid hierarchy and jealously guarded their judicial prerogatives, not only against competition from Islamic courts but also from lay Christian tribunals, monks, and ascetic holy men, who also claimed judicial authority. The bishops' tough rhetoric and the recurring legislation of church councils forbidding recourse to nonecclesiastical courts or judges, often backed up by the weapon of excommunication, indicate how much they had to lose when Christians went "outside" (in their language) the domain of ecclesiastical jurisdiction.

In part, Christian legal philosophy contributed to the legal crisis of Eastern Christianity under Islam. Jesus' dictum "render unto Caesar what is Caesar's and unto God what is God's" (Matt. 22:21) had always justified the emphasis on spiritual, to the exclusion of temporal, matters in ecclesiastical legislation and jurisdiction. Moreover, from the late fourth century on, secular Roman courts adjudicating civil law in the Byzantine realm were no longer presided over by pagans but by fellow Christians. Roman law after Constantine took full cognizance of the preferred position of Christianity as the official religion of the Empire, and this was summed up in the Theodosian and later the Justinian Code. In the Sasanian Persian Empire before the Muslim conquest, insofar as the meager evidence suggests, Nestorian ecclesiastics enjoyed limited judicial autonomy at best, while Christians had access to state courts for mundane legal cases.[35]

The Islamic conquest created a new and, for the Syriac ecclesiastical elite, alarming situation. With the tradition of repairing to nonecclesiastical tribunals for civil matters firmly entrenched in their flock, the elite of the Syriac churches now faced a situation in which Christians were turning to courts that were heathen or pagan in their eyes. In short, their authority and autonomy came under serious threat. In response, the Syriac churches began to develop a corpus of ecclesiastical civil law of their own. The process is most striking in the East Syriac (Nestorian) church, where, even before the Islamic conquests, efforts had been initiated to create an alternative to Sasanian law. These efforts intensified after the Islamic conquest in the project of an eighth-century East Syriac jurist to create a unified religious and civil ecclesiastical code, incorporating Sasanian, Roman, and Islamic elements. Similar efforts were expended in the West Syriac church, although the starting point for this reform in the former Byzantine domains is less clear.[36]

## 9.5 Comparing the Jewish and Christian Cases

Comparison with the Syriac Christians is instructive for understanding the legal situation of the Jews under the Geonim. At the dawn of Islam, Judaism was already equipped with a nearly comprehensive civil law in the Talmud. This corpus adequately suited most mundane legal matters, with the important exception of commercial law, owing to the predominantly agrarian character of Jewish society. This compelled the Geonim to make certain adjustments, as we have seen. If, nonetheless—as seems to be the case—the Geonim were less strident than the Syriac Christian ecclesiastical elite about recourse to Islamic courts, there are reasons for this. As Simonsohn observes, the Gaonic establishment did not rest on the same kind of hierocratic base as the churches. Its ties with Jewish communities and individuals across the Islamic world formed a looser and more informal pattern of relationships, based on master-disciple relations, the training of provincial judges, instruction through the medium of responsa, loyalties stemming from Babylonian descent, and the dispensing of honorific titles. Consequently, the Gaonate was less invested than the Syriac churches in a strict hierarchical power structure, and the Geonim could show more leniency than the bishops toward their flock seeking Islamic legal jurisdiction.

Furthermore, the Geonim knew full well that agrarian-based Talmudic law was ill-suited for the commercial economy of Islam. As indicated by their ruling on the *suftaja*, they understood why Jewish merchants followed Islamicate market practices—the "merchants' law"—and resorted to Islamic courts, where forms of commercial practice unknown in the Talmudic era had legal currency.[37] Similarly, responsa of the Geonim rule that a creditor might legitimately appeal to an Islamic court to recover a debt from a recalcitrant debtor who refused to appear in the Jewish court, and, more generally, in any case concerning a monetary matter.[38]

## 9.6 A Case from al-Andalus

The Gaonic project, balancing the desire for judicial autonomy with the realities of the Islamicate economy, was part of an ongoing process that extended well beyond their period of ascendancy and well beyond their geographic locale. A fascinating legal opinion written by R. Joseph ibn Migash of Lucena, in Muslim Spain in the twelfth century, illustrates the interplay between the Jewish and Islamic legal systems in far-off al-Andalus as well as the challenges faced by rabbinic scholars trying to walk a thin line between preserving judicial autonomy and the Jewish inclination to reach beyond communal legal boundaries.[39]

The case is especially interesting because it involved matrimonial law. A woman whose husband had promised her the huge sum of 1,000 dinars as her delayed, additional marriage gift in her marriage contract became worried about the guarantee of her monetary rights. According to Jewish law, the additional marriage gift was payable to the wife should her husband divorce her or leave her a widow. The questioner explains that the money was to go to her and to his sons on a fifty-fifty basis, which was the local custom. Her husband owned land, and she was concerned lest he someday sell it to a Muslim and she be unable to collect her due when the time came. To avoid this possibility, she asked her husband to take an oath in an Islamic court to the effect that, should he wish to sell any part of his land—meaning to a Muslim—she could appeal to the Islamic court to prevent him from doing so. In short, she wanted the Muslim judge to guarantee rights that she had in her Jewish marriage contract but rights that would be hard to enforce through the Jewish authorities alone.

A local Jewish *moreh* had rendered his opinion. The husband could be required to take such an oath, provided that neither she nor he nor his property would suffer harm and provided that Islamic law in the matter was the same as Jewish law. He evidently assumed this to be the case because of similar terminology in Jewish and Muslim marriage contracts regarding the "early" and "late" installments of the husband's marriage gift. But this was a misunderstanding, as he soon learned from the Muslim judges. When the *moreh* explained to them that, in Judaism, the "late" installment comes due only if the wife becomes a divorcée or a widow, the Muslim judges explained that in Islamic law, the wife was entitled to receive her postponed installment while still married.[40] The Jewish *moreh* then reversed himself, though someone else upheld his original opinion.

These *morehs* (lit., "teachers"), we learn from another of Ibn Migash's responsa, seem to have been a class of judicial authorities unschooled in the Talmud. Many of them claimed, however, that they understood the Talmud and were able to issue rulings on its basis. They rendered opinions, apparently assuming a role similar to the Islamic *muftī* (the word *moreh* might have been *muftī* in the lost Arabic original of the responsum),[41] though without the

Muslim *muftī*'s depth of learning. Ibn Migash, a towering rabbinic sage, often invalidated their decisions. Other local authorities were more to be trusted, he explained, because they at least relied upon responsa of the Geonim, to which they had access. These were evidently the very handbooks that Jews living far from the eastern center of halakhic learning copied in the Middle Ages and relied upon; these handbooks have preserved much of the Gaonic corpus of juridical rulings that has come down to us in manuscript codices.[42]

Ibn Migash's responsum regarding the wife who wished to use the Islamic court to prevent a possible financial loss in the future shows awareness of the Jews' predilection to take advantage of their access to the Muslim judiciary for protection or enforcement of rights. At the same time, he asserts the prerogatives of Jewish judicial autonomy.

> If it is possible for the husband to swear to the amount in her marriage contract and stipulate that any judgment regarding collection of what is due to her will take place in the Jewish court; and, if, in turn, this is upheld in the Islamic court, then it is permissible to compel the husband to swear to this effect, since no harm will then befall him. If these [stipulations] are not upheld in the Islamic court, but rather, upon swearing about the amount in her marriage contract, he becomes liable to pay it to her [while they are still married], in accordance with the law in their court, then it is not permissible to compel her husband to do something that will cause him harm. If, however, it is possible for him to swear in their court that she possesses a Jewish marriage contract in such and such an amount that she will collect from him after his death or if he divorces her, and that his land is mortgaged to her for this purpose, and this is upheld in the Islamic court, then he should be compelled to do it.
>
> The principle is: if a way can be found for the wife to feel secure without causing harm to her husband should she summon him to the Islamic court, then her husband should be compelled to comply. But if there is a possibility that she will actually sue him in the Islamic court, it is not permissible to compel him.

Matrimonial law constituted a sacred domain of Jewish life and was central to the principle of personality of law that acknowledged each person's right to be governed by the laws of his own religious community. Ibn Migash sought to ensure that the halakhic purpose of the deferred installment of the additional marriage gift would not be compromised by Islamic law. Yet he was also sensitive to the economic issue: alienating the land from the family patrimony by sale to a Muslim could result in economic loss to the wife, who could not rely on the Jewish court to extract the land from a Muslim purchaser in order to pay what was due her as a divorcée or a widow. If, however, the Islamic court recognized all the halakhic conditions, then Ibn Migash would allow the husband to take an oath there that would protect his wife. It seems that Ibn Migash considered it a realistic possibility that the Muslim judge would accept these terms.

## 9.7 Maimonides' Position on Recourse to Islamic Courts

Like Ibn Migash and the Geonim, Maimonides confronted the reality of Jewish recourse to the Muslim judiciary on a regular basis. In his Commentary on the Mishna, completed in 1168, soon after his arrival in Egypt from the West, he took note of Jewish merchants' penchant for registering commercial documents in Islamic courts. Echoing the Geonim and commenting on Mishna Giṭṭin 1:5, he acknowledged the validity of business contracts (*ʿuqūd al-buyūʿ wa'l-ashriya*, "deeds of sale and purchase") drawn up in an Islamic court (*majlis al-qāḍī*) "on the condition that it is well known among the Jews that the [professional] witnesses and that particular *qāḍī* do not take bribes."[43] Concerning the Mishna's exclusion of divorce documents and the like, Maimonides explains, further, that since these entail "acknowledgment and denial" (*al-iqrār wa'l-inkār*), they "cannot be attested by Gentiles under any circumstances." As his career in Egypt progressed, the great legist received numerous questions involving Jews who had resorted to the Islamic courts, either to register and validate contracts or for actual litigation.[44]

Maimonides approved of notarization of contracts in the Islamic court if the document conformed with and reinforced Jewish law, which was possible because of the many similarities between the two legal systems. This is illustrated by a case described in one of his responsa. A recently divorced woman demanded that her former husband draw up in a Muslim court a separate deed of indebtedness for the late installment of her additional marriage gift. Her purpose was to put pressure on him from the "civil" authorities. Maimonides responded that, whatever indebtedness a person has in Jewish law may be backed up by registering the indebtedness in a Gentile (Muslim) court, to be invoked if, as in the case at hand, the husband refused to pay what he owed his wife. The Islamic deed should be used against him in the Muslim court to enforce his obligation.[45] On the other hand, Maimonides chastised Jewish judges for referring litigants without cause to a Muslim court to resolve a dispute.[46]

The lure of the Muslim legal system might have been even more pervasive in Egypt than in Maimonides' native Andalusia. In Spain, powerful and deeply learned rabbinic leaders like Joseph ibn Migash and his teacher, Isaac Alfasi, held sway and could discourage the practice,[47] whereas in Egypt before Maimonides' arrival, rabbinic leaders of such high intellectual caliber and judicial authority were few and far between. Prior to Maimonides' arrival in the mid-1160s, only a handful of rabbinic scholars boasting his advanced level of rabbinic learning and accompanying prestige were to be found.[48] In this light, and given the receptiveness of Islamic courts toward *dhimmī* access to their jurisdiction, it is not surprising that he should have fretted over such latitude among Egyptian Jews.

Maimonides gazed incredulously at other lax habits of his new countrymen. We have already described his campaign to reform synagogue decorum. Along with other judges, he also promulgated *taqqanot* to eliminate additional "unorthodox" practices, including the loose habits of some Jews in the practice of family purity laws, under the influence of the Karaites.[49] In the matter of Jewish recourse to Islamic courts, he, like the Geonim before him, took pains both to adapt the halakha to accommodate merchant custom and to protect the integrity of Jewish judicial autonomy.

Emblematic of Maimonides' concern for this halakhic laxity is his *taqqana* of 1187, which included a provision prohibiting recourse to Islamic tribunals. In a responsum mentioning the *taqqana*, he makes an exception, however, for "a person who is unable to go to [alt. trans. "is prevented from going to"] [*tamanna'a min*] a Jewish court."[50] This proscription, with the exception noted, was already anticipated by him a decade earlier in the Code (Laws of Lender and Borrower 27:1). There, in a strict constructionist interpretation of the law of the Mishna, he codified the law singling out deeds of sale and debt as satisfying the criteria for Jewish appearance before a Muslim judge, but ruling out all others by name. Indeed, halakha 27:1 amounts to a vigorous diatribe against exceeding the parameters of Jewish law in this matter.

Maimonides adopts a similarly stern position in this matter in the Laws of the Sanhedrin (26:7). He signals the importance of this halakha by making it the climax of twenty-six chapters dealing with every conceivable aspect of courts of law, adjudication, and punishments.

> Whoever adjudicates by Gentile law [*dinei goyim*][51] and in their courts, even if their law is similar to Jewish law, is a wicked person. It is as if he cursed and blasphemed and raised his hand against the Torah of Moses our master. As is stated: "These are the rules that you shall set before them" (Exod. 21:1), "before them" and not before the Gentiles, "before them" and not before lay judges. If the Gentiles possess coercive power and a Jewish litigant's contending party is defiant [*allam*] and [the plaintiff] cannot get his due in a Jewish court, he should first summon [the other party] to the Jewish court, and if the latter refuses to appear, he should obtain permission from the Jewish court and extract his due from the contending party in a Gentile court.

The Talmud (Giṭṭin 88b) is Maimonides' source, but the language and rhetoric, according to which the violator is said to have "cursed and blasphemed and raised his hand against the Torah of Moses our master," goes well beyond the language of the Talmud and hints at the scope and gravity of the problem in his own day. In a kind of mirror image of the Muslim debate regarding jurisdiction over *dhimmī* affairs, he ruled in this halakha that recourse to Muslim courts was permissible—with the authorization of the Jewish court. He doubtless knew that most Islamic law schools extended *sharīʿa* jurisdiction to non-Muslims even if only one of the contending parties wished to appeal to the *qāḍī*.[52] His innovative halakha discussed in Chapter 6, in which he drew an analogy between an unpaid business agent and the partner of the Mishna called "son of the house," thereby holding an agent liable to the same oath of absolution as the Mishnaic "oath of partners,"[53] was doubtless motivated by the same desire: to discourage disputing Jewish merchants from resorting to Muslim tribunals.

Like the Geonim, Maimonides knew that Jews, especially Jewish merchants, regularly applied to Islamic courts, and, like the Geonim, he presumably knew that Islamic courts had a fairly decent record in meting out justice to *dhimmīs*. In this fluid environment of legal pluralism, in which non-Muslims could more or less freely choose between parallel legal systems, in which Muslim judges normally dealt fairly with non-Muslims, and, finally, in which *sharīʿa* law, the law of the land, in many ways represented civil law for the non-Muslim religious minorities, Maimonides' *taqqana* of 1187 and, especially, his ruling at the end of the Laws of Sanhedrin in the Code, were meant to impose a measure of control over a widespread and seemingly irreversible phenomenon.[54]

Not surprisingly, people continued to follow their old ways. A Geniza letter from the early thirteenth century tells a story about a dispute between two Jewish merchants. One of them insisted that their case be heard by the Muslim court. Naturally, the Muslim judge insisted on using Muslim witnesses. The writer had Jewish witnesses whom he could summon to adjudication in the Jewish court. He asked the Jewish judge and communal leader (*muqaddam*) of Alexandria, Isaac b. Khalfon, to enforce his own (unpopular) injunction against repairing to "Gentile courts," which the letter writer's co-litigant had ignored.[55]

Maimonides' solution for preserving and protecting Jewish judicial autonomy was to reserve authority for the Jewish judges to determine when and under what circumstances the principle of exclusive Jewish adjudication could be waived. If the Jewish judicial establishment could not prevent Jews, particularly Jewish merchants, from going to Muslim courts, at least they could regulate the practice by monitoring it.[56]

Generations later, in the mid-fourteenth century, Maimonides' great-great grandson, the Nagid Joshua (d. 1355), the administrative and judicial leader of the Jewish community of Egypt, presided over a special Jewish tribunal that screened cases before they could be submitted to a Muslim judge. It is possible—indeed, likely—that this institution, called *beit din li'l-mutaḥaddithīn*, "the court for 'informers,'" owed its origins to Maimonides' *taqqana* of 1187 and particularly his ruling in the Code at the end of the Laws of Sanhedrin. Like his illustrious ancestor, and responding to the many transformations in Jewish life under Islam, Joshua Nagid used this court to assert Jewish autonomy in face of powerful centrifugal forces.[57]

### *9.7.1 Embeddedness in Islamicate Society*

For Jewish merchants, in particular, access to Islamic courts was an aspect and expression of their embeddedness in Islamicate society. They spent enormous amounts of time outside the bounds of the community, buying from and selling to Muslims, engaging in partnerships with Muslims, traveling with Muslims on ships and in caravans, regularly crossing confessional barriers to interact with Muslim members of their profession, and sharing with them a common mercantile custom in the Islamicate marketplace. As part of this life outside the community, they arranged and registered business contracts in Islamic courts and sought resolution of disputes in their precincts. In this way, they learned the ins and outs of Islamic commercial law and customary practice and internalized *ṣuḥba*-agency. Gideon Libson has proposed that recourse to Islamic courts was the channel through which Islamic legal procedures were mediated (legal historians, following Alan Watson, would use the word "transplanted") into Jewish practice in the Gaonic period. We have proposed here that the Judaeo-Arabic "oath on fulfillment of the trust," uniting under its umbrella partnership and its affiliate, commercial agency, constitutes a legal transplant that migrated from Islamic into Jewish judicial procedure.

By updating the halakha and modifying it where necessary, Maimonides hoped to bring the merchant back into the halls of Jewish justice rather than have him cross the line to plead his case in the Islamic courtroom.[58] In his multiple roles as leader of Egyptian Jewry, jurisprudent, and codifier, Maimonides evidently sensed, and labored to counteract, what historians familiar with the totality of Jewish life in the Islamic world know: the pervasive embeddedness of Jews in Islamicate society, acting as a centrifugal force and standing in tension with the separate and centripetal force of religious identity and self-government that Islam officially conceded to all its religious minorities.[59]

In the *longue durée*, the centrifugal forces were not easily overcome. Jews in Muslim countries continued to capitalize on the opportunity to benefit from Islamic law as administered in Islamic courts right down into the twentieth century. Studies of Ottoman-period court records, the *sijillāt*, in addition to the invaluable light that they cast on Jewish life in Islamic lands in later medieval and early modern times, offer clear, unequivocal and persistent evidence of the fundamental equality of the Jews before Islamic law, an extension of their legal status as *ahl al-dhimma*, "protected people." The same can be said for Moroccan Jewry in the nineteenth century and for the Jews in modern Egypt.[60] The Jewish sources for the period examined in the present study, for which any Islamic court records that may have once existed have not survived,[61] reflect the same comfort level and confidence in choosing Islamic over Jewish courts and the same challenge to judicial autonomy.

# Conclusion

# Legal Change and Originality

## 10.1 Jewish Law and Society in the Medieval Islamic World

I have constructed this book not only as a study of commercial law in the Mishneh Torah but also as an inquiry into the general subject of law and society. In Chapter 1, I introduced the musings of two learned legal scholars expressing themselves on the role of codification in adapting law to social change. I quoted Roman and English legal scholar Alan Watson, who writes that private law traditionally lags behind societal change but who goes on to ask whether codification can "remove the significant divergence between law and society." I invoked Maimonidean scholar Gerald Blidstein, who asks whether "Maimonidean law . . . remain[s] firmly fixed within the Talmudic reality, both in its resources, rulings, and attitudes," or "[d]o we find extrapolations from Talmudic law to the new situation—or perhaps more than that, or less?"

I believe that the case study presented here answers the speculations of both Watson and Blidstein in the affirmative. It has shown—convincingly, I hope—that Maimonides made adaptations in his Code of Jewish law, the Mishneh Torah, to bring the limited business law of the agrarian-based Talmud up to date with the commercially advanced civilization of the Islamic world. These modifications have hitherto been hidden from view, in part because Maimonides wove them deftly into the fabric of existing halakha, in part because of assumptions that the Mishneh Torah is in essence simply a "repetition of the law" (à la the common understanding of the term *mishneh torah* in Deut. 17:18), and in part because scholars failed to bring quotidian evidence of merchant practice to bear on the subject. The Geniza documents (supported by the responsa literature), portraying in minute detail the activities of the Jewish merchants of the eleventh, twelfth, and thirteenth centuries, have provided the key that unlocks the door to Maimonides' "original" efforts at adaptation.

## 10.2 Originality

My findings raise anew the question of originality in Maimonidean thought.[1] Few would deny the original thinking that went into Maimonides' philosophical writings about Judaism. Nor would anyone gainsay the revolutionary form, structure, style, and scope of the Mishneh Torah that Twersky pointed out long ago.[2] But for many, the idea that Maimonides made changes in the content of the halakha remains problematic. The inclination is strong, particularly among halakhists, to take the great codifier at his word when he insists in the Introduction to the Code and elsewhere that his work was simply a compilation (*ḥibbur*, in his words) of rabbinic law up to his time and contained practically nothing new.[3]

One way to address the question of originality in Maimonidean halakha is well expressed with regard to Islamic law by Wael Hallaq, in words that can usefully be applied to the Jewish case. "It must be stressed that legal change during the pre-modern period was characterized by two qualities, the first of which was its imperceptible nature. No sudden mutability was required, no ruptures . . . but rather a piecemeal modification of particular aspects of the law. . . . The change, therefore, was always eminently organic, naturally arising, as it were, from the adaptive experiences of the past and, most importantly, from within the legal sub-culture of a particular region. . . . The second quality lay in the fact that a modern notion of change . . . was clearly absent from the conceptual world and discourse of the jurists."[4]

My claim regarding Maimonides' Code is that we should not shy away from the search for those imperceptible changes, those "piecemeal modifications of particular aspects of the law" that stem from Maimonides' keen awareness of the custom of the merchants, whose activities are displayed for us in minute detail in the Geniza documents.

We have pointed out such imperceptible changes, for instance, where Maimonides updates halakhot of the Talmud by inserting a brief reference to commerce, *seḥora*, where it was absent in the foundational rabbinic text (several examples are cited above, in Chapter 3). Another nearly indiscernible update, achieved by the addition of just one word to an ancient rabbinic text, concerned a technological improvement of the Islamic world—the use of paper in place of papyrus or animal skin for writing contracts. To account for—and sanction—the ubiquitous use of this "modern" writing surface, Maimonides added the word *'aleh*, "leaf," already approved by the Tosefta for writing divorce decrees, to a Talmudic halakha permitting the use of papyrus or clay shards for contracts. The additional word took the place of the ancient Akkadian derivative, *neyar*, for "papyrus," freeing up the word *neyar* to assume its new meaning of "paper."

A somewhat more obvious change occurs in the halakha regarding partnership with a Muslim. Maimonides altered the context of that law to fit the Islamicate urban setting. Where the Talmud features the example of a partnership with a Gentile to engage in work in a field as sharecroppers, appropriate for a predominantly agricultural society, Maimonides gives pride of place to partnership "in a handcraft, or in commerce, or in a store," making the halakha accord with his own urbanized, commercial Jewish society. Moreover, since, in Maimonides' world, work done for the partnership on the Sabbath by a non-Jew—typically, a Muslim—was the main issue, not the fear that he might, on account of a successful deal, give thanks to his pagan god (one of the reasons given by the Gemara for the Mishnaic injunction), Maimonides placed the halakha among his Laws of the Sabbath, rather than in his Laws of Idolatry, where someone familiar with the Talmud would have expected to find it.

In a world where merchants regularly traveled afar in their quest for profit, Maimonides ruled, in a halakha that seems to have no precedent in classical rabbinic law, that a stationary investor could restrain his itinerant partner from taking risks by traveling to a place where he thought he could get a better price. Resigned, further, to the geographic mobility of long-distance trade and its ill effects on marital harmony, the codifier interpreted a Mishna regarding a Jewish husband's conjugal duties permissively, to sanction merchants' frequent, lengthy separations from their wives, provided the latter gave their consent.

The most innovative—and controversial—legal change in response to the custom of the merchants that I found is Maimonides' treatment of the widespread practice of what Goitein called "formal friendship"; Avrom Udovitch calls "quasi-agency"; Avner Greif calls a closed, self-policing coalition of Maghribī merchants; Jessica Goldberg calls "mutual service agency"; and I call *ṣuḥba*-agency. Maimonides brought this novel form of agency into the halakhic fold by deftly grafting it onto Talmudic partnership law, drawing an analogy with the Mishna's *ben ha-bayit* ("son of the house"). In this way, he made the agent-"friend" subject to the "oath of partners," creating a means of contract enforcement that was absent from the Talmudic law of agency.

Sources indicate that the Geonim—Saadya (d. 942) and possibly Hayya (d. 1038)—had earlier taken account of *ṣuḥba*-agency, though Saadya's solution, relying on the Talmudic oath of bailment, differed from that of Maimonides. The Judaeo-Arabic "oath on fulfillment of the trust," applied to the Mishnaic "oath of partners" and evidently transplanted from Islamic judicial procedure before Maimonides' time, appears in the context of agency relations during the Lebdī lawsuit at the end of the eleventh century and is alluded to in a couple of business letters from the mid-eleventh century.

Maimonides hewed close to classical rabbinic language when accounting for the custom of the merchants. Unlike the Geonim, he does not employ a term like *minhag ha-soḥarim*, a Hebrew phrase mimicking the Arabic equivalent, *ḥukm al-tujjār*, used by the Geonim, though he freely employs the Talmudic phrase *minhag ha-sappanim* in connection with the seafaring laws of non-Jewish society. Rather, he used the time-honored rabbinic locution for "local custom," *minhag ha-medina*, as if to signal—in an original way—that adjusting the halakha to accommodate contemporary merchant practice had the imprimatur of ancient Jewish jurisprudence.

Maimonides' awareness of Jewish adherence to the custom of the merchants could lead him to stringency when he felt that this was warranted. Thus, he strongly objected to Jewish imitation of the Islamic practice of transferring ownership by verbal exchange alone—the method of offer and acceptance prescribed by the *sharīʿa*. In the same vein, he tightened up the Talmudic halakha permitting acquisition by *siṭumta*. When merchants put their signature or label or that of someone else on merchandise that they had purchased, he insisted that they do so in the presence of the seller, at the moment they purchased the goods. Labeling a parcel for identification purposes only, as when loading cargo onto a ship, was not sufficient. *Siṭumta* was a Talmudic concession to local custom in order to enable trade, but Jewish merchants needed to tie it to the actual act of purchase.

Apart from reading the Code through the lens of the Geniza, my search for original features has also been guided by instances where the commentators differ in proposing sources in the Talmudic corpus; or when they pass over a halakha in silence; or when one or another of them, unable to find a precedent in the Talmud, declares the Maimonidean halakha to be "self-evident" (*pashuṭ*). Sometimes what seems self-evident to a commentator, such as the halakha about labeling parcels just mentioned, is patently an original opinion, even if Maimonides does not flag it as his own in the way he explained to the Alexandrian judge Pinḥas b. Meshullam. Sometimes, as I have suggested, the commentators simply misunderstood the realia of Maimonides' time and place (better known to *us*, thanks to the Geniza documents) and hence the "setting in life" of a ruling.[5]

### *10.2.1 Gaonic and Andalusian Background*

To be sure, even piecemeal modifications of particular aspects of the law, to use Hallaq's words, need to be evaluated in the light of opinions by Maimonides' predecessors, the Babylonian Geonim and his teachers in Spain. Meir Havatselet has shown several instances of direct borrowing from the Geonim.[6] Blidstein has emphasized the Code's dependence on the Gaonic and, especially, the North African and Andalusian traditions.[7]

Maimonides refers to "my teachers" or "the rabbis of Spain" (*rabbotai* or *rabbanei sefarad*) some forty times in the Code. He invokes precedents from the Geonim explicitly about thirty-five times, signaled by the formula "the Geonim ruled" (*horu ha-ge'onim*) or "some [or 'one'] of the Geonim ruled" (*horu miqṣat ha-ge'onim*). On other occasions, he adopts rulings without mentioning the Geonim explicitly. An example of a Gaonic opinion that he codifies in the name of "my teachers," namely, his teachers in Spain, without mentioning the Geonim, is the *suftaja*, identified as a "custom of the merchants" in the Gaonic responsum discussed earlier.[8] The gloss "for commerce" in the halakha stipulating the charity obligation of visitors to a town seems to have been based on a ruling of Naḥshon Gaon in connection with a different Talmudic passage. It is likely that Maimonides knew about Gaonic attempts (by Saadya, Hayya?) to accommodate *ṣuḥba*-agency in the halakha, although Robert Brody argues that the Code shows relatively little influence of the halakhic innovations of the Geonim and was largely uninfluenced by the structure of Saadya Gaon's legal writings.[9] We may add the instance, adduced here, of Maimonides' apparent rejection of Saadya's inclusion of reciprocal commercial agency in the Talmudic law of bailment, preferring a solution within agency law. The merchant in Maimonides knew agency when he saw it!

Sometimes, Maimonides borrows material from the Geonim without attribution, adding his own modifications. He seems to have expanded upon (we might say "liberalized") the ruling of Naṭronai Gaon permitting trade on the intermediate days of the festival if transacted in the privacy of one's house, and another responsum of that same Gaon allowing merchants to write letters to accompany merchandise or to convey instructions to a business associate on the same intermediate days in order to send it with a departing caravan. Naṭronai's allowance manifestly served the interests of the international trading community. Showing intimate knowledge of the realities of long-distance trade and the Islamicate marketplace, including the impact that arriving ships and caravans had on market activity, Maimonides goes even further than the Gaon (apparently with the help of a precedent in the Palestinian Talmud), opening the door to trading openly in the marketplace on those days. He may have been influenced by R. Joseph ibn Migash, the Andalusian teacher of his father, who ruled that merchants should be permitted to trade on the intermediate days of the holiday in order not to forfeit a business opportunity.

There are commercial halakhot in the Code for which commentators, like the thirteenth-century German author of the Haggahot Maimuniyot or the early fourteenth-century Spanish commentator Migdal 'Oz, report having found in a Gaonic responsum, which, however, as far as can be determined, is not extant. Huge numbers of these responsa have been completely lost or are only partially quoted in medieval European halakhic sources, and it is conceivable that future discoveries of fragments of lost Gaonic works in the Geniza will uncover Gaonic precedents for some of Maimonides' amendments to the halakha.

Moshe Halbertal adduces instances where Maimonides challenges Gaonic opinions and diminishes their authority vis-à-vis the authority of the Talmud.[10] To Halbertal's examples I have added (in Chapter 7) Maimonides' outspoken rejection of the Gaonic legal fiction of "four cubits of land in the Land of Israel" when appointing a proxy legal agent to collect a debt or a bailment. In an original move, he overruled the artifice, not because he objected to modifications of the halakha to accommodate practices on the ground. Quite the contrary; he objected to the Gaonic novelty because many Jews in his time did, in fact, own land—in the form of urban real estate or agricultural plots, the latter especially in his native Spain. In his view, people could and should use a fraction of their actual property for the notional gift of land to which debt collection by proxy had to be pegged. Maimonides' revision of the Gaonic legal fiction, like his other updates and adjustments, reflects realities of the Islamic world in which he lived. Nonetheless, realistically aware that the legal fiction had become solidly entrenched in Jewish usage—a fact that actual powers of attorney in the Geniza copiously bear out—he left a loophole permitting the use of the Gaonic device under certain conditions.

### *10.2.3 Islamic Law*

Apart from intimate knowledge of marketplace practices, another possible source of some of Maimonides' adaptations of the halakha—the object of Gideon Libson's research—is Islamic law. Libson's findings, both with regard to the Geonim and Maimonides, reveal an original feature of the Code, whether the borrowing resulted from personal study, from familiarity with Islamic court procedure, or, in Maimonides' case, from indirect channels via a predecessor among earlier Jewish jurists. Most of the examples cited in the present book entail changes in the wording or the structure of classical (Talmudic or Gaonic) halakhic texts that, I have proposed, were intended to accommodate merchant practice or otherwise reflect realities of the Islamicate marketplace. My view, further, is that many of Maimonides' adjustments to the halakha reflect mercantile practices that were recognized in Islamic courts.

To be sure, direct borrowing from Islamic law cannot be ruled out, and Libson has illustrated this for the Geonim and for Maimonides more than once. The prime candidate for direct borrowing in my research is represented by the similarity between *ibḍā'*-agency of Islamic Ḥanafī law and Jewish *ṣuḥba*-agency. But Maimonides' formulation in Laws of Agents and Partners 9:5 does not appear to stem directly from Islamic law. Rather, it originates in Muslim and Jewish marketplace practice, which the great sage assimilated into the halakha via an ingenious use of analogy. This exemplifies another instance where Islamic judicial procedure, itself responding to the "custom of the merchants" (*'ādat al-tujjār*), infiltrated Jewish law through the Jewish juristic principle that "custom overrides the law"—in this case, the rabbinic exemption of agents from an oath of trustworthiness.

Even where more direct counterparts in Islamic law to the commercial halakha of the Code exist or might yet be found—ones perhaps better suited to the monetized, mercantile economy than the agrarian law of the Talmud—Maimonides' borrowing should be seen as an original effort to achieve the same goal of accommodating merchant practice that is portrayed in the commercial documents of the Cairo Geniza.[11]

### *10.2.4 Sizing Up Originality*

Beyond the Gaonic and Andalusian background of some halakhot and the possible carryover from Islamic law or judicial procedure, it is my considered opinion that many, if not most, of the changes in commercial law in the

Code represent Maimonides' conscious and—from my perspective, at least—original effort to close the gap between the law of the Talmud and the practice of contemporary Jewish merchants. I suggest, further, that a principal motivation for these modifications stemmed from Maimonides' activity as jurisconsult, regularly answering legal queries arising out of the affairs of the Islamicate marketplace. In regard to his jurisprudential role, it is suggestive to recall Wael Hallaq's theory about the nexus between the respective roles of *muftīs* and "author-jurists" in the evolution of Islamic law. Maimonides, as we have noted earlier, combined both functions in one and the same person. Not to be overlooked, too, is Maimonides' personal experience as head of a merchant family.

Furthermore, we have argued that Maimonides' concern about adapting Jewish commercial law to accommodate the custom of the merchants stemmed from his disquiet over Jewish reliance on the Islamic judiciary and judicial system, a common occurrence among Jewish merchants in his day and for centuries earlier. His *taqqana* of 1187 proscribing this practice and his strident opposition to it at the end of the Laws of Sanhedrin in the Code reflect this concern.

Originality in premodern religious societies was deemed a vice, not a virtue. What people honored was tradition, the "good old law," to capture a phrase. Maimonides must have anticipated that there would be resistance to what was original in his Code, especially since he omitted his sources. In fact, already during his lifetime he faced challenges to the Code, exemplified by the query of the Alexandrian judge Pinḥas ben Meshullam about halakhot that he failed to find in the halakhic tradition. Defense of the Mishneh Torah continued in the writings of Maimonides' son Abraham, who himself encountered accusations of improper innovation (*bid'a*, in Islamic terms) for his program to introduce changes in Jewish prayer. Indeed, virtually the entire, vast literature of commentary on the Code took (and takes) as its purpose to establish the Talmudic and post-Talmudic basis for his rulings, to defend the Code against claims against it on grounds of innovation.

When discussing halakhic adaptations in the Mishneh Torah to accommodate merchant practice, we must ask whether Maimonides thought that he was advancing novel opinions or whether he believed that he was merely eliciting the intended meaning of the halakhot that he "updated" or modified, following the time-honored method of rabbinic exegesis, expecting readers to trust his pious aims. These are questions of intent that we modern mortals cannot hope to answer definitively.

Prima facie, we may hypothesize that, at least on a conscious level, Maimonides did not believe that he was prescribing new law but rather, expanding what he believed (and wanted others to believe) to be the intention of the old law. Accordingly, we would say that he thought (and wanted others to think) that what he was doing was not innovating but, as Twersky puts it, explicating the Talmud, even if this explication was "often invisible."[12] Or we may apply Blidstein's insight: "Rabbinic discussion . . . is not a search to recapture a lost revelation but an *original* attempt to expand revelation into new and unfamiliar territory."[13] That "new and unfamiliar territory" in Maimonides' time was the transformed economy of the Islamic world and the "custom of the merchants" that so thoroughly permeated Jewish trade.[14] Like the Geonim before him but going further, Maimonides accommodated these novel business practices in the halakha in keeping with the principle that custom can override the halakha. Whatever the case, it is difficult to avoid the impression that his efforts—at least, from our modern perspective—bear the distinct stamp of originality.

Here it is useful to call to mind another of Blidstein's observations: "Maimonides' Code responds to contemporary realities when they can be related to Biblical-Talmudic institutions or, put differently, when they bear on norms found in the traditional literature before him, when they can become part of an interpretative process."[15] This statement well describes what Maimonides was doing with his ruling about *ṣuḥba*-agency. He was responding to contemporary reality but relating it to a Talmudic concept via a well-established interpretative process, namely, analogy, likening the *ṣuḥba*-agent to the "son of the house." But in actuality, in this instance Maimonides gave legal ballast to a new but inherently problematic business practice that operated through assumptions that were subjective and sometimes unclear or otherwise ambiguous. As we saw, his ruling seemed so "original" that some later authorities found it unacceptable and rejected it altogether.

A second example of Maimonides' use of a Talmudic concept to bolster a change in the halakha is his treatment of work on the intermediate days of the festival. Rather than deviating from the Talmudic norm that allowed work to avoid lost business opportunity, *praqmaṭia ovedet*, he simply broadened (or stretched) the intent of that halakhic concept. For this move, he had the authority of Naṭronai Gaon's responsum and, likely, the opinion of R. Joseph ibn Migash. He also, as we have seen, seems to have drawn upon a supportive precedent in the Palestinian Talmud.

In adapting the ancient halakha to accommodate contemporary commercial practices, Maimonides could exercise considerable latitude. The Mishneh Torah is, in large measure, detached from the order and structure of the Talmud, unlike the work of his Andalusian predecessor, Isaac Alfasi, which hews closely to the order, structure, and language of the Talmudic text. Unlike Alfasi, too, Maimonides composed his Code in Hebrew, not the laconic and often convoluted Aramaic-Hebrew of the Talmud. Like anyone translating from one language to another, this in itself freed him to go in new directions.[16] Furthermore, by omitting references to rabbinic sources, he made it possible to work new details into old law in such a way that concealed his inventive moves. Lastly, following his practice of organizing the material according to rational categories, Maimonides was free to shift a halakha to a context that made it conform to contemporary realities. We have seen all these methodologies at work in the chapters of this book.

## 10.3 Comparison with Legal Change in Ashkenaz

According to the view that Maimonides was creating a new canon of Jewish law, meant to stand forever as the standard reference book for every aspect of Jewish conduct, it is understandable that he would have wanted to tailor it to accommodate the new commercial economy of the Islamic world. When harmonizing Jewish law with contemporary business practices, he was, in fact, doing what responsible halakhic authorities (and Islamic jurists) have always done: adapt the law to the needs of the time, *taghayyur al-aḥkām bi-taghayyur al-azmān*, to quote the relevant Islamic maxim mentioned in my Introduction. Ashkenazi Talmudists like Rashi in eleventh-century France and Maimonides' own contemporaries in northern Europe in the twelfth and thirteenth centuries, the Tosafist commentators on the Talmud and Rashi, were doing the same for Jewish economic life in northern Europe. Well known, for instance, is the distinction they drew between Trinitarian Christians and the idolaters of old, in order to minimize restrictions on doing business with non-Jews mandated by the Mishna.[17]

In his erudite and nuanced study of Jewish pawnbroking in medieval Europe, Haym Soloveitchik shows how halakhic authorities in Ashkenaz exercised flexibly to enable Jews to borrow and lend money. While sanctioned in the case of loans made to non-Jews, interest-bearing loans between Jews are forbidden by the Torah. However, European Jews could hardly have survived in the medieval economy by relying on credit extended by Christians alone or by lending to Christians alone. They needed to be able to turn to fellow Jews as well. Since, generally speaking, people do not like to lend money for nothing, halakhic masters, beginning in the eleventh century, adapted the law to allow for intra-Jewish interest-bearing loans through a Gentile strawman or some other legal fiction. The most radical adaptation was achieved by R. Jacob Tam (d. 1171), grandson of Rashi, who removed all barriers to this practice, which, by his time, constituted by far the most common form of Jewish business activity in northern Europe.[18]

Ashkenazi halakhists also showed adaptability where ritual law affected economic well-being, Soloveitchik argues. Wine (along with beer) was the beverage of choice in the Middle Ages, and Jews needed Gentile labor to be able to produce it in sufficient quantities so that they could sell it to Christians and use it for themselves. Rashi and the Tosafists amended the halakha regarding wine production to enable Jews to benefit from Christian labor, at least in the early stages of production, despite Talmudic restrictions on the wine processed or touched by Gentiles. Non-Jewish labor was also necessary to produce a sufficient annual supply of wine for Jewish ceremonial use during the short window of time, around the beginning of the Jewish year in the fall, when grapes were harvested. Because wine was a commercial commodity, Christian borrowers often deposited it with Jewish moneylenders as collateral. Therefore, Soloveitchik argues, the Tosafists relaxed the injunction against deriving benefit from the sale of wine that served as Christian collateral.[19]

Rather than through commentary on the Talmud, in the manner of Rashi and the Tosafists, Maimonides registered his halakhic adaptations through codification: updating Talmudic laws written for an agrarian society to make them compatible with the commercial, monetized society of the Islamic world and weaving changes into the fabric of the ancient halakha in order to give halakhic sanction to entrenched business practices, what people were doing on the ground. Like Rabbenu Tam in France, Maimonides wished to reassure merchants as well as Jewish judges that the custom of the merchants that Jews were following in the marketplace or bringing to the Jewish court was in keeping with Jewish law.[20] The most radical case of adaptation I could find—his extension of the oath of partners to commercial agents—satisfies Soloveitchik's criterion for identifying instances where "halakhic texts talk history," namely, "the crucial angle of deflection that is necessary for any demonstration that extraneous factors were impinging upon the course of immanent developments."[21] Nothing indicates this "crucial angle of deflection" better than the strong rejection of this halakhic innovation by Rashba;

by the skeptical question raised about it by Radbaz; and by Joseph Caro's decision not to incorporate it into his own code, the Shulḥan 'Arukh (in this matter, Maimonides represented a minority view among the three authorities Caro relied upon). The "angle of deflection" in this case is steep, dictated by the need to accommodate a ubiquitous custom of the merchants that the Talmud did not know.[22] The present study has also identified other, shallower angles of deflection in the Code.

Whether incorporating rulings of scholars who came before him, modifying them, or even rejecting them, or, as in most of the cases adduced in this book, updating and adapting Talmudic law on his own, Maimonides' original achievement shines through. He was modifying Talmudic law to make it better serve the post-Talmudic Islamicate economy and forestall merchant flight to Islamic courts, using codification to bring Jewish law and Islamicate society into greater harmony.[23]

# Notes

## INTRODUCTION

1. Mark R. Cohen, *Poverty and Charity in the Jewish Community of Medieval Egypt* (Princeton, NJ: Princeton University Press, 2005) and the companion volume, *The Voice of the Poor in the Middle Ages: An Anthology of Documents from the Cairo Geniza* (Princeton, NJ: Princeton University Press, 2005).

2. The Talmudic period as used in this book refers to the era from the destruction of the Second Temple in Jerusalem in 70 C.E. to the Islamic conquest of Palestine (ca. 640). See Seth Schwartz, "Historiography on the Jews in the 'Talmudic Period' (70–640 CE)," in *The Oxford Handbook of Jewish Studies*, ed. Martin Goodman (Oxford: Oxford University Press, 2002), chap. 5.

3. Mark R. Cohen, "Maimonides and Charity in the Light of the Geniza Documents," in *The Trias of Maimonides/Die Trias des Maimonides*, ed. Georges Tamer (Berlin: De Gruyter, 2005), 65–81 and in *Poverty and Charity*, 24–25 and passim.

4. I know of no claim that Babylonian Jews participated directly in the long-distance Sasanian trade with south Asia and China, notwithstanding the considerable evidence of Babylonian Jews involved in merchandising silk during the Talmudic period. On the silk trade, see Catherine Hezser, *Jewish Travel in Antiquity* (Tübingen: Mohr Siebeck, 2011), 325–332.

5. Isaiah M. Gafni, *Yehudei Bavel bi-tqufat ha-talmud: Ḥayyei ha-ḥevra veha-ruaḥ* (*The Jews of Babylonia in the Talmudic Period: A Social and Cultural History*) (Jerusalem: Merkaz Zalman Shazar, 1990), 130–131. Catherine Hezser, writing about the sources for Jewish "travel for trade" in late antique Roman Palestine, comes to this conclusion: "It remains uncertain to what extent Palestinian Jews were involved in this [overseas] trade, whether they collaborated with the Christian import-export merchants or whether they had their own network of Jewish business partners abroad." Hezser, *Jewish Travel in Antiquity*, 417. An old article by Abraham Kamberg, "Commercial Law According to the Talmud," *Commercial Law Journal* 38 (1933): 239–249, contains very little on the forms of commercial collaboration that we discuss in this book.

6. Mark R. Cohen, *Under Crescent and Cross: The Jews in the Middle Ages* (Princeton, NJ: Princeton University Press, 1994; new ed., 2008), 77–79, 88–90.

7. On the status of *dhimmī*, see, e.g., Antoine Fattal, *Le statut légal des non-musulmans en pays d'Islam* (Beirut: Imprimerie Catholique, 1958); with respect to the temporary

resident coming from outside the Domain of Islam, the *musta'min*, see *Encyclopaedia of Islam*², s.v. *amān* (Joseph Schacht).

8. See Michael Morony, "Commerce in Early Islamic Iraq," *Asien Afrika Lateinamerika* 20 (1993): 699–720, whose description of the vast variety of commodities exchanged and of the geographical scope of this trade shows the broad reach and complexity of commerce over great distances, from Spain to India and China, in this early period of Islamic rule.

9. The foundational study of these developments with regard to the Jewish community is the first volume (1967) of S. D. Goitein's *A Mediterranean Society: The Jewish Communities of the Arab World as Portrayed in the Documents of the Cairo Geniza*, 5 vols. plus index volume by Paula Sanders (Berkeley: University of California Press, 1967–1993) (hereafter, *Med. Soc.*). For a recent discussion of this transformation by two economists that employs a model emphasizing the ancient Jewish value of investing in the education (and hence the general literacy) of (mainly male) children, see Maristella Botticini and Zvi Eckstein, *The Chosen Few: How Education Shaped Jewish History, 70–1492* (Princeton, NJ: Princeton University Press, 2012), esp. chap. 6. The authors are aware, of course, that literacy worked in tandem with other—in my opinion, equally, if not more, important—exogenous factors: the political unification of the former Sasanian and Byzantine Empires, which enabled free-flowing trade between regions formerly considered "enemy territory"; the massive urbanization of the Islamic world in the wake of the vast conquests; Jewish (along with general) migration from east to west in the early Islamic period (see next note), resulting in the establishment of new, necessarily urban, Jewish centers and the thickening of others. This, in turn, facilitated wide-reaching and potentially rewarding travel for long-distance traders.

10. See Moshe Gil, "The Rādhānite Merchants and the Land of Rādhān," *Journal of the Economic and Social History of the Orient* 17 (1974): 299–328, who shows convincingly that the Rādhānites originated in the agricultural hinterland of Baghdad, the very vicinity that archaeologist Robert McCormick Adams (*Land Behind Baghdad: A History of Settlement on the Diyala Plains* [Chicago: University of Chicago Press, 1965]) discovered was becoming overpopulated in late Sasanian and early Islamic times, causing migration to nearby urban centers like Baghdad. Urbanization meant the rise in importance of nonagricultural pursuits and urban dependence on trade to satisfy the agricultural and other needs of city dwellers. I remain unconvinced by Phillip Ackerman-Lieberman's revisionist argument in "Revisiting Jewish Occupational Choice and Urbanization in Iraq Under the Early Abbasids," *Jewish History* 29 (2015): 113–135. See next note.

11. Eliyahu Ashtor, "Un mouvement migratoire au haut Moyen Âge: Migrations de l'Irak vers le pays méditerranéens dans le haut Moyen Âge," *Annales: économies, sociétés, civilisations* 27 (1972): 185–214; Moshe Gil, "The Sughmar Family" (Hebrew), in *Ha-islam ve-'olamot ha-shezurim bo* (*The Intertwined Worlds of Islam: Essays in Memory of Hava Lazarus-Yafeh*), ed. Nahem Ilan (Jerusalem: Hebrew University, Institute of Asian and African Studies, Makhon Ben-Zvi, and Mossad Bialik, 2002), 149–150. Evidence of this migratory trend from the Mediterranean Islamic lands in the ninth century: Menahem Ben-Sasson, *Ṣemiḥat ha-qehilla ha-yehudit be-arṣot ha-islam: Qayrawan, 800–1057* (*The

*Emergence of the Local Jewish Community in the Muslim World: Qayrawan, 800–1057*) (Jerusalem: Magnes, 1996), 74–84 (hereafter, Ben-Sasson, *Emergence*).

12. I discuss the evidence for this claim later on. The reader will have noticed that I use the adjective "Islamicate" here and elsewhere in this book. This is the term coined by Marshall Hodgson, which "refer[s] not directly to the religion, Islam, itself, but to the social and cultural complex historically associated with Islam and the Muslims, both among Muslims themselves and *even when found among non-Muslims*," Marshall G. S. Hodgson, *The Venture of Islam: Conscience and History in a World Civilization* (Chicago: University of Chicago Press, 1974), 1:59 (emphasis added). The term "Islamicate" is particularly germane to the commercial context, where Jews, while retaining their religious identity, shared fully in marketplace life—not pariahs, not segregated in particular professions, and deeply embedded in the surrounding culture. On the other hand, I retain "Islamic world," "Islamic period," and "Islamic Middle Ages."

13. Baber Johansen, "The Valorization of the Human Body in Muslim Sunni Law," in Devin J. Stewart, Baber Johansen, and Amy Singer, *Law and Society in Islam* (Princeton, NJ: Markus Wiener, 1996), 71. Johansen goes on to quote the eleventh-century Ḥanafī jurist al-Sarakhsī (d. ca. 1096): "The Muslim and the non-Muslim under Muslim rule . . . are all equal in the contract of tenancy because this contract belongs to the contracts of commercial exchange [*min ʿuqūd al-tijāra*] and in these contracts all are equal [*sawāʾ*]"; ibid., 72.

14. By codification, I do not mean codification in its modern understanding, as a body of laws of the state resulting from legislation, but rather, as understood in medieval religious systems like Judaism and Islam, a collection of laws, originating in scripture and subsequently elaborated through interpretation and augmentation in a central corpus. In Islam, an example would be al-Sarakhsī's collection of and commentary upon Ḥanafī law, *al-Mabsūṭ*, 30 vols. (Cairo: Maṭbaʿat al-Saʿadah, 1906–1913), quoted in the previous note.

15. The Code is the only one of Maimonides' major works that he did not write in Arabic.

16. The Book on Inheritance (*Kitāb al-mawārīth*), by Saadya Gaon, we now know, did include sources; the manuscript identified by Moritz Steinschneider and published by J. Müller (Paris: Ernest Laroux, 1897), is an abridgment that omits them. See Robert Brody, *The Geonim of Babylonia and the Shaping of Medieval Jewish Culture* (New Haven, CT: Yale University Press, 1998), 255–256.

17. Isadore Twersky, "The Beginnings of *Mishneh Torah* Criticism," in *Biblical and Other Studies*, ed. Alexander Altmann (Cambridge: Cambridge University Press, 1963), 161–83.

18. *Teshuvot ha-Rambam*, ed. Joshua Blau, vols. 1–3 (Jerusalem: Mekize Nirdamim, 1957–1961); vol. 4 (Jerusalem: Rubin Mass, 1986), 2:306–308 (no. 160), and many other responsa of this type, e.g., ibid., 2:459ff. and 2:538ff. (hereafter, *Teshuvot ha-Rambam*, ed. Blau). On the early dissemination of the Code, see, esp., Menahem Ben-Sasson, "Maimonides' *Mishneh Torah*: On the Creation of a Canon During the Author's Lifetime" (Hebrew), in *Ha-qanon ha-samui min ha-ʿayin: Ḥiqrei qanon u-geniza* (*The Hidden Canon: Studies in Canonization and Geniza*), ed. Ben-Sasson et al. (Jerusalem: Scolion, 2010), 133–201.

19. Isadore Twersky, *Introduction to the Code of Maimonides (Mishneh Torah)* (New Haven, CT: Yale University Press, 1980).

20. See Mark R. Cohen, "Geniza for Islamicists, Islamic Geniza, and the 'New Cairo Geniza,'" *Harvard Middle Eastern and Islamic Review* 7 (2006): 129–145.

21. See ibid., 136–139. Muslims burn their papers, though burial is also an option. See *Fatāwā al-lajna al-dā'ima li-buḥūth al-'ilmiyya wa'l-iftā'* (Riyadh, 2006), 4:100 (no. 176).

22. Among many surveys of the Geniza, the story of its discovery, and its contribution to knowledge, see Stefan C. Reif, *A Jewish Archive from Old Cairo: The History of Cambridge University's Genizah Collection* (Richmond, Surrey: Curzon, 2000) and the more recent book by Adina Hoffman and Peter Cole, *Sacred Trash: The Lost and Found World of the Cairo Geniza* (New York: Next Book/Schocken, 2011). Mark Glickman's *Sacred Treasure—the Cairo Genizah: The Amazing Discoveries of Forgotten Jewish History in an Egyptian Synagogue Attic* (Woodstock, VT: Jewish Lights, 2011) offers a lighter account of the subject. On the Ben Ezra Synagogue, see Phyllis Lambert, ed., *Fortifications and the Synagogue: The Fortress of Babylon and the Ben Ezra Synagogue, Cairo* (London: Weidenfeld & Nicolson, 1994). Several years after the main discovery of the Geniza in the synagogue, other genizot (pl. of geniza) were unearthed in the Jewish cemetery, the so-called Mosseri Collection. These fragments, numbering more than 7,000, formerly in the hands of the Mosseri family, have been given to the Taylor-Schechter Genizah Unit in Cambridge, England, for conservation. A "New Geniza" was unearthed in the late 1980s at the same cemetery. The contents, insofar as known, date from the late nineteenth and first half of the twentieth century. See M. Cohen, "Geniza for Islamicists," 139–141.

23. See Mark R. Cohen and Yedida K. Stillman, "The Cairo Geniza and the Custom of Geniza Among Oriental Jewry: An Historical and Ethnographic Study" (Hebrew), *Pe'amim* 24 (1985): 3–35.

24. The so-called Afghan geniza, first brought to public awareness in 2013, contains dated documents from as early as the beginning of the eleventh century, mostly in Judaeo-Persian. As these documents are studied, we will have much new insight into Jewish life in a region of the premodern Islamic world about which we presently know practically nothing. For the time being, see Ofir Haim, "Legal Documents and Persian Letters in Early Islamic Judaeo-Persian from Islamic Khurasan" (MA thesis, Hebrew University, 2014); idem, "Letters from Afghanistan in the National Library" (Hebrew), *Ginze Qedem* 10 (2014): 9–28.

25. Yaacov Choueka, "Computerizing the Cairo Genizah: Aims, Methodologies and Achievements," *Ginze Qedem* 8 (2012): 11*. This count was arrived at when calculating the number of images to be digitized by the FGP. See Rebecca Jefferson, "The Historical Significance of the Cambridge Genizah Inventory Project," in *Language, Culture, Computation: Studies in Honour of Yaacov Choueka*, ed. Nachum Dershowitz and Ephraim Nissan (Berlin: Springer, 2014), 30.

26. The number 20,000 is a guesstimate. Only when the entire Geniza has been cataloged will we know the actual number.

27. The most important work based on the Geniza documents and the foundation of all research in the field is Goitein's *Mediterranean Society.*

28. See Wael Hallaq, *Authority, Continuity, and Legal Change in Islamic Law* (Cambridge: Cambridge University Press, 2001), 176–183.

29. Brody, *The Geonim of Babylonia*, 249–266.

30. Ibid., 254.

31. This is discussed in detail in Chapters 5 and 6.

32. See above, n. 18.

33. That is why Goitein cites them so frequently in his *Mediterranean Society*; see the index vol. compiled by Paula Sanders (vol. 6), 244–246.

34. The modern edition of the responsa of Abraham, the son of Maimonides, by contrast, contains relatively few that are pertinent to the present study. *Teshuvot Rabbenu Avraham ben ha-Rambam*, ed. A. H. Freimann, trans. S. D. Goitein (Jerusalem: Mekize Nirdamim, 1937). Mordechai A. Friedman is preparing a new edition with new responsa from the Geniza, but they include relatively little on commercial matters (Mordechai Friedman, personal communication, September 21, 2013).

35. Gideon Libson, "Halakhah and Reality in the Geonic Period: Taqqanah, Minhag, Tradition and Consensus: Some Observations," in *The Jews of Medieval Islam: Community, Society, and Identity*, ed. Daniel Frank (Leiden: Brill, 1995), 67–99; idem, *Jewish and Islamic Law: A Comparative Study of Custom During the Gaonic Period* (Cambridge, MA: Harvard University Press, 2003); and his other publications in the list of works cited in the present volume. Of particular relevance to the present study, apart from his book, are two chapters: "Parallels Between Maimonides and Islamic Law," in *The Thought of Maimonides: Philosophical and Legal Studies*, ed. Ira Robinson et al. (Lewiston, NY: E. Mellen, 1990), 209–248; and "Maimonides' Halakhic Writings Against the Background of Muslim Law and Jurisprudence of the Period" (Hebrew), in *Ha-Rambam: Shamranut, meqoriyut, mahapkhanut* (*Maimonides: Conservatism, Originality, Revolution*), ed. Aviezer Ravitzky, 2 vols. (Jerusalem: Merkaz Zalman Shazar, 2008), 1:247–294.

36. Samuel b. Ḥofni has also been studied fruitfully by David Sklare, *Samuel ben Ḥofni Gaon and His Cultural World: Texts and Studies* (Leiden: E. J. Brill, 1996).

37. Libson, *Jewish and Islamic Law*, 103–110.

38. Y. Zvi Stampfer, *Sefer ha-gerushin (Kitāb al-Ṭalāq) le-Rav Shmuel ben Ḥofni Ge'on Sura* (*Laws of Divorce [Kitāb al-Ṭalāq] by Samuel ben Ḥofni Gaon*) (Jerusalem: Makhon Ben-Zvi, 2009) and "An Influence of Islamic Law of Divorce on Rav Samuel b. Ḥofni Gaon and Maimonides" (Hebrew), in *'Alei 'asor: Proceedings of the Tenth Conference of the Society for Judaeo-Arabic Studies*, ed. Daniel J. Lasker and Haggai Ben-Shammai (Beer Sheva: Ben-Gurion University of the Negev Press, 2008), 309–316.

39. Amir Ashur, "Protecting the Wife's Rights in Marriage as Reflected in Pre-Nuptials and Marriage Contracts from the Cairo Genizah and Parallel Arabic Sources," *Religion Compass* 6/8 (2012): 381–389.

40. An example that Libson discusses is the so-called oath of destitution (*yamīn al-'adam*); Libson, *Jewish and Islamic Law*, chap. 6.

41. See Libson, "Maimonides' Halakhic Writings Against the Background of Muslim Law and Jurisprudence of the Period," 272–291.

42. Libson, *Jewish and Islamic Law*, 38–41, 45–46. See also the methodological

discussion in his conclusion, 175ff. (quotation taken from 177–178). Regarding the Gaonic legal fiction allowing a creditor to collect a debt through a proxy agent, which will be discussed below in Chapter 7, Libson writes: "[I]ts emergence may be attributed to the economic upheaval of the time, as suggested by Assaf, and in that respect it should be considered together with other halakhic innovations introduced at the time to deal with economic problems" (39). The work of Mordechai Akiva Friedman on Jewish family law illuminates modifications in Jewish practice taking place in a Muslim context, though he prefers to seek the roots of these changes in older, Jewish sources and to consider the role of Islamic law as secondary, or incidental, rather than as having a direct influence. See the bibliography of his publications by Amir Ashur, "The Publications of Mordechai Akiva Friedman" (Hebrew), *Dine Israel* 26–27 (2009–2010): xix–xxxiii. Libson takes issue with Friedman's more conservative approach. See Gideon Libson, "Legal Status of the Jewish Woman in the Gaonic Period: Muslim Influence—Overt and Covert," in *Developments in Austrian and Israeli Private Law*, ed. Herbert Hausmaninger et al. (Vienna: Springer, 1998), 243; see also idem, *Jewish and Islamic Law*, 157–159, 313 n. 9.

43. On the question of originality versus conservatism in Maimonides' writings in general, see the essays in Ravitzky , ed., *Ha-Rambam: Shamranut, meqoriyut, mahapkhanut*. The present book differs from many "law and society" studies, which use law to illuminate aspects of social history or to illustrate how law (theory) was put into practice in the social realm. See one example of this approach for medieval Islam: Stewart, Johansen, and Singer, *Law and Society in Islam*. The most important journal for this subject is *Islamic Law and Society* 1 (1994–). See also Yaacov Lev, "Law and Society in Medieval Islam: A Review Article," *Jerusalem Studies in Arabic and Islam* 39 (2012): 423–436. I use "society," namely, the social dimension of economic practice as reflected in the Geniza documents and the responsa, to illuminate law itself.

44. S. Mahmassani, *Falsafat al-tashrīʿ fī l-islām* (*The Philosophy of Jurisprudence in Islam*), trans. Farhat J. Ziadeh (Leiden: Brill, 1961), 106–110.

45. Ibid., 110.

46. Frank E. Vogel, "Contract Law of Islam and the Arab Middle East," vol. 7, part 7, in *International Encyclopedia of Comparative Law* (2006), 7 n. 15. I am grateful to Aron Zysow for referring me to this article.

47. Hossein Modarressi, "The Legal Basis for the Validity of the Majority Opinion in Islamic Legislation," in *Under Siege: Islam and Democracy*, ed. Richard W. Bulliet (New York: Middle East Institute of Columbia University, 1994), 85.

48. Hallaq, *Authority, Continuity, and Legal Change in Islamic Law*, 166.

49. Ibid., 115.

50. Chibli Mallat, *Introduction to Middle Eastern Law* (Oxford: Oxford University Press, 2007), 108.

51. Hallaq, *Authority, Continuity, and Legal Change in Islamic Law*, chap. 6, "The Jurisconsult, the Author-Jurist, and Legal Change."

52. *Teshuvot ha-Rambam*, ed. Blau, 2:320 (no. 178).

## CHAPTER 1

1. Gerald Blidstein, "Where Do We Stand in the Study of Maimonidean Halakhah?," in *Studies in Maimonides*, ed. Isadore Twersky (Cambridge, MA: Harvard University Press, 1990), 27.

2. Alan Watson, *Society and Legal Change* (Edinburgh: Scottish Academic Press, 1977), xviii.

3. Ibid., 136–137 and chap. 8, "Legal Scaffolding."

4. Alan Watson, *Legal Transplants: An Approach to Comparative Law* (Edinburgh: Scottish Academic Press, 1974).

5. Alan Watson, "Society's Choice and Legal Change," *Hofstra Law Review* 9 (1980–1981): 1479, http://digitalcommons.law.uga.edu/fac_artchop/790.

6. The article by Hanina Ben-Menahem, "The Second Canonization of the Talmud," *Cardozo Law Review* 28, 1 (2006): 37–51, deals with discrepancies between the responsa of Maimonides and the Code but not with the subject at hand. Some of the articles in Nahum Rakover, ed., *Maimonides as Codifier of Jewish Law* (Jerusalem: Library of Jewish Law, 1987) touch on the historical reality behind the Code, but none of them uses the Geniza documents to illuminate passages in it. Salo Baron recognized that Maimonides shows awareness of the interplay of legal norms from the Talmud and contemporary economic circumstances (Salo W. Baron, "The Economic Views of Maimonides," in *Essays on Maimonides: An Octocentennial Volume*, ed. Salo W. Baron [New York: Columbia University Press, 1941], 127–264). With his characteristic insight, Baron wrote, "in [Maimonides'] reformulation, adaptation, and modification of the traditional law [of the just price] we may perceive what he regarded as desirable and, to a certain extent, as feasible under conditions known to him" (p. 187). Though aware of these new conditions, the study of the documentary Geniza was too underdeveloped in 1941 for Baron to have backed up his speculations with hard evidence from that source. He had many of Maimonides' responsa before him, but he was writing before Goitein came onto the scene and revolutionized the study of the documentary fragments from the Geniza. Goitein had many occasions to refer to sections in the Code that reflect life in the Geniza community. His citations can be found through the index of Maimonidean sources in the index volume (vol. 6) of *Med. Soc.*

7. The limited, general codes include the *Halakhot gedolot* attributed to R. Simeon Qayara (see below, Chapter 2 n. 38). The most prolific author of legal monographs on specific subjects was Samuel b. Ḥofni Gaon (d. 1013). See the catalog of his works, both extant and not, in Sklare, *Samuel ben Ḥofni Gaon*, 19–24.

8. The chapter "Codificatory Method and Jewish Legal Theory," by Haim H. Cohn, in Rakover, ed., *Maimonides as Codifier of Jewish Law*, explains why the Mishneh Torah should be considered a valid code.

9. Moshe Halbertal discusses Maimonides' intention to compile a new canon, absorbing and replacing all previous collections of Jewish law, in "What Is the Mishneh Torah? On Codification and Ambivalence," in *Maimonides After 800 Years: Essays on Maimonides and His Influence*, ed. Jay M. Harris (Cambridge, MA: Harvard University Press,

2007), 81–111, and in his recent biography, *Ha-Rambam: Rabbi Mosheh ben Maimon* (Jerusalem: Merkaz Zalman Shazar, 2009), chap. 4; English trans., *Maimonides: Life and Thought*, trans. Joel Linsider (Princeton, NJ: Princeton University Press, 2014), chap. 4. See also Ben-Sasson, "Maimonides' *Mishneh Torah*: On the Creation of a Canon During the Author's Lifetime."

10. The translation "repetition of the Law" is used by Twersky (*Introduction to the Code of Maimonides*, 30) and others. But it is possible to hear an echo of the phrase *mishneh la-melekh*, applied to Mordechai in the Book of Esther (10:3), where he is called "second to King Ahashverus," an epithet that is also attached to Joseph in the midrash and in biblical commentary, where he is called "second to Pharaoh." In this sense, the translation "second to the Torah" supports Maimonides' expressed intention in his Introduction that the Mishneh Torah would stand second in line to the Torah, with the need for no other book in between. For this translation, see also Nahum Rakover, "Maimonides as Codifier of Jewish Law," in *Sobre la vida y obra de Maimonides*, ed. Jesús Peláez Rosal (Córdoba: Ediciones el Almendro, 1991), 416; and Herbert A. Davidson, *Moses Maimonides: The Man and His Works* (Oxford: Oxford University Press, 2005), 197–198.

11. See Maimonides' letter to Pinḥas the *dayyan* (see below), *Iggerot ha-Rambam* (*Letters and Essays of Maimonides*), ed. Isaac Shailat, 2 vols. (Ma'aleh Adumim: Yeshivat Birkat Mosheh, 1988), 2:440. Also see Yuval Sinai, "Maimonides' Commentary on the Mishnah" (Hebrew), in *Mi-birkat Moshe* (*Essays on the Teachings of the Rambam in Honor of R. Naḥum Eliezer Rabinovitz*), ed. Zvi Hever and Carmiel Cohen, 2 vols. (Ma'aleh Adumim: Ma'aliyot, 2011), 2:209, 254–255, where Maimonides is quoted as having once told a student, "had it been my intention to explain the *ḥibbur* via the Talmud, I would not have compiled a *ḥibbur*."

12. In "Codification and Legal Culture: In Comparative Perspective," *Tulane European and Civil Law Forum* 13 (1998): 136 n. 39, Daphne Barak-Erez, since 2012 a member of Israel's Supreme Court, writes, concerning codes like the Mishneh Torah and the Shulḥan 'Arukh, that "these so-called codifications did not profess to introduce reform, merely to rewrite doctrines in an organized and accessible forms [*sic*]."

13. "As for your (critical) statement that you found in my composition certain matters which appear unclear (hidden) because they are without proof, and that your own mind is not deep enough to comprehend (them), it would have been correct for you to make this criticism if there were indeed matters in my composition which I myself had deduced on the basis of my sharp reasoning (*pilpul*) and my own opinion, and then recorded them unqualifiedly, without giving proof or reason for them. However, I have never done this. Let your own reason reveal them, and know that every unqualified statement which I made in my composition is based upon an explicit unqualified statement either in the Babylonian Talmud or in the Palestinian one, is drawn from Sifra or Sifre, or from an explicit unqualified statement in the Mishnah or in the Tosefta. If I derived a law from the responsa of the Geonim, I explicitly introduced it with the remark, 'The Geonim have taught,' 'This is an ordinance of the later Rabbis,' or a similar note. *And anything which I myself originated (from my sharp reasoning), I introduced with the note 'It appears to me that the matter is as follows';* this is the proof, inasmuch as I had announced in the introduction

to the work that all the material in it is drawn from the Babylonian or Palestinian Talmuds, Sifra, Sifre, or Tosefta." *Iggerot ha-Rambam*, ed. Shailat, 2:442–443; trans. in Isadore Twersky, *Introduction to the Code of Maimonides*, 35–36 (emphasis added). Twersky (20–47) cites seven statements by Maimonides, including this one, about the purpose of his Code.

14. *Teshuvot ha-Rambam*, ed. Blau, 2:459 (no. 251).

15. Among those who take Maimonides at his word are Benjamin Zeev Benedikt, *Ha-Rambam le-lo seṭiya min ha-talmud: Asufat ma'amarim* (*Maimonides, Without Straying from the Talmud: Collected Articles*) (Jerusalem: Mossad Harav Kook, 1985); Menachem Elon, *Jewish Law: History, Sources, Principles*, trans. Bernard Auerbach and Melvin J. Sykes, 4 vols. (Philadelphia: Jewish Publication Society, 1994), 3:1145: "Nor did Maimonides entertain even the slightest idea of introducing any change in the law through his work"; Davidson, *Moses Maimonides*, 259: "Considered separately, the features and components of Maimonides' *Mishneh Torah* disclose little that is original. . . . Its originality lies primarily in the overall conception and its execution"; Sherwin B. Nuland, *Maimonides* (New York: Next Book/Schocken, 2005), 229: "Maimonides allows his personal views only very limited latitude, and they do not lead him to make rulings in opposition to what the classic rabbinic sources indicate the halakic norm should be." Jacob Levinger, *Darkhei ha-maḥshava ha-hilkhatit shel ha-Rambam* (*Maimonides' Techniques of Codification: A Study in the Method of the Mishneh Torah*) (Jerusalem: Magnes, 1965), concludes in chap. 4, "Maimonides' Attitude Toward His Sources," that, at least with regard to actual rulings, Maimonides did not deviate from the rabbinic sources. In an appendix (pp. 210–225), Levinger provides a convenient list of 123 opinions in the Code that Maimonides marked as his own and another forty-eight in which he states that he differs with or agrees with predecessors—mainly, the Geonim or his own teachers (in Spain). In regard to halakhot that reflect philosophy and science, apart from the explicit sections, Levinger finds that Maimonides did, however, add things without marking them as his own view; Levinger, "Maimonides as Philosopher and Codifier," *Jewish Law Annual* 1 (1978): 133–145. For Libson, see above, Introduction sec. 0.5. And see Sarah Stroumsa's apposite remarks in her *Maimonides in His World: Portrait of a Mediterranean Thinker* (Princeton, NJ: Princeton University Press, 2009), 13: "The prevalent tendency is therefore that, in halakhic matters, [Maimonides'] source of inspiration must have been solely his predecessors, previous halakhic authorities. This approach leaves many of Maimonides' legal innovations unexplained." Her own argument is that, in both his halakhic and his philosophical writing, Maimonides was influenced by the Almohad environment, in which he lived from 1148 until his departure from Morocco for the East around 1165.

16. Blidstein's tendency in this matter is cautious, as Stroumsa points out in *Maimonides in His World*, 65. The question of adaptation of the halakha in response to new economic conditions has been posed with respect to the response of medieval Ashkenazic Jewry and answered in the affirmative. See Haym Soloveitchik, "Religious Law and Change: The Medieval Ashkenazic Example," *AJS Review* 12 (1987): 205–221; repr. in his *Collected Essays* (Oxford: Littman Library of Jewish Civilization, 2013), 1:239–257. I shall return to Soloveitchik in the Conclusion.

17. S. D. Goitein, "Maimonides, Man of Action: A Revision of the Master's Biography in Light of the Geniza Documents," in *Hommage à Georges Vajda*, ed. G. Nahon and Ch. Touati (Louvain: Peeters, 1980), 155–167. See also Joel Kraemer, *Maimonides: The Life and World of One of Civilization's Greatest Minds* (New York: Doubleday, 2008), chap. 16.

18. Ibn al-Qifṭī, *Ta'rīkh al-ḥukamā'*, trans. in Bernard Lewis, *Islam: From the Prophet Muhammad to the Capture of Constantinople*, 2 vols. (New York: Harper and Row, 1974), 2:190; Kraemer, *Maimonides*, 161–162, 243–258. On Ibn al-Qifṭī, see *Encyclopaedia of Islam*², s.v. *Ibn al-Ḳifṭī* (A. Dietrich).

19. Twersky, *Introduction to the Code of Maimonides*, 124–134.

20. Ya'akov Blidstein, review of Twersky's *Introduction*, *Pe'amim* 11 (1982): 140; cf. Libson, *Jewish and Islamic Law*, 196 n. 56. Twersky's index (p. 632) shows that he had little occasion to comment on parts of the Code that deal most directly with matters of commercial partnership and agency (*Hilkhot sheluḥin ve-shutafin*, "Laws of Agents and Partners"), where the impact of the custom of the merchants, as we shall see, was considerable.

21. Twersky, *Introduction to the Code of Maimonides*, 311–320.

22. See, e.g., *Teshuvot ha-Rambam*, ed. Blau, 3:142–148 (no. 464).

23. Isadore Twersky, *Rabad of Posquières, a Twelfth-Century Talmudist* (Cambridge, MA: Harvard University Press, 1962). A characteristic comment by Rabad is his statement, "[W]hen I looked into the Talmud I did not find his statements to be tenable," cited in ibid., 162. Twersky downplays Rabad's assault on the Code, contextualizing it within a common discourse of argumentation that was not necessarily meant to destroy the work. For a different view, see Davidson, *Moses Maimonides*, 272–276. I strongly suspect that, had he heard about the Provençal rabbi's criticisms, Maimonides would have considered them hostile.

24. A convenient summary of critics of Maimonides' Code can be found in Davidson, *Moses Maimonides*, 265–280. Abraham defended his father's Code in his *Birkat Avraham*, ed. Ber Goldberg (Lyck, 1859; repr., Jerusalem: n.p., 1960).

25. For the verb *rattaba* applied by Maimonides to *taqqanot*, see *Teshuvot ha-Rambam*, ed. Blau, 2:393–395 (no. 221).

26. On Jewish use of the term *qibla*, see M. Cohen, *Under Crescent and Cross*, 115.

27. *Teshuvot Rav Naṭronai bar Hilai Gaon*, ed. Robert (Yeraḥme'el) Brody, 2 vols. (Jerusalem: Ofek Institute, 1994), 1:131–132 (no. 25). Gerald Blidstein, "Maimonides' *Taqqanah* Concerning Public Prayer," in *Maimonidean Studies* 3 (1992–1993): 14–19, notes that the Geonim took cognizance of problems arising from the Talmudic arrangement of the double 'Amida, though not on account of the *ḥillul ha-shem* that prompted Maimonides to enact his *taqqana*. See also Blidstein's *Ha-tefilla be-mishnato ha-hilkhatit shel ha-Rambam* (*Prayer in the Halakhic Teaching of Maimonides*) (Jerusalem: Mossad Bialik, 1994), 169–181, where he shows that Maimonides was not the first halakhist to evince concern about the habits of congregants during the synagogue service and that his concerns went beyond the purely ephemeral impression made on Muslim passersby.

28. *Teshuvot ha-Rambam*, ed. Blau, 2:474–475 (no. 256), 483–484 (no. 258), 548 (no. 291). See Naphtali Wieder, *Hashpa'ot islamiyot 'al ha-pulḥan ha-yehudi* (*Islamic Influences*

*on the Jewish Worship*) (Oxford: East and West Library, 1947), 27–28, and Blidstein, "Maimonides' *Taqqanah* Concerning Public Prayer," 3–28; idem, *Ha-tefilla be-mishnato ha-hilkhatit shel ha-Rambam*, 169–174. Maimonides refers elsewhere in his responsa to violation of decorum in the synagogue; see references in *Teshuvot ha-Rambam*, ed. Blau, 2:475 n. 11. See also *Med. Soc.*, 2:168, 223. Maimonides' son, Abraham, had similar reformist views and tried to institute changes in the service of the synagogue, but experienced serious opposition. See Wieder, *Hashpa'ot islamiyot*, 28–29; and Elisha Russ-Fishbane, "Between Politics and Piety: Abraham Maimonides and His Times" (PhD diss., Harvard University, 2009), 262ff., his "The Maimonidean Legacy in the East: A Study of Father and Son," *Jewish Quarterly Review* 102 (2012): 190–223, and his *Judaism, Sufism, and the Pietists of Medieval Egypt: A Study of Abraham Maimonides and His Times* (Oxford: Oxford University Press, 2015). On the significance of *ḥillul ha-shem* in this context, see Menahem Ben-Sasson, "Remembrance and Oblivion of Religious Persecutions: On Sanctifying the Name of God (*Qiddush ha-Shem*) in Christian and Islamic Communities During the Middle Ages," in *Jews, Christians and Muslims in Medieval and Early Modern Times: A Festschrift in Honor of Mark R. Cohen*, ed. Arnold E. Franklin et al. (Leiden: Brill, 2014), 185–187.

29. Based on Ps. 119:126: "It is time to act for the Lord [*'et la'asot la-adonai*], for they have violated Your teaching" (*heferu toratekha*), which, with a slight change of vocalization, was understood as a command: *haferu toratekha*, "[you should] violate your law." This was taken to mean that, when it is necessary to do something for God, it is permissible to deviate from the law, i.e., by enacting a *taqqana*. See Mishna Berakhot 9:5, among many places.

30. *Teshuvot ha-Rambam*, ed. Blau, 2:475 (no. 256).

31. *Hilkhot tefilla u-virkat kohanim* (Laws of Prayer and the Priestly Blessing), chap. 9. I agree with Blidstein, who opines that Maimonides adhered to the status quo in the Code because the Code was meant as a new canon of Jewish law to remain in force forever. Blidstein, "Maimonides' *Taqqanah* Concerning Public Prayer," 13–14.

32. *Hilkhot tefilla u-virkat kohanim*, 9:3. I have not found an earlier rabbinic source that includes the final clause. The major commentators pass over the halakha without comment.

33. *Hilkhot tefilla u-virkat kohanim* 4:10–11. See Mordechai A. Friedman, "Abraham Maimuni's Prayer Reforms: Continuation or Revision of His Father's Teachings?" in *Traditions of Maimonideanism*, ed. Carlos Fraenkel (Leiden: Brill, 2009), 142–143 and the references cited there.

34. Meir Havatselet, *Ha-Rambam veha-ge'onim* (*Maimonides and the Geonites* [*sic*]) (Jerusalem: Sura, 1967), 168–169, 172–174.

35. *Hilkhot tefilla u-virkat kohanim* 11:4. *The Tosefta*, ed. Saul Lieberman. Seder Mo'ed, Megilla 3:21, and idem, *Tosefta Ki-fshuṭah*, Seder Mo'ed, 1199–1200; see also idem, *Tosefet rishonim*, 4 vols. in 2 (New York: Jewish Theological Seminary, 1999), 1:237–238. The Tosefta passage that Maimonides augmented states: "The elders sit facing the people with their backs toward the holy ark [*qodesh*]. When they put the Torah box [*teiva*] down, it should face the people with its back toward the holy ark. When the priests raise their hands (to pronounce the priestly blessing) they face the people, with their backs toward

the holy ark. The cantor of the synagogue faces the people, and all the people face the holy ark." Maimonides elaborates with a significant addition: "How do people sit in the synagogue? The elders sit facing the people with their backs toward the holy ark [here the word is *heikhal*, the common term among Jews from Arab lands to this day]. *The people sit one row in front of the other, each row facing the backs of the row in front of it, such that all the people are facing the holy ark* [here, the word is *qodesh*, as in the Tosefta], *the elders, and the Torah box*. When the prayer leader stands for the prayer of the Eighteen Benedictions, he stands on the floor in front of the Torah box facing the holy ark like all the other people." For a discussion of the word for "Torah box," which differed from the reader's platform called *bima*, see the commentary Kesef Mishneh on *Hilkhot tefilla*, and see Lieberman, *Tosefta Ki-fshuṭah*, 1199. The passage placed in italics above represents a significant elaboration of the Tosefta and illustrates Maimonides' effort, building on a classical rabbinic source, to dictate with absolute clarity how the seating in the synagogue should look. It is hard to escape the conclusion that he is drawing a diagram that mimics the well-ordered arrangement of Muslims at prayer in the mosque on Friday.

36. Kraemer, *Maimonides*, 116–124; Mordechai A. Friedman, *Ha-Rambam ha-mashiaḥ be-teiman veha-shemad* (*Maimonides, The Yemenite Messiah, and Apostasy*) (Jerusalem: Makhon Ben-Zvi, 2002), 31–37; Stroumsa, *Maimonides in His World*, 59; Amir Mazor, "Maimonides' Conversion to Islam: New Evidence" (Hebrew), *Pe'amim* 110 (2007): 5–8. But see Davidson, *Moses Maimonides*, 17–28, defending the traditional opinion. Maimonides' reforms of religious practice failed, as far as we know, to elicit the serious opposition that confronted the Sufi-like pietists of the generation of his son, Abraham. See, among the numerous discussions of Abraham Maimonides' pietistic reforms, Wieder, *Hashpa'ot islamiyot*, 28–29; S. D. Goitein, "Documents on Abraham Maimonides and His Pietist Circle" (Hebrew), *Tarbiz* 33 (1964): 181–197; idem, "Abraham Maimonides and His Pietist Circle," in *Jewish Medieval and Renaissance Studies*, ed. Alexander Altmann (Cambridge, MA: Harvard University Press, 1967), 145–164; idem, "A Treatise in Defense of the Pietists by Abraham Maimonides" (Hebrew), *Journal of Jewish Studies* 16 (1965): 105–114; Russ-Fishbane, "Between Politics and Piety"; idem, *Judaism, Sufism, and the Pietists of Medieval Egypt*; Paul Fenton, "Maimonides—Father and Son: Continuity and Change," in *Traditions of Maimonideanism*, ed. Carlos Fraenkel, 103–137; Marina Rustow, "At the Limits of Communal Autonomy: Jewish Bids for Intervention from the Mamluk State," *Mamlūk Studies Review* 13 (2009): 140–146; Friedman, "Abraham Maimuni's Prayer Reforms"; idem, "Abraham Maimonides on His Leadership, Reforms, and Spiritual Imperfection," *Jewish Quarterly Review* 104 (2014): 495–512.

## CHAPTER 2

1. This is discussed exhaustively by Libson, *Jewish and Islamic Law*. See, esp., chap. 4. Cf. also Menachem Elon, *Ḥerut ha-peraṭ be-darkhei geviyat ḥov ba-mishpaṭ ha-'ivri* (*Freedom of the Debtor's Person in Jewish Law*) (Jerusalem: Magnes, 1964), 38. On the Geonim, see Brody, *The Geonim of Babylonia*.

2. Libson, *Jewish and Islamic Law*, 87.

3. See Walter J. Fischel, *Jews in the Economic and Political Life of Mediaeval Islam* (London: Royal Asiatic Society, 1937), 17–21; *Med. Soc.*, 1:242–245; Libson, *Jewish and Islamic Law*, 84–85, 96–97, 262 n. 34, 270–271 n. 30; *Encyclopaedia of Islam*², s.v. *suftadja* (M. Y. Izzi Dien). The *suftaja* may have originated in the seventh century; see Morony, "Commerce in Early Islamic Iraq," 711.

4. *Encyclopaedia of Islam*², s.v. *suftadja* (M. Y. Izzi Dien).

5. The language of the question is not wholly clear. See the discussion in Elimelech Westreich, "Elements of Negotiability in Talmudic and Geonic Sources," in *Elements of Negotiability in Talmudic and Geonic Times: Jewish Commercial Law—Essays in Memory of George Webber*, ed. J. Cohen, *Jewish Law Association Studies* 29 (2008): 266–272. Below, I translate only the answer.

6. The Babylonian Talmud explains that money cannot be transferred via an agent if the document (a power of attorney) bears a *diyoqne*, even if there are signatures. Scholars correctly identified the etymology of this word as coming from the Greek term for "image" (cf. English: "icon"), though they were mystified by the initial *d*. See the summary of views in J. Ostersetzer, "The דיוקני [*diyoqne*] in Legal Documents in Talmudic Jurisprudence" (Hebrew), *Tarbiz* 11 (1940): 39–55, and the earlier discussion in Asher Gulak, *Das Urkundenwesen im Talmud im Lichte der griechisch-aegyptischen Papyri und des griechischen und roemischen Rechts* (Jerusalem: Rubin Mass, 1935), 145 (updated by Ranon Katzoff in the Hebrew translation, *Ha-sheṭarot ba-talmud* [*Legal Documents in the Talmud*] [Jerusalem: Magnes, 1994], 172). Setting aside the philological difficulty of the prefixed *d*, Ostersetzer explains how legal documents among the Greek papyri from Hellenistic Egypt included, for authenticating purposes, the physical description of the parties concerned. This was rejected for powers of attorney by the Babylonian Amoraim. As to the philological problem, Professor Roxani Eleni Margariti of Emory University kindly researched the term for me and informed me that the word apparently derives from the Greek phrase found, for instance, in Plato and Plutarch, *di'eikon os* (lit., "through an image"). Thus, when the Talmud says, "one may not send money *with a diyoqne*" (*be-diyoqne*), the Hebrew prefix *be-* ("with") is actually pleonastic, indicating that the rabbis (also modern scholars) did not understand the structure of the original loanword. A *suftaja* is called *diyoqne* in an eleventh-century letter, TS 13 J 8.14 line 10, Menahem Ben-Sasson et al., eds., *Yehudei siṣilia 825–1068: Te'udot u-meqorot* (*The Jews of Sicily 825–1068: Documents and Sources*) (Jerusalem: Makhon Ben-Zvi, 1991), 154–155 (no. 35) (hereafter, Ben-Sasson, *Jews of Sicily*); Moshe Gil, ed., *Ereṣ yisra'el ba-tequfa ha-muslemit ha-rishona (634–1099)* (*Palestine During the First Muslim Period [634–1099]*), 3 vols. (Tel Aviv: Tel Aviv University and Ministry of Defense, 1983), 2:596–598 (no. 326) (hereafter, Gil, *Palestine*). The document is translated into English in Shlomo Simonsohn, *The Jews in Sicily, Volume 1, 383–1300* (Leiden: Brill, 1997), 81–83 (hereafter, Simonsohn, *Jews in Sicily*).

7. *Teshuvot ha-ge'onim*, ed. Abraham Eliyahu Harkavy (Berlin: Tsvi Hirsch Itskovski, 1887), 216 (no. 423). See *Med. Soc.*, 1:242–245 and, on this responsum, see 2:328, quoted in Libson, *Jewish and Islamic Law*, 84–85, 96–97; and M. Cohen, *Under Crescent and Cross*, 93.

8. ENA 4020.26, lines 2–3; cf. S. D. Goitein, "The Interplay of Jewish and Islamic Laws," in *Jewish Law in Legal History and the Modern World*, ed. Bernard S. Jackson (Leiden: Brill, 1980), 70–71. The custom in question was confirmed by the testimony of Jewish witnesses. For the meaning "practice, custom, norms" for *ḥukm*, see Elsaid M. Badawi and Muhammad Abdel Haleem, *Arabic-English Dictionary of Qur'anic Usage* (Leiden: Brill, 2008), 227.

9. A. L. Udovitch, "The 'Law Merchant' of the Medieval Islamic World," in *Logic in Classical Islamic Culture*, ed. G. E. von Grunebaum (Wiesbaden: O. Harrassowitz, 1970), 113–130. See also Mallat, *Introduction to Middle Eastern Law*, 313, where several terms for the custom of the merchants are given: *'ādat al-tujjār, ta'āmul al-nās, ta'āruf bayn al-nās, wajh al-tijāra*.

10. See Albrecht Cordes, "The Search for a Medieval *Lex Mercatoria*" (2003), Oxford University Comparative Law Forum 5, at ouclf.iuscomp.org and, more recently, Emily Kadens, "The Myth of the Customary Law Merchant," *Texas Law Review* 90 (2012): 1153–1206, summarizing in her notes previous discussions of this controversial issue.

11. See sec. 2.2 below.

12. *Teshuvot ha-ge'onim sha'arei ṣedeq* [Salonika, 1792; repr., Jerusalem: Kelal U-Ferat, 1966], part 4, chap. 6:8, cited in Libson, *Jewish and Islamic Law*, 270 n. 30 (emphasis added).

13. Recourse by Jews to Islamic courts is discussed below, esp. Chapter 9.

14. Alfasi, Bava Qamma 37b in the pages in the printed Talmud; Maimonides, *Hilkhot sheluḥin ve-shutafin* (Laws of Agents and Partners), 1:8.

15. *Ḥemda genuza*, ed. Ze'ev Wolf Wolfensohn and Schneur Zalman Schneersohn (Jerusalem: n.p., 1860), 13b (no. 65); Chaim Tykocinski, *Taqqanot ha-ge'onim*, trans. Meir Havatselet (Jerusalem and New York: Sura and Yeshiva University, 1960), 30–50 (but see also Ackerman-Lieberman, "Revisiting Jewish Occupational Choice" and below, Chapter 4, n. 44). These examples of Gaonic responses to changes in society call into question Israel Ta-Shma's categorical contrast between the so-called unbending halakhic approach to legal change of the "Babylonian-Spanish" school, limited, as it was, by Babylonian Talmudic law, and the more flexible and adaptive approach of the medieval Ashkenazic rabbinic scholars, who lived far away from the Gaonic center, and where custom, more than written law, governed daily life. Israel Ta-Shma, *Creativity and Traditions: Studies in Medieval Rabbinic Scholarship, Literature, and Thought* (Cambridge, MA: Harvard University Press, 2006), 105–106. The Geniza documents abundantly show the extent to which, in economic affairs, custom governed the activities of Jewish merchants, necessitating flexible adaptation not only by the Geonim but also, as we shall see, by Maimonides.

16. In *Cahiers d'Histoire Mondiale* 3 (1956–1957): 583–604, repr. in Goitein, *Studies in Islamic History and Institutions* (Leiden: Brill, 1966; new ed. with an introduction by Norman A. Stillman, 2010), 217–241. Goitein's student Hayyim Cohen followed up with a dissertation on the occupational *nisbas* of more than 4,000 Muslim jurists and traditionists in the first half-millennium of Islamic rule, finding that a substantial majority of them worked in commercial or related business pursuits, such as handicrafts. Summarized in Hayyim J. Cohen, "The Economic Background and the Secular Occupations of Muslim

Jurisprudents and Traditionists in the Classical Period of Islam (Until the Middle of the Eleventh Century)," *Journal of the Economic and Social History of the Orient* 13 (1970): 16–61.

17. Joseph Schacht, *Introduction to Islamic Law* (Oxford: Clarendon, 1964), 6–7.

18. See A. L. Udovitch, *Partnership and Profit in Medieval Islam* (Princeton, NJ: Princeton University Press, 1970); Imran A. K. Nyazee, *Islamic Law of Business Organization: Partnerships* (Islamabad: International Institute of Islamic Thought, 1999), 232.

19. Robert (Yeraḥme'el) Brody, "Were the Geonim Legislators?" (Hebrew), *Shenaton ha-mishpaṭ ha-'ivri* 11–12 (1984–1986): 290–304.

20. I am grateful to Intisar Rabb, who called my attention to this maxim and its similar application in Islamic law.

21. Bava Meṣi'a 7:1, Venice edition 11b; and Yevamot 12:1, Venice edition 12c. Cf. also *Massekhet Soferim B*, 14:16, ed. Michael Higger (New York: Debei-Rabbanan, 1937), 271.

22. Bava Meṣi'a 74a, and Rashi, s.v. *siṭumta*. See Elon, *Jewish Law*, 2:913–920. On the lexical item, see Michael Sokoloff, *A Dictionary of Jewish Babylonian Aramaic of the Talmudic and Gaonic Periods* (Baltimore: Johns Hopkins University Press, 2002), 801.

23. R. Solomon b. Adret (Rashba), *Ḥiddushim* (*Novellae*) to Bava Meṣi'a 74a; cf. Ron S. Kleinman, *Darkhei qinyan u-minhagei misḥar ba-mishpaṭ ha-'ivri* (*Methods of Acquisition and Commercial Customs in Jewish Law: Theory, Practice and History*) (Ramat Gan: Bar-Ilan University Press, 2013), 100 n. 5 (emphasis added). Rabbinic authorities, right down to modern times, have applied *qinyan siṭumta* broadly to cover new methods of acquisition, such as the handshake, or making a small down payment. See the thorough study by Kleinman. Contemporary concerns discussed by halakhic scholars include the validity of purchase by credit card over the telephone. See Ilan Kaplan, "*Qinyan Siṭumta* (the Custom of the Merchants): Its Validity and Meaning" (Hebrew), *Avnei Mishpaṭ* 2 (2003): 174–192 (on credit-card purchase, see p. 183), and idem, "*Qinyan Siṭumta*: In the Case of Real Property and the Case of Objects That Do Not Exist" (Hebrew), *Avnei Mishpaṭ* 3 (2004): 168–184. Several cases in contemporary Israel concerning the application of *siṭumta* to monetary matters are discussed by Dov Katz, "*Qinyan Siṭumta*" (Hebrew), *Morasha* (Sivan 1971): 79–86.

24. With respect to medieval European commercial law, Udovitch quotes Levin Goldschmidt, author of *Handbuch des Handelsrechts* (1874): "The grandeur and significance of the medieval merchant is that he creates his own law out of his own needs and his own views." Udovitch, "The 'Law Merchant' of the Medieval Islamic World," 113.

25. This is the view of Daniel Sperber in his *Nautica Talmudica* (Ramat Gan and Leiden: Bar-Ilan University Press and Brill, 1986), though in a subsequent article, he slightly revised his opinion. See his "*Nautica* in Talmudic Palestine," in *Seafaring and the Jews*, ed. Nadav Kashtan (London: Cass, 2001), 29–32.

26. These are discussed, along with some medieval sources, in Steven F. Friedell, "Admiralty and the Sea of Jewish Law," *Journal of Maritime Law and Commerce* 27 (October 1996): 647–660. See also Stephen M. Passamaneck, "Traces of Rabbinical Maritime Law and Custom," *Revue d'histoire du droit* 34 (1966): 525–551, and Raphael Patai, "Ancient Jewish Seafaring and Riverfaring Laws," in *By Study and Also by Faith: Essays in*

*Honor of Hugh W. Nibley on the Occasion of His Eightieth Birthday, 27 March 1990*, ed. Stephen D. Ricks and John Lundquist (Salt Lake City: Desert Book, 1990), 389–416.

27. See Hezser, *Jewish Travel in Antiquity*, 189–196 and chap. 6.

28. David Goodblatt, "*Medinat Hayam*: The Coastal District" (Hebrew), *Tarbiz* 64 (1994–1995): 13–37, and refinements in Hezser, *Jewish Travel in Antiquity*, 285–286.

29. Bava Qamma 116b, discussed as a trace of rabbinic maritime law in Passamaneck, "Traces of Rabbinical Law and Custom," 536–544. Cf. *The Tosefta*, ed. Saul Lieberman, 5 vols. (New York: Jewish Theological Seminary, 1955–1988), Seder Neziqin, Bava Meṣi'a 7:13–14, and idem, *Tosefta Ki-fshuṭah*, 10 vols. (New York: Jewish Theological Seminary, 1955–1988), Seder Neziqin, 255–256. For the Talmud's "they must not deviate from the custom of the ass-drivers," the Tosefta substitutes a more general phrase, "they must not deviate from the custom of those who travel by caravan." Through a slight variation in the word there, the caravan is said to have been "attacked by armed men *who plundered it*" (*u-ṭerafah*), suggesting that the travelers share the loss already incurred, rather than, as in the Talmud's version, paying "protection money"—ransom, actually—to the marauders in advance to forestall the depredation. In the case of jettison from a ship, the Tosefta says, "they reckon according to the weight of the cargo and not according the number of souls." The latter option presumably would include travelers who were not accompanying cargo, even the seamen themselves. The passage concerning caravan travel is discussed in Stephen M. Passamaneck, "Caravan Custom in Early Rabbinic Sources," *Revue d'histoire du droit* 36 (1968): 76–78. Gaonic responsa retrieved from the Geniza describe attacks by brigands on caravans and on ships run aground or wrecked. See *Teshuvot ha-ge'onim*, ed. Simḥa Assaf (Jerusalem: Mekize Nirdamim, 1942), 84–85 (no. 74); Louis Ginzberg, *Geonica*, 2 vols. (New York: Jewish Theological Seminary, 1909), 2:150–151 (no. 502); *Teshuvot ha-ge'onim*, ed. Simḥa Assaf (Jerusalem: Darom, 1929), 77–78 (no. 152) (also in *Teshuvot ha-ge'onim sha'arei ṣedeq*, part 4, chap. 8:1). The juxtaposition of sea travel and land travel in the Talmud shows, further, that the rabbis considered laws of seafaring to be analogous to laws governing travel on land. This principle of jurisprudence, too, was carried over to the Islamic period and incorporated into Islamic law. Writing about the medieval Islamic Mediterranean, A. L. Udovitch observes: "The maritime practices on the Islamic coasts of the Mediterranean were a simple and direct extension and application of land based notions and institutions to the affairs of the sea"; Udovitch, "Time, the Sea and Society: Duration of Commercial Voyages on the Southern Shores of the Mediterranean During the High Middle Ages," in *La Navigazione Mediterranea nell'alto Medioevo* (Spoleto: Presso la sede del Centro, 1978), 520 and 546.

30. The text was edited and translated by Walter Ashburner, *The Rhodian Sea Law* (Oxford: Clarendon, 1909).

31. Boaz Cohen, *Jewish and Roman Law: A Comparative Study*, 2 vols. (New York: Jewish Theological Seminary, 1966), 2:469.

32. Hassan Khalilieh, *Islamic Maritime Law: An Introduction* (Leiden: Brill, 1998), and idem, *Admiralty and Maritime Laws in the Mediterranean Sea (ca. 800–1050): The Kitāb akriyat al-sufun vis-à-vis the Nomos Rhodion Nautikos* (Leiden: Brill, 2006), 250–254, in the conclusions.

33. Khalilieh, *Islamic Maritime Law*, 97–100, and his *Admiralty and Maritime Laws*, chap. 4. The merchants on board are said to have become *shurakā' bi-thamanihā*, "partners in [the jettisoned cargo's] value" (*Islamic Maritime Law*, 98 n. 182), what Udovitch calls an "involuntary partnership"; Udovitch, "An Eleventh-Century Islamic Treatise on the Law of the Sea," *Annales Islamologiques* 27 (1993): 51. On jettison, see also Olivia Remie Constable, "The Problem of Jettison in Medieval Mediterranean Maritime Law," *Journal of Medieval History* 20 (1994): 207–220.

34. Constable, "The Problem of Jettison," 213–214.

35. For a different interpretation, see Lieberman, *Tosefta Ki-fshuṭah*, Seder Neziqin, 256.

36. Constable, "The Problem of Jettison," 217–220.

37. For Maimonides, see *Hilkhot gezela va-aveda*, Laws of Theft and Lost Items 12:14.

38. *Halakhot gedolot*, ed. Ezriel Hildesheimer, 2 vols. (Jerusalem: Mekize Nirdamim, 1971–1988), 2:409–412. *Halakhot gedolot*, a legal compendium of the ninth century by Shimon Qayara of Basra, Iraq, consolidates laws in a practical form but adheres to the language of the Talmud. It brings laws of seafaring and the analogous situation of transport by land in his chapter containing halakhot from the Talmudic tractate Bava Meṣi'a and in his section on Bava Qamma, which includes the law of jettison (see above). Maimonides codifies the same laws as does *Halakhot gedolot*; though, in keeping with the rational organization of the Code, he makes them more accessible by placing them in his Laws of Hire (*Hilkhot sekhirut*), chaps. 4 and 5, and his Laws of Theft and Lost Items (*Hilkhot gezela va-aveda*), chap. 12.

39. For a discussion of Gaonic responsa about Jewish agrarian pursuits and legal adjustments to the halakha, see Jacob Mann, "The Responsa of the Babylonian Geonim as a Source of Jewish History," *Jewish Quarterly Review* n.s. 10 (1919): 310–319.

40. On Spain, see Olivia Remie Constable, *Trade and Traders in Muslim Spain: The Commercial Realignment of the Iberian Peninsula 900–1500* (Cambridge: Cambridge University Press, 1994), a book relying heavily on Geniza documents.

41. Above, Chapter 1 n. 18

42. The statement is quoted by Libson, *Jewish and Islamic Law*, 77, from the eleventh-century collection of and commentary on Islamic positive law by the Ḥanafī jurist al-Sarakhsī (d. ca. 1096), *al-Mabsūṭ*. For other authorities, see Libson, *Jewish and Islamic Law*, 78.

43. *Med. Soc.*, 1:178. A responsum attributable to R. Isaac Alfasi (Spain) regards a partnership in which the stationary, investing partner stipulated "that [the active partner] shall not go any place other than the place he is about to travel to." *Teshuvot ha-ge'onim*, ed. Assaf in *Makhon le-Madda'ei Ha-yahadut*, 2:126 (no. 142). For the Islamic *commenda*, see Udovitch, *Partnership and Profit*, chap. 6. When a Geniza merchant-agent decided to change his destination, he wrote to his principal, informing him so that the latter could decide whether the agent should transport his goods there instead. See Jessica L. Goldberg, "The Use and Abuse of Commercial Letters from the Cairo Geniza," *Journal of Medieval History* 38 (2012): 136 (TS 13 J 27.9).

44. *Teshuvot ha-Rambam*, ed. Blau, 1:156–158 (no. 95). On the function of the oath in

Islamic courts, see Robert Brunschvig, "Le système de la preuve en droit musulman," in *Etudes d'Islamologie*, 2 vols. (Paris: Maisonneuve et Larose, 1976), 2:210.

45. Nyazee, *Islamic Law of Business Organization: Partnerships*, 26–27, 86–87, 263–264, and in the index, s.v. *istidānah*.

46. See Libson, *Jewish and Islamic Law*, 38–39, 98.

47. *Teshuvot ha-ge'onim sha'arei ṣedeq*, part 4, chap. 8:4. On the rule, see Bava Meṣi'a 108a and discussion in M. Cohen, "A Partnership Gone Bad: Business Relationships and the Evolving Law of the Cairo Geniza Period," *Journal of the Economic and Social History of the Orient* 56 (2013): 230 n. 48.

48. TS NS J 6, lines 13–14; Phillip I. Ackerman-Lieberman, "A Partnership Culture: Jewish Economic and Social Life Seen Through the Legal Documents of the Cairo Geniza" (PhD diss., Princeton University, 2007), 1.4.4.4 and doc. no. 58.

49. See below, Chapter 5, sec. 5.7.

50. *Sefer ha-'iṭṭur*, ed. Meir Yonah, 2 vols. (Vilna-Warsaw, 1874–1885), 1:42b–43a.

51. Libson, *Jewish and Islamic Law*, 17.

52. I owe this suggestion to Avrom Udovitch.

53. Cf. the expression in Islamic jurisprudence regarding custom: *al-ma'lūm bi'l-'urf ka'l-ma'lūm bi'l-sharṭ*, "what is known by virtue of custom is like what is known by virtue of an agreed condition," quoted in Libson, *Jewish and Islamic Law*, 77. Cf. Udovitch, *Partnership and Profit*, 180.

54. See R. Yosef ha-Levi ibn Migash, *Ḥiddushei Ha-RY Migash*, ed. Moshe Shmuel Shapira (Benei Beraq: Lippa Friedman, 1973), 4a.

55. See Laws of Sale 17:6 and Laws of Hire 4:8; see also Laws of Sale 28:15. The word *yadua'* occurs about twenty times in the Code, with a range of meanings. The expression *zeman ha-yadua'* occurs in two halakhot in Agents and Partners 4:4 and 5:5. The latter states: "If there is a recognized season [*zeman yadua'*] for selling the merchandise [*li-mekhirat otah ha-seḥora*], each of them has the right to restrain the other, so that they do not divide [the proceeds]." Well aware of the range of meanings of the word *yadua'*, Maimonides carefully restricts its meaning in Agents and Partners 4:4 by adding the words "recognized season [lit., 'time'] *for it to be sold.*" *Yadua'* has the meaning of "recognized" in Agents and Partners 5:8: "A thing that is recognized [*davar ha-yadua'*] as belonging to two partners." The expression *minhag yadua'* occurs profusely in the halakhic literature of the Rishonim after Maimonides.

## CHAPTER 3

1. See the Introduction, sec. 0.1.

2. A. L. Udovitch, "Credit as a Means of Investment in Medieval Islamicate Trade," *Journal of the American Oriental Society* 87 (1967): 262.

3. M. Cohen, "Maimonides and Charity in the Light of the Geniza Documents," 66–67. My discussion in this section represents a revision of what I wrote in that essay, based on further reflection while writing the present book.

4. See Olivia Remie Constable, *Housing the Stranger in the Mediterranean World: Lodging, Trade, and Travel in Late Antiquity and the Middle Ages* (Cambridge: Cambridge University Press, 2003).

5. I owe this suggestion to Gerald Blidstein.

6. M. Cohen, *Poverty and Charity*, 72–108 (chap. titled "The Foreign Poor").

7. Ibid., 220–224.

8. See *Med. Soc.*, 4:248.

9. Maimonides' interpretation was adopted by Rashba, *'Avodat ha-qodesh, beit netivot*, 4:72: *shittuf seḥoratam 'oleh lahem mishum shittuf*, "their commercial partnership counts as their joint ownership" (reference courtesy of Zvi Stampfer).

10. *Ḥilluf ha-minhagim bein benei bavel li-vnei ereṣ yisrael*, ed. Joel Müller (Vienna: n.p., 1878), 36–37 (no. 39).

11. See Adams, above, Introduction n. 10.

12. *Teshuvot Rav Naṭronai bar Hilai Gaon*, ed. Brody, 1:295–296 (no. 169).

13. Ibid., 1:293–294 (no. 167). See also *Teshuvot ge'onei mizraḥ u-ma'arav*, ed. Joel Müller (Berlin: P. Deutsch, 1888), 37a (no. 150), the same ruling about transacting business in the privacy of one's home, repeated by the early tenth-century Gaon Kohen Ṣedeq.

14. *Teshuvot Rav Naṭronai bar Hilai Gaon*, ed. Brody, 1:296–297 (no. 170).

15. See Jessica L. Goldberg, *Trade and Institutions in the Medieval Mediterranean: Geniza Merchants and Their Business World* (Cambridge: Cambridge University Press, 2012), chap. 3, sec. 3. And see Chapter 5 below.

16. Eva Mira Grob, *Documentary Private and Business Letters on Papyrus: Form and Function, Content and Context* (Berlin: De Gruyter, 2010), 223 (appendix B1).

17. In rabbinic parlance, a "fence" (around the Torah) that prevents people from committing a more serious transgression.

18. *She'elot u-teshuvot R. Yosef ha-Levi ibn Migash*, ed. Simḥa Ḥasida (Jerusalem: Makhon Lev Sameaḥ, 1991), 138–139 (no. 145).

19. *Teshuvot ha-Rambam*, ed. Blau, 2:579 (no. 311), one of the responsa preserved only in a Hebrew version. On ships and caravans and the sending of letters, see *Med. Soc.*, 1:275–281.

20. Mo'ed Qaṭan 2:3, Venice ed. 80c. Cf. Shulḥan 'Arukh, Oraḥ Ḥayyim 539:5.

21. On the economic relationship between Fustat and Alexandria, see A. L. Udovitch, "A Tale of Two Cities: Commercial Relations Between Cairo and Alexandria During the Second Half of the Eleventh Century," in *The Medieval City*, ed. David Herlihy et al. (New Haven, CT: Yale University Press, 1977), 143–162. On Aden and the India trade, see Roxani Eleni Margariti, *Aden and the Indian Ocean Trade: 150 Years in the Life of a Medieval Arabian Port* (Chapel Hill: University of North Carolina Press, 2007) and the volumes of the Goitein-Friedman *Sefer hodu* listed in the works cited in the present book.

22. M. Cohen, *Poverty and Charity*, chap. 2.

23. Ibid., 163–166, 227–232; idem, *The Voice of the Poor in the Middle Ages*, 107–152.

24. M. Cohen, *Poverty and Charity*, 115–118; idem, *The Voice of the Poor in the Middle Ages*, 69–71.

25. *Med. Soc.*, 1:316, on the sailing season.

26. Translation, with minor changes, taken from Herbert Danby, *The Mishnah* (Oxford: Oxford University Press, 1933), 252.

27. *Mishna 'im perush rabbenu Moshe ben Maimon*, ed. and trans. Joseph Kafiḥ, 6 vols. (Jerusalem: Mossad Harav Kook, 1964–1969), Seder Nashim, 82 (there, the Mishna is 5:5). Kafiḥ translates *lā yatjurūna* correctly, "do not engage in trade," but his rendition of *yakhdumūna* as *'ovdim*, "work," misses the important nuance of the verb *khadama* and the noun *khidma*, which refer to commercial agency, a special type of commercial collaboration, to be discussed in Chapter 5.

28. As early as the ninth century, the Geonim permitted husbands to be away from their wives for long periods of time, with their wives' consent. Absent such permission, the court was instructed to order the husband to return, especially if he was traveling for trade. *Teshuvot Rav Naṭronai bar Hilai Gaon*, ed. Brody, 2:454–455 (no. 303), citing the same Mishna; also in *Ḥemda genuza*, ed. Wolfensohn and Schneersohn, 16a (no. 81).

29. TS 8 J 5.7. Eve Krakowski, *Coming of Age in Medieval Egypt: Women's Adolescence, Jewish Law, and Ordinary Culture* (Princeton, NJ: Princeton University Press, forthcoming), chap. 7.

30. *Med. Soc.*, 3:189.

31. The plight of the wife whose husband remained absent for an excessive period of time occupied Muslim jurists as well. See Khalilieh, *Admiralty and Maritime Laws*, 245–246.

32. TS 8 J 10.17, ed. Goitein, but not published, in the Princeton Geniza Project (PGP) browser, http://etc.princeton.edu/genizaproject. Many other documents concerning traveling husbands can be located by searching the English word "travel" in PGP.

33. TS 8 J 23.23, ed. M. A. Friedman, "Divorce upon the Wife's Demand as Reflected in Manuscripts from the Cairo Geniza," *Jewish Law Annual* 4 (1981): 122–123.

34. The Seleucid Era (also called the Era of Documents) dates from the accession year of the Hellenistic ruler of Babylonia, Seleucus I Nicator, upon his return from exile in Ptolemaic Egypt in the fall of 312 B.C.E., which for the Jews meant the fall of the Jewish year that began on Rosh Hashanah, in September 312 B.C.E.

35. TS 8 J 34.1, ed. Goitein, in PGP.

36. Ashur, "Protecting the Wife's Rights in Marriage," 386.

37. *Teshuvot ha-Rambam*, ed. Blau, 2:358–359 (no. 202). Cf. Mordechai A. Friedman, "The Monogamy Clause in Jewish Marriage Contracts," *Perspectives in Jewish Learning* 4 (1972): 20–40; *Med. Soc.*, 3:147–150.

38. *She'elot u-teshuvot R. Yiṣḥaq Alfasi*, ed. Wolf Leiter (Pittsburgh: Makhon Ha-Rambam, 1954), 43a–b (no. 120).

39. *Teshuvot ha-Rambam*, ed. Blau, 2:358–359 (no. 202); ibid., 426–428 (no. 234). Cf. *Med. Soc.*, 3:147–150 and Friedman, "The Monogamy Clause in Jewish Marriage Contracts," 20–40.

40. So Rashi on Giṭṭin 2a (where he excludes Babylonia). See Goodblatt, "*Medinat Hayam*: The Coastal District," 13–37.

41. Commenting on the passage in Yevamot 64a, in discussing the amount of time a man may be away from his wife, R. Hayya Gaon writes that "her husband went to the land

across the sea" (*Teshuvot ha-ge'onim sha'arei ṣedeq*, part 4, chap. 4:30, reference courtesy of Zvi Stampfer). With long-distance trade in mind, Maimonides specifies "for commerce."

42. On the relationship between Maimonides and Alfasi, see Zvi Stampfer, "Maimonides *Hilkhot ha-yerushalmi* on Tractate Ketubbot" (Hebrew), in *Mi-birkat Moshe* (*Essays on the Teachings of the Rambam in Honor of R. Naḥum Eliezer Rabinovitz*), ed. Zvi Hever and Carmiel Cohen (Maʿaleh Adumim: Maʿaliyot, 2011), 1:12–108.

## CHAPTER 4

1. Ackerman-Lieberman's "A Partnership Culture" provides a handy summary of partnership in Jewish law. See now his book, *The Business of Identity: Jews, Muslims, and Economic Life in Medieval Egypt* (Stanford, CA: Stanford University Press, 2014); see also his "Commercial Forms and Legal Norms in the Jewish Community of Medieval Egypt," *Law and History Review* 30 (2012): 1007–1052.

2. The expression used in Arabic legal documents can be seen by searching the database "Islamic Law Materialized," http://cald.irht.cnrs.fr/php/ilm.php.

3. The percentage could vary as long as the active partner received a greater percentage of the profit than his share of possible loss.

4. On the *'isqa*, based on both Jewish law and Geniza documents, see *Med. Soc.*, 1:171–179 and Ackerman-Lieberman, "A Partnership Culture," 1.4.4.2.

5. Menahem Ben-Sasson makes this point with regard to Jewish commerce in North Africa as early as the ninth century, using evidence from Gaonic responsa of flexible adjustment to the needs of the marketplace. Ben-Sasson, *Emergence*, 78–80.

6. Cf. A. L. Udovitch, "At the Origins of the Western Commenda: Islam, Israel, Byzantium?," *Speculum* 37 (1972): 198–207; idem, *Partnership and Profit*, chap. 6; cf. *Med. Soc.*, 1:171. Samuel ben Ḥofni's mini-code, *Kitāb al-sharika wa'l-muḍāraba*, uses the Islamic legal term *muḍāraba* to designate the Talmudic-Aramaic term *'isqa*. In another of his partially extant halakhic mini-codes, he cites this book, and it is clear from that reference that by *muḍāraba*, he means the Jewish *commenda*, based on half loan and half deposit, not the Islamic type. Shraga Abramson, "From One of the Books of R. Samuel b. Ḥofni: B. from the Book of Acquisition?" (Hebrew), *Tarbiz* 18 (1946–1947): 39.

7. According to Morony, "Commerce in Early Islamic Iraq," 710, the Islamic *qirāḍ* "seems to have its genesis in the Arabian caravan trade." See also Udovitch, *Partnership and Profit*, 172.

8. Udovitch, *Partnership and Profit*, chap. 6; Nyazee, *Islamic Law of Business Organization: Partnerships*, 243–276.

9. The Ḥanafī legist al-Sarakhsī says of the *muḍāraba* that it is mutually beneficial because "[t]he owner of the wealth may not have the opportunity for a profitable investment, while the person who has such an opportunity may not have wealth, and profit is acquired through both, that is, wealth and the ability to transact. In permitting this contract, the goals of both are achieved." Quoted in Nyazee, *Islamic Law of Business Organization: Partnerships*, 247.

10. *Med. Soc.*, 2:294.

11. Ibid., 1:171.

12. The evidence for this in the Geniza is legion (see ibid., 2:398–402). And see below, Chapter 9.

13. Such a contract, drawn up in the Jewish court of Fustat in 1106/07, is contained in ENA NS 21.4, ed. and trans. in S. D. Goitein and Mordechai A. Friedman, *Sefer hodu I: Yosef al-Lebdi soḥer hodu ha-gadol: Te'udot mi-gnizat Qahir* (*Joseph Lebdī Prominent India Trader: Cairo Geniza Documents*) (Jerusalem: Makhon Ben-Zvi and Rabbi David and Amalia Rosen Foundation, 2009), 221–223 (hereafter, Goitein-Friedman, *Sefer hodu I: Lebdı*). It is called *muḍārabat al-tujjār*, "the merchants' *commenda*," and assigns the traveling merchant responsibility for "whatever loss there may be" (*khasāra kā'ina mā kāna*, line 16).

14. S. D. Goitein, "What Would Jewish and General History Benefit by a Systematic Publication of the Documentary Geniza Papers?," *Proceedings of the American Academy for Jewish Research* 23 (1954): 34.

15. A responsum of Maimonides deals with two Jews, one of whom was owed money by the other pursuant to a *commenda* agreement drawn up in an Islamic court according to "Islamic law rather than Jewish" (*bi-madhhab al-goyim dūna al-yahūd*); *Teshuvot ha-Rambam*, ed. Blau, 1:39–40 (no. 27). *Qirāḍ al-goyim* brought before a Jewish court and stipulating that the active party bore no responsibility for loss: ibid., 46–47 (no. 32), 120–121 (no. 78), 2:676–677 (no. 400). In no. 400, Maimonides is queried about a litigation stemming from a *commenda* partnership. The traveling partner had died in a shipwreck, and the investor claimed money from the dead man's son and heir, namely, money that the deceased merchant had earlier sent to his son and that the investor now claimed belonged to him. Maimonides upheld the freedom from responsibility for loss clause in the Islamic *commenda* agreement. In the Code, *Hilkhot malveh ve-loveh* (Laws of Lender and Borrower) 27:1, he honors financial deeds drawn up in Gentile courts, following the exception established by the Mishna (Giṭṭin 1:5; see Chapter 9 below), as long as Jewish witnesses testified that the Muslim witnesses and judge were known not to take bribes. Cf. Udovitch, "At the Origins of the Western Commenda," 200–201. Partnership and *commenda* are discussed together in *Med. Soc.*, 1:169–183.

16. Goitein describes the challenges and perils of commercial travel by land and by sea in *Med. Soc.*, 1:275–281 and 319–323. See also S. D. Goitein and Mordechai A. Friedman, *India Traders of the Middle Ages: Documents from the Cairo Geniza ("India Book")* (Leiden: Brill, 2008), 157–164 (hereafter, Goitein-Friedman, *India Traders*); S. D. Goitein and Mordechai A. Friedman, *Sefer hodu II: Maḍmūn negid ereṣ teman ve-saḥar hodu: Te'udot mi-gnizat qahir* (*India Book II: Maḍmūn Nagid of Yemen and the India Trade: Cairo Geniza Documents*) (Jerusalem: Makhon Ben-Zvi and Rabbi David and Amalia Rosen Foundation, 2010), 53–59 (hereafter, Goitein-Friedman, *Sefer hodu II: Maḍmūn*); and Goldberg, *Trade and Institutions in the Medieval Mediterranean*, 117–119.

17. A typical responsum about losses due to brigandage: *Teshuvot ha-ge'onim*, ed. Naḥman Nathan Coronel (repr., Jerusalem, 1967), 1b (no. 7).

18. See S. D. Goitein, *Letters of Medieval Jewish Traders, Translated from the Arabic*

(Princeton, NJ: Princeton University Press, 1973), 207–212; Kraemer, *Maimonides*, 243–258.

19. On banking in the Geniza, see *Med. Soc.*, 1:229–266 and A. L. Udovitch, "Bankers Without Banks: Commerce, Banking, and Society in the Islamic World of the Middle Ages," in *The Dawn of Modern Banking*, ed. Fredi Chiapelli (New Haven, CT: Yale University Press, 1979), 255–273.

20. Goitein, *Med. Soc.*, 1:186–192.

21. Goitein-Friedman, *India Traders*, 62. Cf. Nyazee, *Islamic Law of Business Organization: Partnerships*, 108.

22. One very good example among many of a merchant with multiple partnerships as well as items on his "personal account" (*khāṣṣatī*; on the term *khāṣṣa*, see Chapter 5 at n. 38) is the long account of the great eleventh-century merchant Nahray b. Nissim's business deals with various other traders in the Geniza letter, ENA 1822 A.9, Ben-Sasson et al., eds., *Jews of Sicily*, 621–629 (no. 125); Moshe Gil, ed., *Be-malkhut yishmael bi-tqufat ha-ge'onim* (*In the Kingdom of Ishmael*), 4 vols. (Tel Aviv: Tel Aviv University, Mossad Bialik, and Ministry of Defense, 1997), 2:885–896 (no. 294) (hereafter, Gil, *Be-malkhut yishmael*); trans. Simonsohn, *Jews in Sicily*, 296–298 (no. 139).

23. Nyazee, *Islamic Law of Business Organization: Partnerships*, 141.

24. *She'elot u-teshuvot R. Yiṣḥaq Alfasi*, ed. Leiter, 38a–b (no. 98).

25. Bava Meṣi'a 72b. Also in Tosefta Bava Meṣi'a 4:7 and Palestinian Talmud Bava Meṣi'a 5:5, Venice ed. 10a. Person A is traveling from one place to another, where the price for the merchandise is higher and Person B proposes to buy it from him and later pay him at the higher price, and the Talmud considers whether this would be a veiled form of interest.

26. *Med. Soc.*, 1:178.

27. TS NS J 6, line 11.

28. *Teshuvot ha-ge'onim*, ed. Assaf, *Makhon le-Madda'ei Ha-yahadut* 2, 126 (no. 142).

29. See Goldberg, *Trade and Institutions in the Medieval Mediterranean*, esp. chap. 3.

30. Sanhedrin 63b; Bekhorot 2b; Mishneh Torah, Laws of Agents and Partners 5:10.

31. 'Avoda Zara 2a.

32. As explained by Rashi, if, without formally stipulating conditions, the Jew instructs his non-Jewish partner to take the Sabbath earnings for himself, it is as if he appoints him his agent for half the work that day, which is forbidden. If, however, they stipulate this in advance, the partnership is valid, unless they wait each week to settle accounts.

33. My thanks to Christine Hayes for checking the manuscripts for me. The printed first editions are now displayed in synoptic form on the Friedberg Jewish Manuscript Society's online database, www.jewishmanuscripts.com.

34. See Tosafot on 'Avoda Zara 2a, s.v. *lifnei eideihem shelosha yamim*, and Jacob Katz, *Exclusiveness and Tolerance: Studies in Jewish-Gentile Relations in Medieval and Modern Times* (Oxford: Oxford University Press, 1961), 32–36. The medieval German commentator on Maimonides' Code, *Haggahot maimuniyyot*, explains these things in his comments to Laws of Agents and Partners 5:10.

35. Mann, "The Responsa of the Babylonian Geonim," *Jewish Quarterly Review* n.s. 10 (1919): 332.

36. *Med. Soc.*, 2:294.

37. M. Cohen, *Under Crescent and Cross*, 96.

38. On interfaith commercial arrangements, see *Med. Soc.*, 2:293–296. Goitein notes (ibid., 297) that "the Geniza documents contain hardly anything indicative" of a double standard when Jews did business with Muslims.

39. See *Teshuvot ha-Rambam*, ed. Blau, 2:725–728 (no. 448), his letter to the Muslim proselyte Obadiah; also in *Iggerot ha-Rambam*, ed. Shailat, 1:238–241; and Mishneh Torah, *Hilkhot ma'akhalot asurot*, Laws of Forbidden Foods 11:7 and 13:11. See Ya'akov (Gerald) Blidstein, "The Status of Islam in Maimonidean Halakha" (Hebrew), in *Rav-tarbutiyut bi-mdina demoqraṭit vi-yhudit* (*Multiculturalism in a Democratic and Jewish State*), ed. Menachem Mautner et al. (Tel Aviv: Ramot, 1998), 465–476, with references to other literature. Eliezer Schlossberg, "Maimonides' Attitude Toward Islam" (Hebrew), *Pe'amim* 42 (1990): 42–45, notes that in other, non-halakhic writings, Maimonides' appraisal of Muslims was harsher.

40. E.g., Ginzberg, *Geonica*, 2:187, 194–195; *Teshuvot ge'onei mizraḥ u-ma'arav*, ed. Müller, 14b (no. 50) (partnership in handcraft); *Teshuvot ha-ge'onim*, ed. Ya'akov Mussaphia (Lyck: Rudolph Siebert, 1864), 24–25 (nos. 65, 67, and 68).

41. *Teshuvot Rav Naṭronai bar Hilai Gaon*, ed. Brody, 1:168–169 (no. 62). Brody (168 n. 2) suggests that the substitution of the word "purchased" (*laqeḥu*) for the word "received" (*qibbelu*, in contract as sharecroppers) found in the Talmud has to do with the specific circumstances of this particular partnership.

42. Ginzberg, *Geonica*, 2:195; also discussed in Shraga Abramson, *'Inyanot be-sifrut ha-ge'onim* (Jerusalem: Mossad Harav Kook, 1974), 263–264. Some twenty Gaonic responsa regarding economic dealing with Gentiles that impinge on the commandment to rest on the Sabbath were found by B. M. Lewin, *Oṣar ha-ge'onim, Volume 2: Shabbat* (Haifa: N. Warhaftig, 1930), 10–17.

43. *Teshuvot ha-ge'onim*, ed. Mussaphia, 24 (no. 65).

44. Libson, *Jewish and Islamic Law*, 41. These responsa, documenting continued Jewish activity in agriculture during the early Gaonic period, would seem to support Phillip Ackerman-Lieberman's view, expressed in his "Revisiting Jewish Occupational Choice," 113–135, that Jews continued in their traditional role as farmers in Babylonia, though now as sharecroppers rather than as landholders, as before. I find less convincing his hypothesis challenging the consensus view that Jews underwent rapid urbanization in Iraq following the Arab conquests. See Ben-Sasson, *Emergence*, which describes urbanized Jewry in Tunisia already in the ninth century, including Jews who had migrated from the eastern Islamic lands.

45. *Teshuvot ha-Rambam*, ed. Blau, 2:360 (no. 204); *Med. Soc.*, 2:296.

46. Reflecting the orientation of Jews from Christian lands, in some commentaries the term is *nokhri*, "heathen foreigner"; e.g., Maggid Mishneh, by Vidal of Tolosa, Spain, fourteenth century, and Leḥem Mishneh, by the sixteenth-century Salonikan rabbi Abraham de Boton, whose ancestors had been expelled from Christian Spain. In some late commentaries, the term *kuti* (Cuthean), a name for the sect of the Samaritans, is found. On *kuti* as a euphemism for expurgated *goy* in the Talmud, see William Popper, *The*

*Censorship of Hebrew Books* (New York: Burt Franklin, 1899), 59. The Gaon of Vilna, Elijah ben Shlomo Zalman Kremer (1720–1797), whose comments are printed in the margin of the Talmud page, had *goy* in his printed Talmud.

47. *Med. Soc.*, 2:278. Characteristically, a query to Maimonides concerning two sisters who owned a portion of a courtyard house in Alexandria with a *goy* refers to him in the next sentence as a Muslim. *Teshuvot ha-Rambam*, ed. Blau, 1:145 (no. 90). Juxtaposition of *goy* and *'arel*: ibid., 10 (no. 7). Cf. also Goitein-Friedman, *India Traders*, 133 n. 55. See also Libson, *Jewish and Islamic Law*, 283 n. 21.

48. *Med. Soc.*, 1:99.

49. Ibid., 1:362–367, appendix C, Industrial Partnerships.

50. *Med. Soc.*, 1:116–127.

51. *She'elot u-teshuvot R. Yiṣḥaq Alfasi*, ed. Leiter, 38b (no. 100; sale of a field); 38b–39a (no. 101; a vineyard); 43b–44a (no. 131; fig-tree grove in Granada); 54a (no. 177; a fruit grove). *She'elot u-teshuvot R. Yosef Migash*, ed. Ḥasida, 149–150 (no. 156; sale of a garden to a son); 86–87 (no. 100; two brothers, partners in a field).

52. P. 7b in the pages of Alfasi's epitome in the printed Talmud.

53. Summarized by Joseph Kafiḥ in his modern commentary on the Code, *Sefer Mishneh Torah*, 23 vols. (Kiryat Ono: Makhon Mishnat Ha-Rambam, 1984–1996), 3:132–134.

54. Oraḥ Ḥayyim 245:1. If the amount of Sabbath earnings was known, the Gentile was entitled to that, but if not, Maimonides' solution is to award one-seventh of the entire week's income to him.

55. In the Mishna there (Giṭṭin 31a), Rabbi Judah is quoted as saying that wine set aside to be donated to priests as *teruma*, "heave-offering" (Lev. 22:10–17), must be examined to determine its value at three seasons of the year. The Gemara (Giṭṭin 31b), commenting on the Mishna, cites a similar statement by Rabbi Judah relating to commerce and stipulating the times of the year when produce or wine should be sold. This ruling, in turn, is interpreted as having practical legal implications in partnerships, when, as Rashi explains in his gloss on the passage, sale at the established time fixes the proceeds to be shared, even if the price spikes upward.

56. In the Palestinian Talmud Bava Meṣi'a 5:3, 11b.

57. R. David ibn Abi Zimra, *Yeqar tif'eret 'al hilkhot sheluḥin ve-shutafin ve-hilkhot 'avadim*, ed. Shemuel Barukh Werner (Jerusalem: Mossad Harav Kook, 1945), 32, quoting R. Abraham b. David. Radbaz's commentary on Laws of Agents and Partners is not found in the standard printed editions of the Code.

58. *Med. Soc.*, 1:121, 4:246, 441 n. 155.

59. See M. Cohen, *Poverty and Charity*, 208–209.

## CHAPTER 5

1. Samuel b. Ḥofni Gaon's *Kitāb al-sharika wa'l-muḍāraba* (*Book on Partnership and Commenda*), only parts of which have thus far been recovered from the Geniza and published, by B. M. Lewin and by Israel Friedlander, *Ginze Kedem* 6 (1944): 41–73, dealt with

Talmudic partnership and Talmudic *'isqa*, and not with the Muslim *qirāḍ* or with the form of commercial agency that we are about to describe.

2. Nahum Rakover, *Ha-sheliḥut veha-harsha'a ba-mishpaṭ ha-'ivri* (*Agency and Legal Proxy in Jewish Law*) (Jerusalem: Mossad Harav Kook, 1972), 11–29; Israel H. Levinthal, "The Jewish Law of Agency," *Jewish Quarterly Review* n.s. 13 (1922): 117–191.

3. Qiddushin 41a–41b, the basic discussion of agency in the Talmud.

4. See *Hilkhot ishut* 3:18; *Hilkhot gerushin*, chap. 6.

5. Goitein notes that, second only to marriage contracts, the power of attorney is the most commonly found document in the Geniza. *Med. Soc.*, 2:276.

6. Levinthal, "The Jewish Law of Agency," 176–177. See also M. Cohen, "A Partnership Gone Bad," 235–236. An example of an agent held responsible because he acted negligently is recounted in a Gaonic responsum. The agent sold merchandise entrusted to him on credit, without permission of the owner of the goods, and to a person known to be "defiant" (*allam*)—from whom he was likely to have had difficulty collecting the debt. *Teshuvot ge'onei mizraḥ u-ma'arav*, ed. Müller, 3a–b (no. 6).

7. See, e.g., the "Book of Agency (*Wakāla*)," in Ibn Rushd, *Bidāyat al-mujtahid* (*The Distinguished Jurist's Primer*), trans. I. A. K. Nyazee, 2 vols. (Reading: Garnet, 1994–1996), 2:362–367; Liaquat Ali Khan Niazi, *Islamic Law of Contract* (Lahore: Research Cell, Dyal Sing Trust Library, n.d.), 155–174; Wael Hallaq, *Sharī'a: Theory, Practice, Transformations* (Cambridge: Cambridge University Press, 2009), 261–264.

8. Ibn Rushd, *Bidāyat al-mujtahid*, trans. Nyazee, 2:366.

9. Al-Sarakhsī, *Al-mabsūṭ*, 22:38. See Udovitch, "The 'Law Merchant' of the Medieval Islamic World," 122 ("quasi-agency"); idem, *Partnership and Profit*, 101–104; Nyazee, *Islamic Law of Business Organization: Partnerships*, 250 and n. 30 there, 252, 332. Nyazee (268–269) argues that agency differs from *muḍāraba* (he eschews the comparison with the European *commenda*, differing with Udovitch on this matter [244]), which, according to Nyazee, can be an ongoing relationship, whereas agency proper (*wakāla*) is a one-time stage that terminates with the purchase by the agent. Nyazee considers the possibility, however, that agency in Islam could be an ongoing arrangement, "especially if it is a general agency and is concluded as a continuing affair for a general purpose, or even for a series of specific purposes." Ibid., 269.

10. *Med. Soc.*, 1:164–169. Vol. 1 was published in 1967. There, Goitein called it "friendship" and "informal 'cooperation.'" He introduced the term "formal friendship" in his "Formal Friendship in the Medieval Near East," *Proceedings of the American Philosophical Society* 115 (1971): 484–489. He refers to it as "the organizational backbone of international trade." *Med. Soc.*, 5:277.

11. See the citations in n. 7 above and also A. L. Udovitch, "Formalism and Informalism in the Social and Economic Institutions of the Medieval Islamic World," in *Individualism and Conformity in Classical Islam*, ed. Amin Banani and Speros Vryonis (Wiesbaden: Harrassowitz, 1977), 61–81.

12. See below in sec. 5.5.

13. Goldberg, *Trade and Institutions in the Medieval Mediterranean*.

14. On Goitein's general view of the importance of the Geniza for general Islamic and

Mediterranean history, see M. Cohen, "Geniza for Islamicists." For a recent challenge to this claim, see Ackerman-Lieberman, *The Business of Identity*. For the "vocabulary of reciprocity" shared by Jewish and Muslim merchant-agents, see secs. 5.10 and 5.11 below.

15. *Med. Soc.*, 1:169ff.; 2:484, 487. The word *wadād*, also meaning "friendship," occurs as well: see TS 13 J 25.12, right margin line 14 (*al-wadād wa'l-ṣuḥba*), Ben-Sasson, *Jews of Sicily*, 302 (no. 69); Gil, *Palestine*, 3:223 (no. 497). The phrase, a hendiadys, is imprecisely translated as if the terms represented two different things, *ha-yedidut veha-shutafut*, "friendship and partnership," by both Ben-Sasson and Gil and, following them, by Simonsohn, *Jews in Sicily*, 212 (no. 105). In another letter a merchant writes, using hendiadys, that his business arrangement was "a partnership between us, not 'friendship' [*mawadda*] and not 'companionship' [*ṣuḥba*]"; Ben-Sasson, *Jews of Sicily*, 66–67 (no. 12). It is worthwhile mentioning, as Gideon Libson pointed out to me when I lectured on the subject at a conference on trade and legal pluralism in the era of the Geniza at Tel Aviv University in 2013, that the term *ṣuḥba* occurs in Sufi texts to describe the companionship of master and disciple. See, e.g., Eric Geoffrey, *Introduction to Sufism: The Inner Path of Islam*, trans. Roger Gaetani (Bloomington, IN: World Wisdom, 2010), 51. As a term from commercial life, it has had a *longue durée*, right down to modern times. See M. Cohen, "A Partnership Gone Bad," 232. Of course, in the vast majority of cases in the Geniza, the word *ṣuḥba* serves simply as a preposition meaning "with"/"along with"/"in the company of."

16. *Med. Soc.*, 1:183–184. Confusingly, in the Geniza documents, the term *biḍā'a* occurs more often in its simple root meaning of "goods," even in the same letter. Thus, in Bodl. MS Heb. a 3.13, line 57, we have *lam yabqā laka 'indī lā biḍā'a wa-lā dīn(ār) wa-lā dirh(am)*, "nothing belonging to you remains with me, neither *goods* nor cash," as translated by Goitein, *Letters*, 124 (emphasis added), and in the very next line and the one following that (lines 58–59), *fa-lam yabqā laka ghayruhu lā min al-khulṭa wa-lā min al-biḍā'a*, which Goitein (ibid.) translates "nothing should remain either on account of the partnership or *your own account*" (emphasis added). Neither edition of the letter, Ben-Sasson, *Jews of Sicily*, 371 (no. 82) or Gil, *Be-malkhut yishmael*, 3:941 (no. 581), nor the English translation in Simonsohn, *Jews in Sicily*, 173 (no. 91), which adheres to the Hebrew translations of both Ben-Sasson and Gil, captures the nuance preserved in Goitein's translation. A similar misunderstanding of *biḍā'a* occurs in connection with a Gaonic responsum existing in three versions. The story relates how a merchant, A, was transporting fifteen dinars in *biḍā'a* (spelled in Hebrew letters בידעה in phonetic Hebrew transcription, in one case; and בצאעה in another, in Arabic) on behalf of B. When the caravan in which he was traveling (a Berber caravan in one of the responsa, perhaps originating in Spain or North Africa) encountered brigands, and the thieves threatened his life, A decided to use B's dinars, which were tucked away in a chest, to buy his safety. Later, he returned to B half the amount because of "the affection there was between us" (an allusion to their *ṣuḥba*-"friendship"?), but B demanded the full amount. The halakhic issue hinged on whether A had disclosed the dinars to the thieves or not. *Teshuvot ha-ge'onim*, ed. Assaf (Jerusalem, 1942), 84–85 (no. 74); Ginzberg, *Geonica*, 2:150–151 (no. 502); *Teshuvot ha-ge'onim*, ed. Coronel, 5a (no. 41). Coronel explains the Arabic as meaning "merchandise" (*seḥora*), but from the context, it is clear that A was carrying B's money, not goods, and that the word

represents the commercial institution of *ibḍāʿ/biḍāʿa*, as it is called in Islamic law. The stock formula, *lā biḍāʿa wa-lā tijāra*, appearing regularly in releases dissolving a partnership and settling accounts in a Jewish court, may be a hendiadys, both words referring to the *ṣuḥba* institution and distinguished from other forms of business. See, e.g., the sequence of doublets in a mutual release by two partners dated 1077: "neither goods [*biḍāʿa*] nor merchandise [*tijāra*], neither equipment [*athāth*] nor material [*qamash*] . . . neither a 'mixing' of capital [*khulṭa*] nor a partnership [*sharika*], neither a deposit [*wadīʿa*] nor a pledge [*rahīna*], neither a consignment [*irsāl*] nor a shipment [*tawjīh*] . . . neither a loan [*qarḍa*] nor a *commenda* [*qirāḍ*]"; TS 16.138, ed. and trans. Ackerman-Lieberman, "A Partnership Culture" (no. 47) (and other releases in that appendix of documents). Samuel Stern made the same suggestion, intuitively, about the meaning of *tijāra* in a petition, where it is differentiated from *qirāḍ* and denotes "goods," *tijāra*, on the merchant's own account. See Stern, "Three Petitions of the Fatimid Period," *Oriens* 15 (1962): 181. *Irsāl* in the passage quoted must refer to *risāla*, one of the stock terms for commercial agency; the Arabic *tawjīh* has the same meaning as *irsāl*.

17. Described in Mauss's influential book *Essai sur le don* (*The Gift: The Form and Reason for Exchange in Archaic Societies*), trans. W. D. Halls (London: W. W. Norton, 2002), and one earlier translation. For two appreciations of the impact of Mauss's work, see Natalie Zemon Davis, *The Gift in Sixteenth-Century France* (Madison: University of Wisconsin Press, 2000), and Harry Liebersohn, *The Return of the Gift: European History of a Global Idea* (Cambridge: Cambridge University Press, 2011). In an interesting parallel, Davis explains that "friendship" played an important semantic role in gift exchange in sixteenth-century France (*The Gift in Sixteenth-Century France*, 20).

18. Avner Greif, "Reputation and Coalitions in Medieval Trade: Evidence on the Maghribi Traders," *Journal of Economic History* 49 (1989): 857–882 (quotation taken from pp. 865–866, where the context is Jewish courts); idem, "Contract Enforceability and Economic Institutions in Early Trade: The Maghribi Traders' Coalition," *American Economic Review* 83 (1993): 525–548; idem, "Cultural Beliefs and the Organization of Society: A Historical and Theoretical Reflection on Collectivist and Individualist Societies," *Journal of Political Economy* 102 (1994): 912–950; idem, "Contract Enforcement and Institutions Among the Maghribi Traders: Refuting Edwards and Ogilvie," CESifo, Working Paper Series no. 2350 (2008); idem, "The Maghribi Traders: A Reappraisal?," *Economic History Review* 65 (2012): 445–469, a rejoinder to the second article by Edwards and Ogilvie mentioned in the next note. See also Greif, *Institutions and the Path to the Modern Economy: Lessons from Medieval Trade* (Cambridge: Cambridge University Press, 2006), chap. 3. Udovitch, "Formalism and Informalism in the Social and Economic Institutions of the Medieval Islamic World," spoke earlier about webs of relationships "whose skeins could tie together a fairly large number of people; but those bonds were never expressed in terms of membership in a group abstractly defined" (74–75). Miriam Frenkel, who studied Geniza documents relating to Alexandria, concludes that the merchant community of that city fit Udovitch's description, *Ha-ohavim veha-nedivim: 'Illit manhiga be-qerev yehudei Alexandria bimei ha-beinayim* (*The Compassionate and Benevolent: The Leading Elite in the Jewish Community of Alexandria in the Middle Ages*) (Jerusalem: Makhon Ben-Zvi, 2006), 209.

19. See Jeremy Edwards and Sheilagh Ogilvie, "Contract Enforcement, Institutions and Social Capital: The Maghribi Traders Reappraised," CESifo, Working Paper Series no. 2254 (2008); idem, "Contract Enforcement, Institutions, and Social Capital: The Maghribi Traders Reappraised," *Economic History Review* 65, 2 (2012): 421–444. Goldberg and Ackerman-Lieberman join other critics, such as Edwards and Ogilvie, questioning Greif's insistence on the predominance of extralegal informalism and challenging Greif's theory about a closed coalition and the exclusivity of informal contract enforcement. Goldberg discusses methodological problems in Greif's work in *Trade and Institutions in the Medieval Mediterranean*, intro., sec. 4, and pp. 41, 148–150. The influence that Greif's work, based on data from a minority community in the Islamic Middle Ages, has had on economists and economic historians is quite astonishing, as a Google search of Greif's name reveals.

20. See the bibliography in Greif's *Institutions and the Path to the Modern Economy* and the bibliography in Goldberg's *Trade and Institutions in the Medieval Mediterranean.*

21. A similar, even more overwhelming, preference for outside agents (over family members) characterizes Genoese traders in the twelfth century. Greif, *Institutions and the Path to Modernity*, 274. A major difference between the Italian and Mediterranean Jewish merchants is that the former received monetary compensation for their agency services, whereas the Geniza agents were "compensated" with reciprocal agency favors, not with money, and hardly ever with a commission. *Med. Soc.*, 1:184.

22. Goldberg, *Trade and Institutions in the Medieval Mediterranean*, esp. secs. 5.2, 5.3, and 5.4; and idem, "Choosing and Enforcing Business Relationships in the Eleventh-Century Mediterranean: Reassessing the 'Maghribī Traders,'" *Past and Present* 216 (2012): 1–40. In her book, she writes (155): "The reciprocity of services in a *ṣuḥba* relationship was indeed 'informal' in that it was not subject to legal contract; each assumption of *agency*, on the other hand, *was* a binding legal relationship. Both Goitein's initial description of the *ṣuḥba* system and Udovitch's further analysis unfortunately use the word 'informal' without noting this distinction." Her assumption that the Geniza merchants made use of the Jewish law of agency and Jewish courts needs to be modified in light of evidence about evolving Jewish law discussed later on in the present chapter.

23. Goitein, *Med. Soc.*, 1:179, came to this conclusion based on the assumption that the Islamic *commenda* was the marketplace institution preferred by Jews and that Islamic *commenda* was not recognized by Jewish courts. My point relates to *ṣuḥba*-agency relations, which Jewish law and Jewish courts also did not recognize.

24. Ibid., 1:362–367, appendix C, Industrial Partnerships.

25. Ibid., 1:176. What we have is largely legal documents concerning the dissolution of such partnerships. See Ackerman-Lieberman, "A Partnership Culture," and his *The Business of Identity*.

26. Libson, *Jewish and Islamic Law*, 98.

27. Goldberg, *Trade and Institutions in the Medieval Mediterranean*, 126, 156–157; Ackerman-Lieberman, "A Partnership Culture," 128–129; Ackerman-Lieberman, *The Business of Identity*, 96–97. See also Jessica Goldberg, "On Reading Goitein's *A Mediterranean Society*: A View from Economic History," *Mediterranean Historical Review* 26 (2011): 173.

28. See, among many publications on this subject, *The Islamic City: A Colloquium*, ed. Albert H. Hourani and Samuel M. Stern (Oxford: Cassirer; and Philadelphia: University of Pennsylvania Press, 1970), esp. Samuel Stern's essay, "The Constitution of the Islamic City."

29. See M. Cohen, "A Partnership Gone Bad." Also see Goldberg, "Choosing and Enforcing Business Relationships in the Eleventh-Century Mediterranean" and her "Geographies of Trade and Traders in the Eleventh-Century Mediterranean: A Study Based on Documents from the Cairo Geniza" (PhD diss., Columbia University, 2005), 153: "This system of mutual agency . . . operated alongside formal, legally bounded forms of cooperation represented by various forms of contractual partnership." Also Goldberg, *Trade and Institutions in the Medieval Mediterranean*, chap. 5.

30. On such Islamic formularies, see Jeanette A. Wakin, *The Function of Documents in Islamic Law: The Chapters on Sales from Ṭahāwī's Kitāb al-shurūṭ al-kabīr* (Albany: State University of New York Press, 1972). See also Menahem Ben-Sasson, "Remnants of the Book of Testimony and Formularies by R. Saadya Gaon," *Shenaton ha-mishpaṭ ha-'ivri* 11–12 (1984–1986): 17–21. Al-Ṭaḥāwī was an older contemporary of Saadya and, like him, was born in Egypt. See also Udovitch, *Partnership and Profit*, 86–96.

31. Contracts or, rather, testimonies regarding the formation or dissolution of partnerships, releasing one or another or all of the partners from future claims, include the 105 legal documents constituting the appendix to Ackerman-Lieberman's dissertation on partnership in the Geniza (see above, Chapter 2 n. 48), the majority of which, however, are "industrial," not commercial, partnerships. His *The Business of Identity* includes a sampling of fifteen of these documents. See also his "Contractual Partnerships in the Geniza and the Relationship Between Islamic Law and Practice," *Journal of the Economic and Social History of the Orient* 54 (2011): 646–676. Other examples of partnership contracts drawn up in the Jewish court include: TS 12.5 recto and TS 20.152, Gil, *Palestine*, 2:721–733 (nos. 394–395), also published in Ben-Sasson, *Jews of Sicily*, 157–165 (nos. 37–38); ENA NS 21.4, a *commenda* contract (*bi-ḥukm muḍārabat al-tujjār*), Goitein-Friedman, *Sefer hodu I: Lebdī*, 221–223, cf. Goitein-Friedman, *India Traders*, 251; TS 12.830 +TS 8 J 5.13, a partnership (*sharika*) contract, ed. S. D. Goitein and Mordechai A. Friedman, with the assistance of Amir Ashur, *Sefer hodu IV/B: Ḥalfon ve-Yehuda ha-Levi* (*Ḥalfon and Judah Ha-Levi: The Lives of a Merchant Scholar and a Poet Laureate According to the Cairo Geniza Documents*) (Jerusalem: Makhon Ben-Zvi and Rabbi David and Amalia Rosen Foundation, 2013), 142–147 (doc. VIII 26) (hereafter, Goitein-Friedman, *Sefer hodu IV/B: Ḥalfon*); TS 8.81, fragment of a partnership (*sharika*) contract, Goitein-Friedman, *Sefer hodu IV/B: Ḥalfon*, 163–165 (doc. VIII 29).

32. See, e.g., Menahem Ben-Sasson, "Remnants of the Book of Testimony," 72–73.

33. *Teshuvot ha-ge'onim*, ed. Harkavy, 112 (no. 234); *Teshuvot ha-Rambam*, ed. Blau, 1:38–39 (no. 26), two contracts, one drawn up in a Jewish and the other in an Islamic court; *She'elot u-teshuvot R. Yiṣhaq Alfasi*, ed. Leiter, 66b (no. 243). A responsum of R. Joseph ibn Migash describes a "silent" partnership (*'isqa*) in which the active partner was accused of misusing the stationary investor's funds to pay for his daughter's dowry. Ibn Migash prescribed the means of verifying the matter, which had to be through irrefut-

able eyewitness testimony. *She'elot u-teshuvot R. Yosef ha-Levi ibn Migash*, ed. Ḥasida, 155 (no. 169).

34. A perusal of the letters translated in Goitein, *Letters of Medieval Jewish Traders*, illustrates this. See also Goldberg, *Trade and Institutions in the Medieval Mediterranean*, chap. 3, sec. 2.

35. *Ginze Kedem* 1 (1924): 1–2; *Teshuvot ha-ge'onim*, ed. Harkavy, 27 (no. 59 and for the date, p. 32 n. 1) (a shortened version); Ginzberg, *Geonica*, 2:284–285. As precedent, Hayya cited a statement in the Talmud (Shevu'ot 41b) permitting repayment of a loan without witnesses being present. See also Ben-Sasson, *Emergence*, 80 and n. 158 there, and 98; and his "The Jewish Community of Gabes in the 11th Century," in *Communautés juives des marges sahariennes du Maghreb*, ed. Michel Abitbol (Jerusalem: Makhon Ben-Zvi, 1982), 271–272, containing a partial English translation of the responsum. Libson, *Jewish and Islamic Law*, 98. Also Goldberg, *Trade and Institutions in the Medieval Mediterranean*, 64.

36. This is my distinct impression, differing from Ben-Sasson's assumption that the father-in-law and son-in-law were partners.

37. See, e.g., *Teshuvot ha-Rambam*, ed. Blau, 1:135 (no. 87): "Reuben and Simeon had a *ṣadāqa* between them. Whenever Simeon came to Alexandria and was about to return to Sicily, Reuben would give him gold [dinars] with which to buy some merchandise. He would travel with this as a 'consignment' [*risāla*, i.e., on agency, for which he bore no responsibility in case of loss], and the profit belonged to Reuben alone." For the participle *marsūl*, see Mosseri VII, 101 (L 101), line 14, Ben-Sasson, *Jews of Sicily*, 364 (no. 80); Gil, *Palestine*, 2:337 (no. 193). The letter is translated in Simonsohn, *Jews in Sicily*, 93–95 (no. 60), where *marsūl* is rendered "ordinary agency."

38. See above, sec. 5.3.

39. See A. de Biberstein Kazimirski, *Dictionnaire Arabe-Français*, 2 vols. (Paris: Maisonneuve, 1860), 1:508 (e.g., *lī 'indaka ḥāja*, "J'ai quelque chose à vous demander").

40. See http://etc.princeton.edu/genizaproject (PGP).

41. Goitein pointed out the meaning of *khidma* as "service" to the Jewish community or to the government (see index vol. to *Med. Soc.*, 60). I wrote about the significance of the concept of *khidma* in the context of charity in *Poverty and Charity*, 187–188: "*Khidma* is one of those expressions from the vocabulary of everyday life that mirrors the social mentality of the Judaeo-Arabic world, deeply embedded in its Muslim-Arabic and general Near Eastern setting, in which the poor and the charitable could interact in a nexus of patronage complementing the reciprocity between giver and taker conferred by religious precept." The role of *khidma* in daily life has been expounded further by Marina Rustow, "Formal and Informal Patronage Among Jews in the Islamic East: Evidence from the Cairo Geniza," *Al-Qanṭara* 29 (2008): 356–357, and "Benefaction (Ni'ma), Gratitude (Shukr), and the Politics of Giving and Receiving in Letters from the Cairo Geniza," in *Giving in Monotheistic Religions*, ed. Miriam Frenkel and Yaakov Lev (Berlin: De Gruyter, 2009), 384–385; and by Goldberg, *Trade and Institutions in the Medieval Mediterranean*, chap. 5. The example quoted is a Judaeo-Arabic letter, Heidelberg 29 recto, lines 8–9, ed. Werner Diem, *Arabische Briefe auf Papier aus der Heidelberger Papyrus-Sammlung* (Heidelberg: Universitätsverlag Winter, 2013)

(no. 47). The meaning and function of *khidma* in Geniza society adds a dimension to the concept as it appears in sources for a different region of the Islamic world. See Jürgen Paul, "*Khidma* in the Social History of Pre-Mongol Iran," *Journal of the Economic and Social History of the Orient* 57 (2014): 392–422.

42. An example in ENA 2805.11A, lines 13–14, ed. A. L. Udovitch in the PGP browser: *wa-naḥnu nas'al rabbenu sh(emaro) ṣ(uro) an lā yukhliyanā min al-ḍu'ā wa-bi-ḥāja in takūn lahu wa-bi-khidma an nakhdumahu fa-innī la-atasharraf bihā*, "I ask our master, (may your) R(ock) [i.e., God] preserve you, not to deprive me of your prayers, and if you should have a request or a service you wish me to serve, I shall be very honored to do so" (the last word, *bihā*, is misplaced in the transcription).

43. TS 13 J 13.11, line 11, Ben-Sasson, *Jews of Sicily*, 597 (no. 121); Gil, *Be-malkhut yishmael*, 3:592 (no. 479) (since *khadama* and *khudima* are written exactly the same in both Hebrew and Arabic unvocalized texts, the writer added the Hebrew vowel sign for *u* in the second verb to make clear that it was to be understood as passive). The letter is discussed and translated by Goldberg, *Trade and Institutions in the Medieval Mediterranean*, 56–61, with a facsimile of the manuscript; she presents the translation in a layout mimicking the manuscript; also trans. Simonsohn, *Jews in Sicily*, 199–201 (no. 102).

44. CUL Or 1080 J 13r, lines 17–20, right margin line 1, Gil, *Be-malkhut yishmael*, 3:696 (no. 509); quoted and discussed at length by Goldberg, "Choosing and Enforcing Business Relationships," 13–17. The letter is translated into English in Simonsohn, *Jews in Sicily*, 283–286 (no. 133). In a letter from the eleventh-century merchant Nahray b. Nissim, he writes: *fa-yashraḥu lahu fīhi ṣurat ḥālī bi-ihtimāmī wa-ḥirṣī fī qaḍā' ḥāja takhuṣṣuhu akthar mimmā yata'allaqu bi'l-khulṭa*, "explain to [a third merchant] in [a letter] how I have diligently taken greater care to fulfill the request on his personal account than with the partnership." ENA 2805.14A, lines 20–21, ed. A. L. Udovitch in the PGP browser. The locution is not restricted to Geniza letters. In a literary context, it occurs, for instance, in Nethanel al-Fayyūmī's *Bustān al-'uqūl* (twelfth century). When the pagan king Nimrod casts Abraham into the fire, God instructs the angel Gabriel to ask Abraham "if he has a request for you to fulfill on his behalf" (*hal lahu ḥāja taqḍīhā lahu*). *Bustān al-'uqūl*, ed. and trans. Joseph Kafiḥ (Kiryat Ono: Agudat Halikhot Am Yisra'el, 1984), 49. CUL Or 1080 J 13r, lines 17–20, right margin line 1, Gil, *Be-malkhut yishmael*, 3:696 (no. 509); quoted and discussed at length by Goldberg, "Choosing and Enforcing Business Relationships," 13–17.

45. Halper (Dropsie) 397, lines 15–16, Gil, *Palestine*, 3:76 (no. 451): *in yakūn lahu ḥāja aw laka ya sayyidī aw li-ṣadīq tusharrifnī bihā innī usarru bi-dhālika kathīr*; cf. TS 12.58, line 16: *in yakūn laka ḥāja aw li-ṣadīq*, ed. ibid., 3:57 (no. 444). Another example in Goitein, *Letters of Medieval Jewish Traders*, 49–51.

46. TS 8 J 15.24, margin at the top of the page: *wa-kitābuhu lā yukhlīnī minhu bi-khidmatihi wa-ḥājātihi*, Goitein-Friedman, *Sefer hodu II: Maḍmūn*, 65 (doc. II, 1); trans. into English in Goitein-Friedman, *India Traders*, 286 (*ḥāja* is translated as "errand" there). Other examples: ENA 2805.11A, line 14 (in PGP); TS 8 J 9.7, line 7 (in PGP); TS 8 J 38.6, lines 7–8 (in PGP).

47. TS 12.371, lines 17–18. My interpretation of *ahl al-ḥawā'ij* differs from Goitein's, *Med. Soc.*, 1:149.

48. Bodl. MS Heb. d 76.57v, lines 17–18, *wa-in ṣalaḥtu li-[m]awlayā fī ḥāja aw khidma yusharrifunī bihā fa-yafʿal*, Gil, *Be-malkhut yishmael*, 3:748 (no. 523). Cf. at the end of a business letter from Aden from the merchant Khalaf ben Isaac to the merchant Abraham ibn Yijū in India: *wa-mā kāna li-mawlayā min ḥāja aw khidma sharrifnī bihā*, "If my master has a request or service [to fulfill], please honor me with it." Jewish National and University Library 4° 577.3/6, Goitein-Friedman, *Sefer Hodu III: Avraham ben Yiju soḥer ve-yaṣran be-hodu: teʿudot mi-gnizat qahir* (*Abraham ben Yijū India Trader and Manufacturer: Cairo Geniza Documents*) (Jerusalem: Makhon Ben-Zvi and Rabbi David and Amalia Rosen Foundation, 2010), 157 lines 25–26 (hereafter, *Sefer hodu III: Abraham b. Yijū*). English trans. in Goitein-Friedman, *India Traders*, 630.

49. TS 13 J 15.7, lines 23–26, right margin, lines 1–3; cf. *Med. Soc.*, 1:299.

50. TS NS 184.45 verso, line 4 (in PGP): *fī sheṭar lā ḥāja*.

51. See the discussion in Goldberg, *Trade and Institutions in the Medieval Mediterranean*, 23–29.

52. Gladys Frantz-Murphy calls for comparison between Muslim documents and the Geniza documents in her review of Ackerman-Lieberman's *The Business of Identity*, in *Journal of Economic History* 75 (2015): 611, though she does not mention Arabic merchant letters. Indeed, very few such letters exist. I discuss them in what follows. See the titles by Rāġib, Diem, Kaplony, and Guo.

53. Many examples are readily accessible through the Arabic Papyrology Database (APD), housed at the Ludwig-Maximilians University in Munich, www.naher-osten.lmu, s.v حاجة (*ḥāja*) (accessed August 3, 2015).

54. Yūsuf Rāġib, *Marchands d'étoffes du fayyoum au IIIe/IXe siècle d'après leurs archives (actes et lettres) II: La correspondance administrative et privée des Banū ʿAbd al-Muʾmin* (Cairo: Institut Français d'Archéologie Orientale, 1985), 59 lines 16–17 (doc. no. 24).

55. Werner Diem, *Arabische Briefe aus dem 10.–16. Jahrhundert* (Berlin: De Gruyter, 2011), no. 9, lines 16–17: *wa-lā taqṭaʿ kutubaka ʿannī muḍammanatan akhbāraka wa-aḥwālaka wa-ḥāja in ʿaraḍat asraʿtuhā bi-ʿawn allāh sarraka*. The expression at the end is found frequently in this very meaning and context in the Geniza; see, e.g., AIU VII E 4, verso lines 11–12, Gil, *Palestine*, 3:257–261 (no. 504); PGP; and the Arabic Papyrology Database (above, n. 53).

56. *Med. Soc.*, 1:164, TS 13 J 25.18 verso, lines 2–3: *lā yaqṭaʿ kutubahu ʿanni muḍammatan bi-akhbār salāmatihim wa-ḥawāʾijihim li-aqūma bihi ḥisbat al-wājib in shāʾa allāh*. This document has been much discussed in scholarship; see the bibliography in the FGP database, https://fgp.genizah.org.

57. Werner Diem, *Arabische Privatbriefe des 9. bis 15. Jahrhunderts aus der Österreichischen Nationalbibliothek in Wien* (Wiesbaden: Harrassowitz , 1996), no. 24r, line 7.

58. Andreas Kaplony, *Fünfundzwanzig arabische Geschäftsdokumente aus dem Rotmeer-Hafen al-Quṣayr al-Qadīm (7./13. Jh.)* (Leiden: Brill, 2014), doc. no. 1, line 7; and see other examples from Arabic papyri and from the Geniza cited by Kaplony, ibid., 19–20. Also idem, "The Interplay of Different Kinds of Commercial Documents at the Red Sea Port al-Quṣayr al-Qadīm (13th c CE)," in *Verbal Festivity in Arabic and Other Semitic Languages: Proceedings of the Workshop at the Universitätsclub Bonn on January 16, 2009*, ed. Lutz

Edzard and Stephan Guth (Wiesbaden: Harrassowitz, 2010), 94–115. Kaplony can freely mix and compare evidence from al-Quṣayr and from the Geniza, since the documents and the merchants who wrote them reflect the same *Weltanschauung*. Also see Li Guo, *Commerce, Culture, and Community in a Red Sea Port in the Thirteenth Century: The Arabic Documents from Qusair* (Leiden: Brill, 2004), and Mordechai A. Friedman, "Quṣayr and the Documents on the Indian Ocean Trade," *Journal of the American Oriental Society* 126 (2006): 401–409.

59. See M. Cohen, "A Partnership Gone Bad," 232.

60. Had the evidence of the "vocabulary of reciprocity," shared by Muslim and Jewish merchants, been available to him, it might have modified Ackerman-Lieberman's revisionist challenge to the "Goitein hypothesis" in his *The Business of Identity*. The argument of his dissertation and his book is based on *partnership*, which has a well-established foundation in Talmudic law and, from there, in Maimonides' Code. *Ṣuḥba*-agency, on the other hand, lacked a basis in Talmudic law and therefore required accommodation by halakhists. It is here that the embeddedness of Jewish merchants in their Islamicate environment and their "identity" as "Islamicate" merchants are to be encountered and where the evidence of their commercial correspondence can, in consequence, be taken as typical of Islamicate trade in general.

61. Roxani Margariti, "*Aṣḥābunā l-tujjār*—Our Associates, the Merchants: Non-Jewish Business Partners of the Cairo-Geniza's India Traders," in *Jews, Christians and Muslims in Medieval and Early Modern Times: A Festschrift in Honor of Mark R. Cohen*, ed. Arnold E. Franklin et al. (Leiden: Brill, 2014), 40–58.

62. See *Med. Soc.*, 2:295–296.

63. *Teshuvot Rabbenu Avraham ben ha-Rambam*, ed. A. H. Freimann, trans. S. D. Goitein (Jerusalem: Mekize Nirdamim, 1937), 53–54 (no. 51).

64. See Chapter 9 below.

65. Ibid.

66. Bodl. MS Heb. c 28.61, lines 16–17, Ben-Sasson, *Jews of Sicily*, 276 (no. 65); Gil, *Be-malkhut yishmael*, 3:916 (no. 576); trans. Simonsohn, *Jews in Sicily*, 357 (no. 156). See also M. Cohen, "A Partnership Gone Bad." Goitein writes: "More often than not, informal cooperation was accompanied by one or more partnerships concluded between the correspondents. . . . Almost any larger accounts in the Geniza contain items such as 'you personally,' 'I personally,' 'our partnership with so-and-so.'" *Med. Soc.*, 1:167. Elsewhere, he adds: "[T]he Geniza records teem with cases in which the parties were not sure on what conditions they had collaborated, or who made contradictory statements about the subject." Ibid., 186.

67. TS K 2.32, Gil, *Be-malkhut yishmael*, 3:163–170 (no. 354); trans. Simonsohn, *Jews in Sicily*, 213–217 (no. 106).

68. M. Cohen, "A Partnership Gone Bad."

69. Ben-Sasson, *Emergence*, 310, citing *Teshuvot ha-ge'onim*, ed. Harkavy, 113–115 (no. 235). The case concerns a dispute between two merchants in a partnership. When their dispute reached an impasse, "some merchants [*taggarim*, a Hebraized form of Aramaic *tagarei*, meaning "merchants"] gathered to decide between them but were unable." The

dispute remained unresolved for twenty years, until the original investor summoned his partner to court, whereupon a new confrontation ensued.

70. Bodl. MS Heb. a 3.7 line 10, see *Med. Soc.*, 1:363 (no. 8), Ackerman-Lieberman, ed., "A Partnership Culture" (no. 4), and others in the appendix there.

71. *Teshuvot ha-Rambam*, ed. Blau, 1:36–37 (no. 24); cf. *Med. Soc.*, 2:383.

72. *Teshuvot ha-Rambam*, ed. Blau, 1:30–31 (no. 20).

73. Ibid., 1:147–149 (no. 91) and 153–154 (no. 93). Goitein discusses and translates a portion of no. 93 in *Med. Soc.*, 1:183–184, calling it "a good illustration of the different conditions under which a merchant could carry with him goods given to him by a business correspondent."

74. *Teshuvot ha-Rambam*, ed. Blau, 1:147 (no. 91).

75. A had purchased the indigo for 37 1/3 dinars (see below). This was evidently a sale on *ṣabr*, "patience," sold on credit for a higher price later on. Maimonides sanctioned this form of veiled interest. See below, Chapter 7 at n. 21.

76. Ibid., 1:153 (no. 93). The entire responsum is translated in Simonsohn, *Jews in Sicily*, 436–437 (no. 202).

77. Ibid., 1:149 (no. 91).

78. Wael Hallaq, "Notes on the Term *Qarīna* in Islamic Legal Discourse," *Journal of the American Oriental Society* 108 (1988): 475–480; idem, *Sharīʿa: Theory, Practice, Transformations* (Cambridge: Cambridge University Press, 2009), 88–90, 241, 314, 348.

## CHAPTER 6

1. Rakover, *Ha-sheliḥut veha-harsha'a*, 37. See also *Hilkhot mekhira* (Laws of Sale), 5:11–12, where Maimonides mentions exceptions to the rule.

2. Libson, *Jewish and Islamic Law*, 98.

3. See the discussion in Arnold E. Franklin, "More than Words on a Page: Letters as Substitutes for an Absent Writer," in *Jews, Christians and Muslims in Medieval and Early Modern Times: A Festschrift in Honor of Mark R. Cohen*, ed. Arnold E. Franklin et al., 287–305.

4. Laws of Agents and Partners 9:1.

5. Similarly, in Islamic court procedure, an oath by an accused amounted to exoneration. See Hallaq, *Sharīʿa: Theory, Practice, Transformations*, 352–353; for a twentieth-century case of oath-taking in a *sharīʿa* court, see Brinkley Messick, "Commercial Litigation in a Sharīʿa Court," in Muhammad Khalid Masud et al., *Dispensing Justice in Islam: Qadis and Their Judgements* (Leiden: Brill, 2006), 216–217.

6. TS 13 J 13.11, lines 9–10, Gil, *Be-malkhut yishmael*, 3:592 (no. 479); trans. into English and discussed by Goldberg, *Trade and Institutions in the Medieval Mediterranean*, 56–61, with a facsimile of the manuscript, and in Simonsohn, *Jews in Sicily*, 199 (no. 102). That the two men had a *ṣuḥba* is indicated in another letter, quoted by Goldberg, *Trade and Institutions in the Medieval Mediterranean*, 127. In a third letter, written in the 1060s, a correspondent of the same Nahray informs him that he had insisted that a merchant

swear that he was telling the truth about the intended recipients of a shipment that he had brought from Sicily. TS 12.380 verso, line 5, Gil, *Be-malkhut yishmael*, 3:515–519 (no. 453), partially trans. into English by Udovitch, "Formalism and Informalism in the Social and Economic Institutions of the Medieval Islamic World," 76. The letter does not state whether this oath was administered in the Jewish court or before Muslim officials.

7. The words "or part of it," *o miqṣatah*, seem to be missing from the manuscript fragment ENA NS 29.12 recto (bottom), an apparent omission by the scribe due to homoioteleuton.

8. That Maimonides was analogically creating a sixth category of businessman subject to an oath on suspicion of malfeasance, rather than simply redefining *ben ha-bayit*, becomes clear in 9:7, where he distinguishes between *shaliaḥ* and *ben ha-bayit*.

9. I am grateful to Gideon Libson for pointing out to me this hermeneutical use of the preposition *ke* in Maimonides' Code.

10. *Encyclopaedia of Islam*², s.v. *ḳiyās* (M. Bernand). See also Mohammad Hashim Kamali, *Principles of Islamic Jurisprudence*, rev. ed. (Cambridge: Islamic Texts Society, 1999), chap. 9. On Maimonides' use of analogy with respect to Islamic *qiyās*, see Moshe Halbertal, "Sefer Ha-Miṣvot of Maimonides: His Architecture of Halakha and Theory of Interpretation" (Hebrew), *Tarbiz* 59 (1989–1990): 471. Also Aviram Ravitzky, "Saadya Gaon and Maimonides on the Logic and Limits of Legal Inference in Context of the Karaite-Rabbanite Controversy," *History and Logic of Philosophy* 32 (2011): 29–36.

11. A responsum of R. Joseph ibn Migash (no. 162) dealing with a different matter mentions, in passing, a "son of the house" as being either paid or unpaid. Thanks to Zvi Stampfer for bringing this source to my attention. Maimonides was, of course, heir to the Andalusian tradition.

12. See Libson, *Jewish and Islamic Law*, 85. For Islamic judicial oaths, see the "Book of Oaths (*Aymān*)," in Ibn Rushd, *Bidāyat al-mujtahid*, trans. Nyazee, 1:488–505; and on agents' oath-taking, ibid., 2:366–367, in the "Book of Agents (*Wakāla*)."

13. The passage comes from one of many Geniza fragments of Saadya's halakhic works that have been collected over the years by Brody (see Robert [Yeraḥme'el ] Brody, "The Influence of Sa'adyah Gaon's Halakhic Monographs on Maimonides' *Mishneh Torah*" [Hebrew], in *Ha-Rambam: Shamranut, meqoriyut, mahapkhanut*, 1:216, 218). I am grateful to Professor Brody for sharing it with me before publication in his *Ḥibburim hilkhatiyim shel Rav Saadya Gaon* (*Halakhic Works of Rav Saadya Gaon*) (Jerusalem: Yad Ha-Rav Nissim, 2015), 196–197. The passage, which, Brody explains, has no precedent in the Talmud and is absent also from Maimonides' Code (see the second chart in Brody, "Influence of Sa'adyah Gaon's Halakhic Monographs on Maimonides' *Mishneh Torah*," 218), alludes to *ṣuḥba*-agency. Professor Brody's transcription of the relevant passage from TS Arabic 48.238, 2 verso left-hand side lines 8–10: *wa'l-thāniyya an yubrīyahu al-mustawdī' fī 'amal lahu 'amal aw ya'idahu annahu ya'malu lahu al-'amal fa-inna dhālika ayḍān shomer sakhar*. If we substitute the word *khidma*, "service," for the word *'amal*, "task," this passage exactly describes the reciprocity of mutual service that defines the *ṣuḥba* system, which Saadya sought to subsume under the halakha of bailments. I was unaware of the Saadya passage when I published my "A Partnership Gone Bad"; it strengthens my claim about the

absence of a Talmudic mechanism for enforcing mutual service agency, a manifestly new form of Jewish commercial collaboration in the post-Talmudic Islamic world.

14. *Teshuvot ha-Rambam*, ed. Blau, 2:451–452 (no. 248).

15. The word *risāla* in the query should be understood in its core sense of something "sent," a "shipment," not in its technical meaning of a consignment on agency.

16. Goldberg, *Trade and Institutions in the Medieval Mediterranean*, 68.

17. However, a passage in an earlier chapter of Laws of Agents and Partners (2:9) might contain an allusion to Saadya's opinion: "An agent [*shaliaḥ*] who claims that he incurred a loss owing to some unavoidable occurrence takes the bailee's oath [*shevu'at ha-shomerim*] regarding his claim and is held exculpable." The pertinent passage in the Talmud (Bava Meṣi'a 83a) applies this to a bailee [*shomer*], and discusses whether a remunerated or unremunerated bailee is meant. Radbaz (*Yeqar tif'eret*, 13) reconciles 2:9 with 9:4–5 by stating that the Talmudic discussion applies to "all bailees as well as to agents and partners."

18. Goldberg argues, *pace* Greif, that Jewish traders—whether partners or agents—made use of the legal system, both the Jewish *beit din* and the Muslim *sharī'a* court, to resolve disputes. Ackerman-Lieberman's work documents this effectively for *partnerships*, which were arranged or dissolved in the Jewish court, but firsthand evidence of Jewish recourse to the *beit din* to adjudicate disputes stemming from *commercial agency* relations is sparse (see the next section of this chapter). It is reasonable to conclude, as Goldberg herself suggests (in *Trade and Institutions in the Medieval Mediterranean*, 150–164), that Jewish traders went to Islamic courts in such cases. I argue that Maimonides, who, like other rabbinic authorities, objected to this practice, instituted his reform of the halakha to make it easier for merchants in agency relations to adjudicate their disputes in the *beit din*.

19. Many examples are in Ackerman-Lieberman's corpus in "A Partnership Culture": see, e.g., docs. no. 51, 70, 71, 81, all from the twelfth century. Often the phrase "fulfillment of the trust" is paired with the expression "avoidance of betrayal" (*khiyāna*).

20. Udovitch, *Partnership and Profit*, 93 n. 140. The term for violation of the trust is *ta'ddī al-amāna* (ibid., 98). Cf. Nyazee, *Islamic Law of Business Organization: Partnerships*, 58–59.

21. Quoted in Ackerman-Lieberman, "A Partnership Culture," 3.2; see n. 11 there. I have slightly modified his translation of the Arabic *adā' al-amāna* (emphasis added).

22. See above, Chapter 5, sec. 5.12.1.

23. Goitein-Friedman, *Sefer hodu I: Lebdī*, 88 (doc. I, 10a, line 8) and 133 (doc. I, 18b, lines 10, 16); cf. Goitein-Friedman, *India Traders*, 196. On the Lebdī lawsuit, see the documents with Hebrew translations in Goitein-Friedman, *Sefer hodu I: Lebdī*, 30–31, 45–122; English translations or summaries of documents with English introduction in Goitein-Friedman, *India Traders*, 30–32, 167–210. Goldberg points to only one other agency lawsuit (from 1040), described in Mosseri VII 101 (L 101), Gil, *Palestine*, 2:336–339 (no. 193). There, witnesses were available to testify to the facts of the case.

24. Goldberg, *Trade and Institutions in the Medieval Mediterranean*, 155.

25. Goitein-Friedman, *Sefer hodu I: Lebdī*, 88–89 (doc. I, 10–11, lines 8, 12ff.); cf. Goitein-Friedman, *India Traders*, 196.

26. Goitein-Friedman, *Sefer hodu I: Lebdī*, 133 (doc. I, 18b, lines 10, 16). On mutual

oaths by plaintiff and defendant and their capacity to terminate disputes, see Hallaq, *Sharīʿa: Theory, Practice, Transformations*, 353.

27. Goitein-Friedman, *Sefer hodu I: Lebdī*, 86.

28. Ibid. (TS 12.830 +TS 8 J 5.13, ed. in *Sefer hodu IV/B: Ḥalfon*, 142–147 [doc. VIII 26]).

29. Goitein-Friedman, *Sefer hodu I: Lebdī*, 87 (TS Arabic 47.206 verso, left-hand folio, lines 2–6).

30. Goitein-Friedman, *Sefer hodu I: Lebdī*, 87.

31. Ibid. (TS Arabic 47.56, left-hand folio, lines 6ff.). Friedman suggested that the legal monograph might be one of the many compiled by Samuel b. Ḥofni Gaon (d. 1013) but one that has not yet been discovered. David Sklare, whom I queried on the matter, suggested that the text in question is Hayya Gaon's (d. 1038) *Adab al-quḍāh*, "since the chapter heading in the ms. does not correspond to the chapter heading found in the table of contents of Samuel ben Ḥofni's book" (e-mail of July 18, 2012). Neri Ariel is working on fragments of R. Hayya's book on judicial procedure for his doctoral dissertation in Talmud at the Hebrew University, under the direction of Robert Brody: "Manuals for Judges (ادب القضاة): A Study of Genizah Fragments of a Judaeo-Arabic Monographic Legal Genre" (Hebrew). He edits the relevant Geniza manuscript folios, TS Arabic 47.56 followed by CUL Or 1080 6.1.

32. Al-Ṭaḥāwī, *Al-shurūṭ al-ṣaghīr*, ed. Rawḥī Ūzjān (Baghdad: Ri'āsat Dīwān al-Awqāf, 1974), 2:736.

33. Udovitch, *Partnership and Profit*, 92–93, citing from a manuscript of the unpublished section "Book of Partnership" (*Kitāb al-sharika*), in Shaybāni's *Kitāb al-aṣl*. Nyazee translates from al-Sarakhsī: "They have participated in this partnership with the fear of Allah in fulfilling their trusts"; Nyazee, *Islamic Law of Business Organization: Partnerships*, 31–32. To the best of my knowledge, that part of *Kitāb al-aṣl* has not been published. Sarakhsī, *Al-mabsūṭ*, 11:156.

34. Hallaq, *Sharīʿa: Theory, Practice, Transformations*, 252 (emphasis added).

35. Legal documents of release typically contain a formula making a business partner exempt from any future claim of *biḍāʿa*, *tijāra*, *qirād*, or *muḍāraba*. In letters as well as legal documents, the word *biḍāʿa* often means, simply, "goods" or "merchandise"; but as we have seen, the term also occurs in the Geniza as a synonym for *ṣuḥba*-agency (see above, Chapter 5, sec. 5.10). It cannot be discounted that the appearance of the term *biḍāʿa* together with other forms of business collaboration in release documents reflects an effort to accommodate mutual service agency within Jewish judicial procedure. For examples, see Ackerman-Lieberman, "A Partnership Culture," doc. 44 and others in the same collection.

36. Goitein-Friedman, *Sefer hodu I: Lebdī*, 86. The citation he gives is *India Traders* VII, 43, but as Professor Friedman kindly informed me, this is a typo and the citation should be VII, 34, which is identified in the index of the English Goitein-Friedman, *India Traders*, 830 as TS Arabic Box 30.258.

37. Libson, *Jewish and Islamic Law*, chap. 6.

38. Ibid., 101, 103.

39. Watson, *Legal Transplants*. I am aware of the debate surrounding the concept of legal transplant and of the fact that it is normally applied to the movement of law between states. I think, however, that the concept is useful in the present context, where Islam can be considered the functional equivalent of the state; and the Jews, with their autonomous community and law, as a kind of "state within a state." I am also particularly mindful of what Watson wrote about the "transplant bias" of mercantile law (see above, p. 16). The very affinity between Jewish and Islamic law may have made the former especially susceptible to transplantation. Islamic legal scholars whom I have queried have not been able to refer me to a source using the term *al-yamīn 'alā adā' al-amāna*, but the description of the Islamic oath of absolution asserting *amāna* (fiduciary duty) given by Wael Hallaq (above at n. 34) fits the terminology found in Judaeo-Arabic Geniza documentary and other texts. A Geniza letter (the longest of its type in the Geniza) mentions the "oath on fulfillment of the trust," which a Muslim who had given money to a Jewish merchant imposed on the latter. It is not clear whether this concerned partnership or agency, but it is safe to assume that this was a judicial procedure recognized by the Muslim, and, if the oath was imposed in a court, it would have been an Islamic court, where mixed litigations took place, not a Jewish one. Halper (Dropsie) 389, verso lines 40–43, Ben-Sasson, *Jews of Sicily*, 73 (no. 12); Gil, *Be-malkhut yishmael*, 4:471 (no. 751); trans. Simonsohn, *Jews in Sicily*, 342 (no. 151); Goldberg, *Trade and Institutions in the Medieval Mediterranean*, 296–300. At a recent conference in Frankfurt am Main (September 2016), the theme was "Migrating Words, Migrating Merchants: Migrating Law." I gave a lecture there based on research done for the present book prior to its publication.

40. Menahem Ben-Sasson notes the phrase *wa-anā 'alā al-ahd muqīm min iqāmat al-emuna* in a merchant's letter around 1060, which he understands to refer to the type of informal business cooperation identified by Goitein. He hypothesizes that the Hebrew term *emuna* stems from a biblical verse. Ben-Sasson, *Jews of Sicily*, 64 n. to line 19. The Hebrew word *emuna* is the cognate of Arabic *amāna* and is used by Maimonides when referring to the oath of partners. See above, p. 97.

41. Migdal 'Oz, ad loc., referring to both 9:5 and 9:6.

42. Radbaz, *Yeqar tif'eret*, ed. Werner, 59.

43. Shraga Abramson, ed., *Sefer mishpeṭei shevu'ot* (*The Laws of Oaths*), prepared for publication by Robert (Yeraḥme'el) Brody and David Sklare (Jerusalem: Makhon Ben-Zvi, 2012), 54–55.

44. *She'elot u-teshuvot ha-Rashba*, vol. 1 (Jerusalem: Makhon Yerushalayim, 1997), no. 920, also cited by Kesef Mishneh, ad loc., Rashi Shevu'ot 48b, s.v. *u-ven*.

45. Radbaz, *Yeqar tif'eret*, 59.

46. Herbert Davidson's comment, "No one, as far as I have seen, has been able to uncover an instance where Maimonides deliberately decided an issue in opposition to what the rabbinic sources indicate the halakic norm to be," needs, therefore, to be qualified. Davidson, *Moses Maimonides*, 260.

47. In Kesef Mishneh, he mentions the Gaonic responsum cited by Migdal 'Oz but does not seem to have had direct familiarity with it.

48. See above, Chapter 5, sec. 5.12.1; see also *Med. Soc.*, 2:334–335.

49. See Amnon Cohen, *Jewish Life Under Islam: Jerusalem in the Sixteenth Century* (Cambridge, MA: Harvard University Press, 1984), 122–123.

50. Out of fear of judicial error, Goitein explains (*Med. Soc.*, 2:335), courts relied on declarations by the parties.

## CHAPTER 7

1. See Bava Qama 38–39; 73a; 104b. See Rakover, *Ha-sheliḥut veha-harsha'a*, 253–254.

2. See Introduction, n. 42.

3. Tykocinski, *Taqqanot ha-ge'onim*, 81–89; Elon, *Jewish Law*, 2:649–651; Libson, *Jewish and Islamic Law*, 39–40, 65–66, 93–94. Israel Schepansky, in his *Ha-taqqanot be-yisra'el*, 4 vols. (New York and Jerusalem: Michael Scharf Publication Trust and Mossad Harav Kook, 1991–1993), 3:228–230, discerns two distinct *taqqanot* here. The first permitted assigning a power of attorney for debts (presumably, as an adjunct of land transfer), and the second allowed this even when the party appointing the agent did not personally own any land. He bases this on Maimonides' language, "they have further ordained," in sec. [c] below.

4. Libson, *Jewish and Islamic Law*, 39–40.

5. See Rakover, *Ha-sheliḥut veha-harsha'a*, 273–274, which does not take into consideration the historical realia discussed below.

6. One long chapter in vol. 4 of *Med. Soc.*, based on a large body of data from the Geniza, is devoted to "the home" and includes discussion of sales and gifts of houses (86–90) and renting of premises in houses owned by Jews (90–97).

7. One example from among many about houses (*dār* in Arabic) or parts of houses owned by Jews: *Teshuvot ha-Rambam*, ed. Blau, 1:8 (no. 6). Share in a house by a Jew and a Muslim (*goy*): ibid., 12 (no. 9); ibid., 145 (no. 90). Jewish perfumery store: ibid., 174 (no. 104). Share in a store by Jews and Muslims: ibid., 2:360 (no. 204); cf. *Med. Soc.*, 1:365. Two stores, a cooperative in silk, one branch in al-Maḥalla and the other in Fustat: *Teshuvot ha-Rambam*, ed. Blau, 1:177–178 (no. 105); cf. *Med. Soc.*, 1:88.

8. *Teshuvot ha-Rambam*, ed. Blau, 1:151 (no. 92). The same responsum and many others mention opposition to renting to Muslims.

9. This might appear in a legal question when a Jewish partner wished to sell his part of a house to a Muslim, which Maimonides sought to discourage; ibid., 2:672 (no. 394).

10. Moshe Gil, *Documents of the Jewish Pious Foundations from the Cairo Geniza* (Leiden: Brill, 1976), part 4 (Use of Revenue). Cf. M. Cohen, *Poverty and Charity*, 200–204. On the Muslim *waqf*, see Amy Singer, *Charity in Islamic Societies* (Cambridge: Cambridge University Press, 2008), 92–114 and passim.

11. Goitein writes: "[P]owers of attorney constitute the type of documents found most frequently in the Geniza"; *Med. Soc.*, 2:335.

12. E.g., Bodl. MS Heb. c 28.11, line 23, ed. and trans. M. Cohen, "A Partnership Gone Bad," 251–255, with English trans. ibid., 223–227; see also Gil, *Be-malkhut yishmael*, 4:63–66 (no. 623).

13. E.g., ENA 4010.3, Goitein-Friedman, *Sefer hodu I: Lebdī*, 292–293 (doc. A43b); TS 10 J 21.1; CUL Or 1080 4.15, line 9, ed. Oded Zinger, "Women, Gender and Law: Marital Disputes According to the Documents from the Cairo Geniza" (PhD diss., Princeton University, 2014), appendix. This formula also appears in the work of a German Tosafist of the twelfth century, R. Elazar b. Nathan; see Rakover, *Ha-sheliḥut veha-harsha'a*, 275.

14. Saadya Gaon and R. Hayya Gaon both compiled formularies that were widely used in the Geniza period, as attested by lists of books from personal libraries. See Nehemya Allony, *Ha-sifriya he-yehudit bimei ha-beinayim* (*The Jewish Library in the Middle Ages: Book Lists from the Cairo Geniza*), ed. Miriam Frenkel and Haggai Ben-Shammai (Jerusalem: Makhon Ben-Zvi, 2006), in the index.

15. On the latter possibility, see Rakover, *Ha-sheliḥut veha-harsha'a*, 260 and 106.

16. A responsum from Spain in the eleventh century (R. Isaac Alfasi) indicates that the formula "four cubits of land in my courtyard" was used in powers of attorney, though the questioner wanted assurance that it was based on Talmudic law. *She'elot u-teshuvot R. Yiṣḥaq Alfasi*, ed. Leiter, 45b (no. 140). The Andalusian formulary book from Lucena published by Joseph Rivlin has two versions of the power of attorney, both containing the clause "four cubits of land" without the addition "in the Land of Israel"; *Shiṭre qehillat al-Yusanah min ha-me'ah ha-aḥat-'esreh* (*Formularies of the Community of Lucena from the Eleventh Century*) (Ramat Gan: Bar-Ilan University Press, 1994), 169–177 (nos. 23–24). The formulary of Judah ben Barzilai of Barcelona contains the realistic formula "four cubits in my courtyard"; *Sefer ha-sheṭarot*, ed. S. J. Halberstam (Berlin: Itskovski, 1898), 43. See also the discussion in Rakover, *Ha-sheliḥut veha-harsha'a*, 271–273. Even the agency document in the book of formularies by R. Hayya Gaon (d. 1038) includes, as an option, the clause "four cubits of land *in such-and-such a place*." *Sefer ha-sheṭarot le-rav Hayya b. Sherira Gaon*, ed. Simḥa Assaf, supplement to *Tarbiz* 1 (1930): 32–33.

17. See Kraemer, *Maimonides*, 125–141.

18. Rakover, *Ha-sheliḥut veha-harsha'a*, 257. On the debate over whether conquest of the Land by Gentiles transfers ownership, see ibid., 259 n. 42.

19. Kesef Mishneh, ad loc., explains this differently, apparently based on a responsum of R. Hayya Gaon, to the effect that the Jew might be a descendant of converts lacking the right to property in the Land of Israel. See Rakover, *Ha-sheliḥut veha-harsha'a*, 274.

20. For credit in the Islamic context, see Udovitch, "Credit as a Means of Investment," 260–264, and his *Partnership and Profit*, 77–86. For the Jewish case, see *Med. Soc.*, 1:197–200.

21. An Islamic legal text calls it *al-bay' bi'l-ta'khīr*; cf. Udovitch, "Credit as a Means of Investment," 261.

22. *Teshuvot ha-Rambam*, ed. Blau, 1:88–89 (no. 53); cf. *Med. Soc.*, 1:197.

23. *Teshuvot ha-Rambam*, ed. Blau, 2:520–521 (no. 272); cf. Kraemer, *Maimonides*, 309.

## CHAPTER 8

1. "He who punished the people of the generation of the Flood and of the Tower of Babel, the inhabitants of Sodom and Gomorrah, and the Egyptians at the [Red] Sea, will exact vengeance upon him who does not stand by his word; and if one enters into a verbal transaction [*ha-nose' ve-noten bi-dvarim*], he acquires no title, but if he retracts (*ha-ḥozer bo*), the spirit of the Sages is displeased with him." Bava Meṣi'a 48a.

2. Ibid. and 49a.

3. Hayya ben Sherira, *Sefer ha-meqaḥ veha-mimkar* (Vienna: Joseph Hraschanzki, [1800]), 27a. Zvi Stampfer, who is collecting fragments of the Arabic original of Hayya's book for publication, informs me that the beginning of chap. 13 lacks this sentence, which he believes was added by the medieval Hebrew translator.

4. Goldberg, *Trade and Institutions in the Medieval Mediterranean*, index, s.v. flax trade.

5. "Pulling" is mentioned in the Mishna Qiddushin 1:5. Characteristically organizing halakhot in his "user-friendly" manner, Maimonides incorporates "lifting" from elsewhere in the Talmud, Bava Qamma 86a.

6. *Med. Soc.*, 1:11, 196.

7. *Encyclopaedia of Islam²*, s.v. īdjāb (Joseph Schacht); Nyazee, *Islamic Law of Business Organization: Partnerships*, 104–105.

8. Vogel, "Contract Law of Islam and the Arab Middle East," 44.

9. Aron Zysow, "The Problem of Offer and Acceptance: A Study of Implied-in-Fact Contracts in Islamic Law and the Common Law," *Cleveland State Law Review* 34 (1985–1986): 75–76. Cf. Nyazee, *Islamic Law of Business Organization: Partnerships*, 248.

10. On offer and acceptance in connection with surety for a loan, see Gideon Libson, "Islamic Influence on Medieval Jewish Law? Sefer Ha'Arevuth ('Book of Surety') of Rav Shmuel Ben Ḥofni Gaon and Its Relationship to Islamic Law," *Studia Islamica* 73 (1991): 13 n. 20.

11. Johansen, "The Valorization of the Human Body in Muslim Sunni Law," 72.

12. Geoffrey Khan, *Arabic Legal and Administrative Documents in the Cambridge Genizah Collections* (Cambridge: Cambridge University Press, 1993), 27. The court records also include the Islamic formula comparable with the Jewish *qinyan*: *ṣafqatan wāḥidatan* (*wa-'aqdan wāḥidan*), "with one clasp (or clap) of the hands (and one contract)" (ibid., passim).

13. Ibid., no. 8 (TS Misc. 29.21), line 16.

14. Amnon Cohen, *A World Within: Jewish Life as Reflected in Islamic Court Documents from the Sijill of Jerusalem (XVIth Century)*, 2 vols. (Philadelphia: Center for Judaic Studies, University of Pennsylvania, 1994), 2:161. A Jew from Cairo buys a house in Jerusalem from another Jew through a Jewish agent, *bi-ījāb shar'ī wa-qabūl mur'ī*, "through a legal offer and valid acceptance" (line 20 in the facsimile); translated into Hebrew in Amnon Cohen and Elisheva Simon-Pikali, *Yehudim be-veit ha-mishpaṭ ha-Muslemi: ḥevra kalkala ve-irgun qehillati bi-Yerushalayim ha-'Otmanit: Ha-me'ah ha-shesh-'esreh (Jews in*

*the Muslim Religious Court: Society, Economy and Communal Organization in the XVIth Century Documents from Ottoman Jerusalem*) (Jerusalem: Yad Izhak Ben-Zvi, 1993), 313.

15. *Med. Soc.*, 2:329.

16. See, e.g., M. Cohen, "Maimonides and Charity in the Light of the Geniza Documents," 74–79.

17. And see, in general, Kleinman, *Darkhei qinyan u-minhagei misḥar*.

18. *Oṣar he-ge'onim 'al Bava Meṣi'a*, ed. Robert (Yeraḥme'el) Brody et al. (Jerusalem: Ofeq Institute, 2012), 235. See also *Med. Soc.*, 1:118–123, and Kleinman, *Darkhei qinyan u-minhagei misḥar*, 78 n. 8.

19. See above, n. 3.

20. Hayya ben Sherira, *Sefer ha-meqaḥ veha-mimkar*, 35a.

21. Maggid Mishneh, ad loc.

22. On the use of the term *pashuṭ* by the Maggid Mishneh, see Gideon Libson, "Chapters of *Sefer ha-Mazranut* of R. Samuel b. Ḥofni Gaon" (Hebrew), *Tarbiz* 56 (1986–1987): 75.

23. *Med. Soc.*, 1:336–337. See Khalilieh, *Admiralty and Maritime Laws*, 113. For a discussion of labeling practices among Geniza merchants, see Goldberg, *Trade and Institutions in the Medieval Mediterranean*, 180–184. For the Quṣayr texts, see Mordechai A. Friedman's review of Li Guo's *Commerce, Culture, and Community in a Red Sea Port in the Thirteenth Century: The Arabic Documents from Qusair* (Leiden: Brill, 2004), "Quṣayr and the Documents on the Indian Ocean Trade," *Journal of the American Oriental Society* 126 (2006): 405.

24. TS 13 J 3.4, lines 9–10, ed. Goitein (in the PGP browser); cf. *Med. Soc.*, 1:336.

25. Goitein-Friedman, *India Traders*, 313 (TS 18 J 2.7).

26. Ibid., 325 (TS 24.66). See also Margariti, *Aden and the Indian Ocean Trade*, 299 n. 72.

27. TS AS 146.12, lines 5–7, part of a letter, Goitein-Friedman, *Sefer Hodu III: Abraham ben Yijū*, 90 (cf. 91, lines 18–19); English translation in Goitein-Friedman, *India Traders*, 574–575.

28. ENA 1822 A.9, lines 9–10, Gil, *Be-malkhut yishmael*, 2:886; Ben-Sasson, *Jews of Sicily*, 623; trans. Simonsohn, *Jews in Sicily*, 296 (no. 139).

29. *Med. Soc.*, 1:336 (picture in Gil, *Be-malkhut yishmael*, 2:720 [TS Misc. 25.19]).

30. On labeling, see, again, Goldberg, *Trade and Institutions in the Medieval Mediterranean*, 180–184.

31. See Elon, *Jewish Law*, 2:916–920.

32. On *ḥeres* as a writing material, see Samuel Krauss, *Talmudische Archäologie*, 3 vols. (Leipzig: G. Fock, 1910–1912), 1:148.

33. Sokoloff, *Dictionary of Jewish Babylonian Aramaic*, 750. I am grateful to Seth Schwartz for clarifying the meaning of *neyar* as papyrus.

34. On paper in the Islamic world, see Jonathan M. Bloom, *Paper Before Print: The History and Impact of Paper in the Islamic World* (New Haven, CT: Yale University Press, 2001), 29.

35. See *Encyclopaedia of Islam*[2], s.v. *kāghad*, *kāghid* (Cl. Huart-A. Grohmann). See

also Neil Danzig's long note on the word *neyar* occurring in another halakha in the Code, "Lining in Holy Texts: The Source of a Halakha and Its Aftermath" (Hebrew), in *'Aṭeret le-Ḥaim: Studies in Talmudic and Rabbinic Literature in Honor of Professor Haim Zalman Dimitrovsky*, ed. Daniel Boyarin et al. (Jerusalem: Magnes, 2000), 339–340 n. 154 (my thanks to Zvi Stampfer for bringing this reference to my attention).

36. Bloom, *Paper Before Print*, 42–47.

37. Ibid., 74. See also Johannes Pedersen, *The Arabic Book*, trans. Geoffrey French (Princeton, NJ: Princeton University Press, 1984), chap. 5.

38. *Med. Soc.*, 2:232; Bloom, *Paper Before Print*, 74–79.

39. Marriage contracts that became lost could easily be replaced by testimony in court. Moreover, upon payment of the money due to a divorcée or a widow, the marriage contract had to be torn anyway (most of the marriage contracts in the Geniza are ripped). It did not have to be as durable as a divorce decree.

40. See *Med. Soc.*, 2:573 n. 25.

## CHAPTER 9

1. In this, I am in agreement with Libson with regard to the Geonim; *Jewish and Islamic Law*, 101–103, 110–111.

2. As Danby recognizes in his translation, *The Mishnah*, 307.

3. The Gemara (Giṭṭin 10b) rationalizes granting permission to conclude pecuniary transactions in a Gentile court since, in Jewish law, the act of exchanging money for a purchase in itself completed the transfer of ownership, making the action of the Gentile court moot.

4. Quoted in Libson, *Jewish and Islamic Law*, 80, from al-Kāsānī (d. 1191), *Kitāb badā'i' al-ṣanā'i' fī tartīb al-sharā'i'*.

5. Néophyte Edelby, "The Legislative Autonomy of Christians in the Islamic World," in *Muslims and Others in Early Islamic Society*, ed. Robert Hoyland (Aldershot: Ashgate, 2004), 53–58 (17–22); Antoine Fattal, "How Dhimmīs were Judged in the Islamic World," in ibid., 92–94 (11–13); Gideon Libson, "Legal Autonomy and the Recourse to Legal Proceedings by Protected Peoples, According to Muslim Sources During the Gaonic Period" (Hebrew), in *Ha-islam ve-'olamot ha-shezurim bo* (*The Intertwined Worlds of Islam: Essays in Memory of Hava Lazarus-Yafeh*), 334–392; Milka Levy-Rubin, *Non-Muslims in the Early Islamic Empire: From Surrender to Coexistence* (Cambridge: Cambridge University Press, 2013), 113–163. On hierarchy in Muslim–non-Muslim relations, see M. Cohen, *Under Crescent and Cross*, chap. 6.

6. *Med. Soc.*, 2:398–402. For a discussion of the Gaonic material, see Uriel I. Simonsohn, *A Common Justice: The Legal Allegiances of Christians and Jews Under Early Islam* (Philadelphia: University of Pennsylvania Press, 2011), chap. 6. See also Jessica M. Marglin, "Jews in *Sharī'a* Courts: A Family Dispute from the Cairo Geniza," in *Jews, Christians and Muslims in Medieval and Early Modern Times: A Festschrift in Honor of Mark R. Cohen*, ed. Arnold E. Franklin et al., 207–225.

7. Fattal, "How Dhimmīs Were Judged," 90–91 (8–9). See also U. Simonsohn, *A Common Justice*, 5–6, and Libson, "Legal Autonomy," 387–388.

8. Mahmassani, *Falsafat al-tashrī' fi l-islām*, 29.

9. *Kitāb al-umm*, 8 vols. (Cairo: Maktabat al-Kulīyāt al-Azharīya, 1961), 4:197–198; English trans. in Lewis, *Islam: From the Prophet Muhammad to the Capture of Constantinople*, 2:219–223.

10. Christian Mueller, "Non-Muslims as Part of Islamic Law: Juridical Casuistry in a Fifth/Eleventh-Century Law Manual," in *The Legal Status of Ḏimmī-s in the Islamic West*, ed. Maribel Fierro and John Tolan (Turnhout: Brepols, 2013), 40.

11. For the first expression, see *Teshuvot ha-Rambam*, ed. Blau, 1:39 (no. 27). For the second, see TS 16.138: "I, Khalaf b. Khalaf b. 'Ezrōn, have an Arabic document witnessed by non-Jews [i.e., Muslims] [*kitāb 'arabī be-'eidei goyim*] concerning a partnership that was between us," ed. and trans. Ackerman-Lieberman, "A Partnership Culture," doc. no. 47; see also idem, "Legal Pluralism Among the Court Records of Medieval Egypt," *Bulletin d'Etudes Orientales* 63 (2014): 85.

12. Khan, *Arabic Legal and Administrative Documents*, 56–285.

13. Ibid., 1.

14. E.g., *al-naql wa'l-ju'l*; ibid., 57 line 7 (doc. no. 1).

15. Ibid., 208–209 (doc. no. 35); 218–220 (doc. no. 39).

16. Goitein, "The Interplay of Jewish and Islamic Laws," 61, 66; cf. Libson, *Jewish and Islamic Law*, 103. Also see Goitein's "The Interplay of Laws," in *Med. Soc.*, 2:395–402.

17. C. Mueller, "Non-Muslims as Part of Islamic Law," 21–63, which begins: "Studies on non-Muslims in Islam usually concentrate on the status of ḏimmī-s as a category apart. . . . I will use a radically different approach and describe legal rules concerning non-Muslims within the legal system as a whole, not as a specific, somehow disconnected part of it." See also the apposite remarks of Ackerman-Lieberman, "Legal Pluralism Among the Court Records of Medieval Egypt," 83: "[O]ne might say that Jewish scribes understood Jewish law to function as yet another *madhhab* in the multivalent legal landscape of medieval Egypt; and Islamic courts' acceptance of documents produced in the Jewish court would suggest a similar understanding on the part of Islamic courts." Also Audrey Dridi, "Christian and Jewish Communities in Fusṭāṭ: Non-Muslim Topography and Legal Controversies in the Pre-Fatimid Period," in *The Late Antique World of Early Islam: Muslims Among Christians and Jews in the East Mediterranean*, ed. Robert Hoyland (Princeton, NJ: Darwin, 2015), 110–113; and Eve Krakowski and Marina Rustow, "Formula as Content: Medieval Jewish Institutions, the Cairo Geniza, and the New Diplomatics," *Jewish Social Studies* 20 (2014): 111–146.

18. Anver Emon, *Religious Pluralism and Islamic Law: Dhimmīs and Others in the Empire of Law* (Oxford: Oxford University Press, 2012), chap. 2.

19. *Teshuvot ha-Rambam*, ed. Blau, 1:145 (no. 90); *Med. Soc.*, 2:298 and 591 n. 33.

20. *Med. Soc.*, 2:402.

21. *Teshuvot ha-Rambam*, ed. Blau, 2:347–348 (no. 191). In a case from the Islamic court of Jerusalem in the sixteenth century, a Jewish *dayyan* was present to help validate

the sale of a property, a sale carried out by a Jewish agent on behalf of a Jewish buyer in Cairo. A. Cohen, *A World Within*, 2:161 (line 23 in the facsimile); trans. into Hebrew in A. Cohen and Pikali, *Yehudim be-veit ha-mishpaṭ ha-Muslemi: Ḥevra kalkala ve-irgun qehillati bi-Yerushalayim ha-ʿOtmanit: ha-me'ah ha-shesh-ʿesreh*, 314.

22. M. Cohen, *Under Crescent and Cross*, 53.

23. A Gaonic responsum confirms the validity of deeds of debt drawn up in Islamic courts in Baghdad, where the Geonim knew from direct experience that Muslim witnesses and judges were honest and fair. The respondent explains: "This [i.e., validating sale and debt documents from Islamic courts and admitting them into evidence in Jewish courts] is our custom now, *and we practice it all the time*." The source is *Teshuvot ha-ge'onim*, ed. Harkavy, 140 (no. 278). See U. Simonsohn, *A Common Justice*, 185–187, for a translation of the responsum. See also Libson, *Jewish and Islamic Law*, 85, 102; and see *Teshuvot ha-ge'onim*, ed. Coronel, 6a (no. 51), where a Gaon writes: "In the case of contracts for sale and purchase of fields, dwellings, or stores, if a Jew sells to another Jew in the Gentile [=Muslim] court, where they have the contract drawn up and signed by Gentiles, if the Gentiles signing the deeds are considered trustworthy [*ne'emanim*] by their judges, then we consider them qualified [*kesherim*] with their testimony as well." The bountiful evidence for Jewish recourse to *sharīʿa* courts in the Jewish responsa and Geniza documents speaks loudly in favor of the fair treatment that Muslim judges normally accorded the Jews.

24. Aharon Nachalon, *Qahal ve-taqqanot qahal be-toratam shel ha-ge'onim* (*The Kahal and Its Enactments in the Gaonic Period*) (Jerusalem: Institute for Research in Jewish Law, Hebrew University of Jerusalem, 2001), 81–90; U. Simonsohn, *A Common Justice*, 138–140.

25. Ibid., 192–193.

26. TS 24.20, ed. Ackerman-Lieberman, "A Partnership Culture," in the appendix, no. 54, one example among many.

27. The principle is stated in the *Adab al-qāḍī* (etiquette for judges) treatise of al-Khaṣṣaf (d. 874), as summarized by Muhammad Khalid Masud, Rudolph Peters, and David S. Powers in "Qāḍīs and Their Courts: An Historical Survey," in *Dispensing Justice in Islam*, 26–27. It is often claimed as one of the discriminatory measures against non-Muslims that, in mixed litigations in Islamic courts, the testimony of Jews and other *dhimmī*s against Muslims was not accepted. They were considered untrustworthy, lacking the attribute of *ʿadāla*, "honesty," "fairness," the ethical quality required of those wishing to serve as professional witnesses (*ʿudūl*) in an Islamic religious court. The authority standardly cited for the intestability of *dhimmī*s is Fattal, *Le statut légal des non-musulmans*, 361–363. But *dhimmī*s could testify against one another in an Islamic court (stated in Fattal, 365) and establish their honesty by taking an oath. In some circumstances, according to one school of law or another, exceptions were made to the rule denying *dhimmī*s the right to testify concerning a Muslim, for instance, when witnessing a last will and testament for a Muslim traveler if no Muslims were available, or giving testimony against a foreigner from outside Dār al-Islām. Ahmed Oulddali, "Recevabilité du témoignage du ḏimmī d'après les jurists mālikites d'Afrique du Nord," in *The Legal Status of Ḏimmī-s in*

*the Islamic West*, ed. Fierro and Tolan, 278–279. On the capacity of a non-Muslim to swear a defendant's oath of innocence, see Brunschvig, "Le système de la preuve en droit musulman," 210–211. For sixteenth-century Jerusalem, see A. Cohen, *Jewish Life Under Islam*, 122–123.

28. At a conference in Córdoba, "Law and Religious Minorities in Medieval Societies: Between Theory and Praxis," in 2014, sponsored by the project on the legal status of religious minorities in the Euro-Mediterranean world (fifth–fifteenth centuries), known as RELMIN (www.relmin.eu) and centered at the University of Nantes, Camilla Adang of Tel Aviv University discussed a medieval *fatwā* recommending that non-Muslims take their oath "in a place they hold in awe" (*yu'aẓẓimūhā*), namely, their own house of worship. See also Fattal, *Le statut légal des non-musulmans*, 365. In practice, a Jew might take the oath in the Muslim court itself. In a case before the Jerusalem *sharī'a* court in 1555, a Muslim claimed a debt owed by a Jewish goldsmith for purchase of wheat. The Muslim could not provide proof, so, instead, the Jew exonerated himself by taking an oath "by God the Exalted who gave the Torah to our master Moses, peace be upon him" (*fa-ḥalafa billāhi ta'alā alladhī anzala al-taurat 'alā sayyidinā mūsā 'alayhi al-salām*). A. Cohen, *A World Within*, 2:178, record 2, line 7 in the facsimile; trans. into Hebrew in A. Cohen and Simon-Pikali, *Yehudim be-veit ha-mishpaṭ ha-Muslemi: ḥevra kalkala ve-irgun qehillati bi-Yerushalayim ha-'Otmanit: ha-me'ah ha-shesh-'esreh*, 276; see also A. Cohen, *Jewish Life Under Islam*, 122–123.

29. When a Muslim once demanded that a Jew swear an Islamic oath in the name of Allah, the Gaon who was consulted in the matter cautioned the Jewish party to treat this as gravely as a Jewish oath. *Teshuvot ha-ge'onim*, ed. Mussaphia, 15 (no. 40); cf. *Teshuvot ha-ge'onim*, ed. Coronel, 5a (no. 40), a case where "the state [*melekh*, usually called *shilṭonot*, 'authorities'], a tax collector, or a [lay] Gentile" wanted someone or the community to impose an oath "by your Torah" on a Jew. The Gaon instructed the inquirer not to impose the oath, and if the Jews came under threat, they should claim that they no longer imposed oaths but rather the "*gezera*" (see further on in this note). Libson comments elsewhere (*Jewish and Islamic Law*, 115): "All oaths in Islamic *courts* were required to be taken in God's name, even by Jews appearing in these (Muslim) courts, to which there is copious evidence in Muslim literature. There was no difference between oaths imposed on Jews and other minorities (*milla*) and those administered to Muslims." See also his nn. 16–17 on pp. 282–283, citing echoes in Gaonic responsa and other halakhic works. Importantly, Libson points out (p. 262 n. 41) that he found no mention in sources he studied (up to the twelfth century) of the offensive "Jews' Oath," allegedly dating from the turn of the ninth century. This oath is quoted in al-Qalqashandī's fifteenth-century epistolographic manual, *Ṣubḥ al-a'shā*, and is often cited as evidence of age-old Muslim hostility toward the Jews by certain modern writers. It is translated into English in Stillman, *The Jews of Arab Lands: A History and Source Book* (Philadelphia: Jewish Publication Society, 1979), 165–166. Elsewhere, Libson has argued persuasively that, in response to the procedure in Islamic courts, "where oaths were imposed almost without limit," the Geonim sought to minimize oath-taking in the Jewish court by substituting the much less severe "oath by imprecation" (*gezerta*); Libson, *Jewish and Islamic Law*, 64–65 and his "*Gezerta* and *Ḥerem*

*Setam* in the Gaonic and Early Medieval Periods" (Hebrew) (PhD diss., Hebrew University, 1979), summarized by him in the *Encyclopaedia Judaica*[2], s.v. *gezerta.*

30. *Med. Soc.*, 2:399. E.g., TS 8 J 6.8 + TS 13 J 30.3, most recent edition, translation, and discussion in Zinger, "Women, Gender and Law," appendix and in the text.

31. Tykocinski, *Taqqanot ha-ge'onim*, 11–29. For an earlier responsum on the *taqqana*, see *Teshuvot Rav Naṭronai bar Hilai Gaon*, ed. Brody, 2:456–457 (no. 304), and Brody, "Were the Geonim Legislators?." See also Libson, *Jewish and Islamic Law*, 111. The concern about wives turning to Islamic courts and threatening to convert to Islam as the motivation for this *taqqana* is inferred from an ambiguous statement by R. Sherira Gaon three hundred years later in one of his responsa; *Ḥemda genuza*, ed. Wolfensohn and Schneersohn, 25a (no. 140); cf. Tykocinski, *Taqqanot ha-ge'onim*, 15–16. For a fresh, critical look at the matter, see Lena Salaymeh, "Every Law Tells a Story: Orthodox Divorce in Jewish and Islamic Legal Histories," *UC Irvine Law Review* 4, 1 (2014): 19–63. The Talmudic *moredet* is very similar to the Islamic *iftidā'*, or "ransom-divorce." See Mordechai A. Friedman, "The Ransom-Divorce: Divorce Proceedings Initiated by the Wife in Medieval Jewish Practice," *Israel Oriental Studies* 6 (1976): 288–307.

32. Aḥmad ibn Yaḥyā al-Wansharīsī, *Al-mi'yār al-mu'rib wa'l-jāmi' al-mughrib 'an fatāwī 'ulamā' ifrīqīya wa'l-andalus wa'l-maghrib*, vol. 10, ed. Muḥammad Ḥajjī (Beirut: Dār al-Gharb al-Islāmī, 1981), 128–130; discussed in Torki Fahad Abdullah A. Al Saud, "Al-Qirqisānī and Maimonides' Polemics Against Islam: An Intercultural Study in Religion and Literature" (PhD diss., Boston University, 2008), 22–24.

33. Aḥmad ibn Yaḥyā al-Wansharīsī, *Al-mi'yār al-mu'rib wa'l-jāmi' al-mughrib 'an fatāwī 'ulamā' ifrīqīya wa'l-andalus wa'l-maghrib*, 128–130; discussed in Al Saud, "Al-Qirqisānī and Maimonides' Polemics Against Islam," 22–24.

34. U. Simonsohn, *A Common Justice*. I draw much of what follows concerning the Eastern churches from that study.

35. Richard E. Payne, "Christianity and Iranian Society in Late Antiquity, ca. 500–700 CE" (PhD diss., Princeton University, 2010), 161–169.

36. U. Simonsohn, *A Common Justice*, 48–50, 109–114, 118–119. Using the Arabic and Greek papyri letters of the Muslim governor of Fustat in the early eighth century, Mathieu Tillier develops an intriguing hypothesis that would explain how Islamic precedence was in the process of replacing Christian (Byzantine) judicial authority over the Coptic majority less than a century following the conquest. "Dispensing Justice in a Minority Context: The Judicial Administration of Upper Egypt Under Muslim Rule in the Early Eighth Century," in *The Late Antique World of Early Islam: Muslims Among Jews and Christians in the East Mediterranean*, ed. Robert G. Hoyland (Princeton, NJ: Darwin, 2015), 133–156.

37. Libson, *Jewish and Islamic Law*, 103, writes: "[T]he geonim sought halakhic dispensations in line with the laws of the host society, enabling the Jewish courts to offer legal solutions similar to those attainable under Islamic law. By doing so they could uphold the Talmudic prohibition on recourse to non-Jewish courts and avert encroachment on the community's judicial autonomy. Nevertheless, the Geonim were sufficiently flexible to permit such recourse in exceptional cases, so as not to damage the delicate fabric of orderly social life and to maintain their own position and authority."

38. Nachalon, *Qahal ve-taqqanot qahal*, 86–89; U. Simonsohn, *A Common Justice*, 192–193.

39. *She'elot u-teshuvot R. Yosef ha-Levi ibn Migash*, ed. Ḥasida, 108–109 (no. 118). For other instances, see ibid., 92–93 (no. 106) and 96–98 (no. 110).

40. Goitein pointed to this difference between Islamic and Jewish marital law (*Med. Soc.*, 3:120); cf. Mordechai A. Friedman, "Division of the Marriage Gift into Immediate and Postponed Portions in the Cairo Geniza Documents" (Hebrew), *Proceedings of the Sixth World Congress of Jewish Studies, Held in 1973* (Jerusalem: World Union of Jewish Studies, 1977), 3:377–387. The Islamic "late (or postponed) payment" (Arabic, *mu'akhkhar*), part of the "bride price," was payable on delay sometime after the wedding, whereas the balance of the Jewish "additional marriage payment," also called *mu'akhkhar* in Arabic (Hebrew, *me'uḥar*), was a "debt" that the husband owed his wife if he divorced or predeceased her, and it only came due in those circumstances.

41. Note the formulaic language in Jewish responsa, *yorenu moreinu* (*ve-rabbenu*) "teach us, *our teacher* (and master)," in Andalusian responsa and in those of Maimonides and his son Abraham.

42. *She'elot u-teshuvot R. Yosef ha-Levi ibn Migash*, ed. Ḥasida, 102–103 (no. 114); Kraemer, *Maimonides*, 64; *Med. Soc.*, 2:208–209.

43. Giṭṭin 1:5, *Mishna 'im perush rabbenu Moshe ben Maimon*, ed. Joseph Kafaḥ, 6 vols. (Jerusalem: Mossad Harav Kook, 1963–1968), 3:205.

44. See, e.g., *Teshuvot ha-Rambam*, ed. Blau, 1:6–8 (no. 5): a Muslim rental contract and litigation in the Islamic court; ibid., 2:350 (no. 193), *iltamasat minhu kitābat ḥujja be-nimmusei goyim*, "she asked him to write the deed [for paying the late marriage payment her divorced husband owed her] in the Gentile [i.e., Muslim] court"); ibid., 2:456 (no. 250), *qad athbata maḥḍar 'inda qāḍī al-muslimīn*, "he had authenticated a deed in the court of the Muslim *qāḍī*"; ibid., 2:488 (no. 260), *wa-aẓharat masṭūr . . . wa-huwa be-'arkha'ot shel goyim fa-athbatathu 'inda al-shofeṭ wa-staḥlafahā al-shofeṭ bi-ḥaḍrat shāhidīn goyim 'adilīn ['ādilīn] 'alā al-masṭūr*, "she produced a deed . . . from the court of the Gentiles [i.e., Muslims] which she had authenticated before the judge. The judge had her swear concerning the deed in the presence of honest [professional] Gentile witnesses." See also the index at the end of vol. 3 of Blau's edition, p. 210, s.v. *'arkha'ot shel goyim*. A quick search of the database of the PGP, using an appropriate keyword like *goyim* ("Gentiles," namely, Muslims) or *dinei goyim* ("Gentile court," i.e., "Muslim court"), dramatically reveals the extent of Jewish recourse to Islamic courts. For Goitein's discussion of the phenomenon, see *Med. Soc.*, 2:398–402. Maimonides chastised a local Jewish judge for referring a dispute between two partners sharing ownership of a courtyard house to the Islamic court when that judge learned that one of the litigants had drawn up the agreement regarding leasing the house to renters in an Islamic tribunal. *Teshuvot ha-Rambam*, ed. Blau, 2:685–686 (no. 408).

45. Ibid., 2:350 (no. 193).

46. Ibid., 2:686 (no. 408).

47. R. Isaac Alfasi firmly denounced Jewish recourse to Islamic courts; see *She'elot u-teshuvot R. Yiṣhaq Alfasi*, ed. Leiter, 62b–63a (no. 221).

48. Mark R. Cohen, *Jewish Self-Government in Medieval Egypt: The Origins of the*

*Office of Head of the Jews, ca. 1065–1126* (Princeton, NJ: Princeton University Press, 1980), chap. 3.

49. Idem, "Maimonides' Egypt," in *Moses Maimonides and His Time*, ed. Eric L. Ormsby (Washington, DC: Catholic University of America Press, 1989), 21–34.

50. On the *taqqana*, see *Teshuvot ha-Rambam*, ed. Blau, 2:624 (no. 347) and n. 4; 2:685 (no. 408); 1:39–40 (no. 27, containing the above-mentioned exception).

51. The reading *dinei goyim* of many manuscripts and some commentaries, rather than *dayyanei goyim*, "Gentile judges," of the printed editions, is to be preferred. See *Mishneh Torah, Shofeṭim*, ed. Shabse Frankel, 12:88 (note in margin) and 12:598.

52. Libson, *Jewish and Islamic Law*, 81–82.

53. I discuss this at the end of my "A Partnership Gone Bad" (above, Chapter 2 n. 47).

54. See John Griffiths, "What Is Legal Pluralism?," *Journal of Legal Pluralism* 24 (1986): 1–55, still regarded as a classic discussion of the concept. On legal pluralism as a framework for evaluating Jewish and Christian autonomy in the Islamic Middle Ages, see U. Simonsohn, *A Common Justice*. Marina Rustow addresses the same issue from a different perspective, showing how Jewish leadership in medieval Egypt actively sought the intervention of Muslim state authorities in inner communal affairs when it served their purposes, despite the negative impact that this could have on Jewish autonomy. Rustow, "At the Limits of Communal Autonomy." In a suggestive article that indirectly impinges on the issue of the autonomy of non-Muslim communities, Timur Kuran uses the concept of legal pluralism as the operative concept to explain why non-Muslims disproportionately dominated economic modernization in the Middle East beginning in the late eighteenth century, since they had access to the jurisdiction of European courts in the Middle East and were able to invoke the protection of European colonial powers. This enabled them to take advantage of the legal structure of modern capitalism and gain an advantage over Muslims, who were unable to take shelter in European courts because of the requirement that they live by Islamic law alone. Timur Kuran, "The Economic Aspect of the Middle East's Religious Minorities: The Role of Legal Pluralism," *Journal of Legal Studies* 33 (June 2004): 475–515. It is worth noting that Jews in medieval Egypt were not alone among the non-Muslims who had access to and resorted to Islamic courts. For the Copts, see the Arabic marriage contract from 948, incorporating stipulations according with Islamic marital law and witnessed by a very large number of Muslim witnesses and, on verso, the wife's release of her husband upon receipt of her late marriage payment (*mu'akhkhar*), dated 989; Nabia Abbot, "Arabic Marriage Contracts Among Copts," *Zeitschrift der Deutschen Morgenländischen Gesellschaft* 95 (1941): 59–81.

55. ENA NS 16.32, ed. Frenkel, *Alexandria*, 280–281; cf. 139–140.

56. R. Joseph Caro quotes (in Beit Yosef, Oraḥ Ḥayyim 26b) a responsum of the Babylonian Gaon R. Palṭoi (Gaon 842–858), ruling that it was permissible to summon a recalcitrant co-litigant to a Gentile (Muslim) court, but the monitoring system codified in *Hilkhot Sanhedrin* 26:7 seems to be Maimonides' own invention. A similar procedure seems to have been instituted in the next century in Germany, as reported by R. Meir of Rothenburg (cited in Beit Yosef, ibid.).

57. Mark R. Cohen, "Correspondence and Social Control in the Jewish Communities

of the Islamic World: A Letter of the Nagid Joshua Maimonides," *Jewish History* 1 (Fall 1986): 39–48. I did not make the connection with Maimonides in that article.

58. For the Geonim, see Libson, *Jewish and Islamic Law*, 103.

59. Sarah Stroumsa has made the case for Maimonides' own immersion in Islamicate society in her *Maimonides in His World*. The question of the Jewish identity of Jewish merchants is taken in a different direction by Ackerman-Lieberman, *The Business of Identity*.

60. The main studies: Amnon Cohen, *Yehudei Yerushalayim ba-me'ah ha-shesh-'esreh lefi te'udot turkiyot shel beit ha-din ha-shar'ī* (*Ottoman Documents on the Jewish Community of Jerusalem in the Sixteenth Century*) (Jerusalem: Yad Izhak Ben-Zvi, 1976); idem, *Jewish Life Under Islam*; idem and Elisheva Simon-Pikali, *Yehudim be-veit ha-mishpaṭ ha-Muslemi: ḥevra kalkala ve-irgun qehillati bi-Yerushalayim ha-'Otmanit: ha-me'ah ha-shesh-'esreh* (*Jews in the Moslem Religious Court: Society, Economy and Communal Organization in the XVIth Century: Documents from Ottoman Jerusalem*) (Jerusalem: Yad Izhak Ben-Zvi, 1993); A. Cohen, *A World Within*; Amnon Cohen and Elisheva Simon-Pikali, *Yehudim be-veit ha-mishpaṭ ha-Muslemi: ḥevra kalkala ve-irgun qehillati bi-Yerushalayim ha-'Otmanit: ha-me'ah ha-shemoneh-'esreh* (*Jews in the Moslem Religious Court: Society, Economy and Communal Organization in the XVIIIth Century: Documents from Ottoman Jerusalem*) (Jerusalem: Yad Izhak Ben-Zvi, 1996); idem, *Yehudim be-veit ha-mishpaṭ ha-Muslemi: ḥevra kalkala ve-irgun qehillati bi-Yerushalayim ha-'Otmanit: ha-me'ah ha-tesha'-'esreh* (*Jews in the Moslem Religious Court: Society, Economy and Communal Organization in the XIXth Century: Documents from Ottoman Jerusalem*) (Jerusalem: Yad Izhak Ben-Zvi, 2003); idem, *Yehudim be-veit ha-mishpaṭ ha-Muslemi: ḥevra kalkala ve-irgun qehillati bi-Yerushalayim ha-'Otmanit: ha-me'ah ha-sheva'-'esreh* (*Jews in the Moslem Religious Court: Society, Economy and Communal Organization in the XVIIth Century: Documents from Ottoman Jerusalem*), 2 vols. (Jerusalem: Yad Izhak Ben-Zvi, 2010); Najwa al-Qattan, "Dhimmīs in the Islamic Court: Legal Autonomy and Religious Discrimination," *International Journal of Middle East Studies* 31 (1999): 429–444; Joseph R. Hacker, "Jewish Autonomy in the Ottoman Empire: Its Scope and Limits. Jewish Courts from the Sixteenth to the Seventeenth Centuries," in *The Jews of the Ottoman Empire*, ed. Avigdor Levy (Princeton, NJ: Darwin and Institute of Turkish Studies, 1994), 153–202; Haim Gerber, *Crossing Borders: Jews and Muslims in Ottoman Law, Economy and Society* (Istanbul: Isis, 2008), 70–71; Élise Voguet, "Les communautés juives du Maghreb central à la lumière des *fatwa*-s mālikites de la fin du Moyen Âge," in *The Legal Status of Ḏimmī-s in the Islamic West*, ed. Fierro and Tolan, 301–305; Jessica Marglin, "In the Courts of the Nations: Jews, Muslims, and Legal Pluralism in Nineteenth-Century Morocco" (PhD diss., Princeton University, 2013); Aomar Boum, *Memories of Absence: How Muslims Remember Jews in Morocco* (Stanford, CA: Stanford University Press, 2013), 43–55 (cases of litigation in *qāḍī* courts involving Jews in southern Morocco, prior to the mass exodus of most of Moroccan Jewry after 1956); Ron Shaham, "Jews and the Sharī'a Court in Modern Egypt," *Studia Islamica* 82 (1995): 113–136.

61. The relatively few extant Islamic court records that have survived from our period had the benefit of being discarded in the Geniza; see Khan, *Arabic Legal and Administrative Documents*. One of the documents, an eleventh-century Muslim marriage contract,

has a note at the top, *thubita fī dīwān al-ḥukm al-muwaffaq*, which Khan translates "It was registered in the archives of the prosperous (i.e., Islamic) court." Ibid., 198 (no. 34).

## CONCLUSION

1. The problem of originality in Maimonides' work has recently been addressed in a broader context in the two-volume publication in Hebrew, *Maimonides: Conservatism, Originality, Revolution* (see Introduction n. 35, above). See, even more recently, Halbertal, *Maimonides: Life and Thought*, and Stroumsa, *Maimonides in His World.*

2. Twersky, *Introduction to the Code of Maimonides.* For Twersky, however, the "external historical motive" or the "response to contemporary need" is limited to Maimonides' avowed intention, as he wrote in the Introduction to the Code, to respond to the "vicissitudes" of his time, including the fact that "[t]he wisdom of our wisemen has disappeared" (ibid., 62). In the present study, we have concerned ourselves with concrete legal changes responding to contemporary need in the sphere of economic life and practice, a subject that Twersky does not address.

3. See above, p. 18, and his correspondence with the Alexandrian judge, Pinḥas b. Meshullam. For the view of contemporary scholars on changes in the halakha in the Code, see Chapter 1 n. 15.

4. Hallaq, *Sharī'a: Theory, Practice, Transformations*, 183.

5. Libson makes this point regarding the southern French commentator Rabad of Posquières; *Jewish and Islamic Law*, 262.

6. Havatselet, *Ha-Rambam veha-Ge'onim.*

7. Blidstein, "Where Do We Stand in the Study of Maimonidean Halakhah?," 28.

8. Also cited in the name of the Geonim as "a custom of the merchants" by the Andalusian R. Isaac Alfasi in his epitome of the Talmud, Bava Qamma 37b.

9. Robert Brody, "Maimonides' Attitude Towards the Halakhic Innovations of the Geonim," in *The Thought of Maimonides: Philosophical and Legal Studies*, ed. I. Robinson et al. (Lewiston, NY: E. Mellen, 1990), 183–208; idem, "The Influence of Sa'adyah Gaon's Halakhic Monographs on Maimonides' *Mishneh Torah*," 211–222.

10. Halbertal, *Maimonides: Life and Thought*, 175–181.

11. Regarding halakhot in the Code that lack precedent in the Talmud but have parallels in Islamic law, Gideon Libson notes with some ambivalence the difficulty of deciding whether Maimonides borrowed from Islamic law directly or through the mediation of lost Gaonic sources. Libson, "Maimonides' Halakhic Writings Against the Background of Muslim Law and Jurisprudence of the Period," 260–267. In my view, Maimonides could just as likely have come upon halakhic solutions to economic problems as a result of his intimate knowledge of the habits of Jewish and Muslim merchants.

12. Twersky writes: "The *Mishneh Torah* is thus a repository of interpretations, some of which it helped preserve or disseminate. This emphasis obviously should not obscure the fact that there are many changes in the *Mishneh Torah* resulting from Maimonides' ongoing reflection and progressive precision in analysis; as his understanding of the

Talmud changed, there would obviously be a corresponding change in his codificatory formulation. Some explication (*perush*), *often invisible*, whether inherited, adapted, or totally original, is at the base of every normative formulation"; *Introduction to the Code of Maimonides*, 161 (emphasis added). Twersky reached his conclusion, however, based on minute comparison of the Code with Maimonides' predecessors in the school of Jewish law, but he did not address the larger question of society as reflected in the Geniza documents and legal change in any substantial way.

13. Blidstein, "Where Do We Stand in the Study of Maimonidean Halakhah?," 13 (emphasis added).

14. Here it is relevant to quote Blidstein's comments in his "*Halakhah*—the Governing Norm," *Jewish Political Studies Review* 8 (spring 1996): "*Halakhah*'s role vis-à-vis economic activity is clearly supervisory rather than constitutive. This sphere more than any other, finally, was shaped by Jewry's integration into the world. . . . *Halakhah* regulates the formal structures through which economic activity takes place. . . . But be all this as it may, *halakhah* recognizes extra-*halakhic* structures in this area. Custom (*minhag*), frequently merchants' custom, has the force of law; indeed "custom abolishes the law" in this realm" (65–66).

15. Idem, "Where Do We Stand in the Study of Maimonidean Halakha?," 27–28.

16. Jacob Levinger, writing about halakhot in the Code that reflect philosophical or scientific views, as distinguished from legal opinions, states: "We know that Maimonides did not copy word for word from his sources; he very often paraphrased. This fact in itself is liable to raise for us the possibility that Maimonides' special wording is his own commentary to the Talmudic halakhot, just as any editor, translator, or rewriter incorporates his own commentary to texts which he gives a new form." Levinger, "Maimonides as Philosopher and Codifier," 135.

17. J. Katz, *Exclusiveness and Tolerance*, chap. 3.

18. Haym Soloveitchik, "Pawnbroking: A Study in *Ribbit* and of the Halakhah in Exile," in his *Collected Essays*, 1:57–166.

19. Haym Soloveitchik, "Can Halakhic Texts Talk History?," *AJS Review* 3 (1978): 153–196, and idem, "Religious Law and Change," 205–221; both reprinted in his *Collected Essays: Volume I*. See also his two books: *Yeinam: Saḥar be-yeinam shel goyim 'al gilgulah shel halakha be-'olam ha-ma'aseh* (*Principles and Pressures: Jewish Trade in Gentile Wine in the Middle Ages*) (Tel Aviv: Alma–Am Oved, 2003) and *Ha-yayin bimei ha-beinayim: Yein nesekh—Pereq be-toledot ha-halakha be-Ashkenaz* (*Wine in Ashkenaz in the Middle Ages: Yein Nesekh—a Study in the History of Halakhah*) (Jerusalem: Merkaz Zalman Shazar, 2008).

20. See Soloveitchik, "Religious Law and Change," 211–213 (in his *Collected Essays*, 1:245–247) and his follow-up article, "'Religious Law and Change' Revisited," *Collected Essays*, 1:258–277. I do not know whether Maimonides assumed that what pious people did in itself somehow reflected the proper halakha, as Soloveitchik surmises in the case of Ashkenazic Jews. We do know that Maimonides considered Jews in the East less learned than Jews in southern France, with whom he exchanged correspondence expressing his dissatisfaction with the level of learning in his own milieu and his admiration for the

educational level of Jews in the West. The approach of the Tosafists to reconciling economic realities with Talmudic halakha is also discussed by Shalom Albeck, "Rabbenu Tam's Attitude Toward the Problems of His Time" (Hebrew), *Zion* 19 (1954): 104–141.

21. Soloveitchik, "Can Halakhic Texts Talk History?," 176; in his *Collected Essays*, 1:198, Soloveitchik uses the phrase "measurable deflection."

22. I am grateful to Haym Soloveitchik for pointing out to me how profound Maimonides' "angle of deflection" is in this case. In his e-mail to me of December 9, 2013, Professor Soloveitchik wrote: "Early Ashkenaz confronted the same problem of adapting an agricultural legal system to a commercial world—a much tinier and infinitely less sophisticated commercial world, to be sure—and they did it their way. They weren't of Maimonidean stature and they weren't writing a *summa*, but still they had to make their adjustments."

23. The methodology underlying the present study has broad implications for studying the Code in its socioeconomic context as portrayed in the documents of the Cairo Geniza. A systematic study of *Hilkhot ishut* (Laws of Marriage) in the Code, for instance, would doubtless uncover many places where Maimonides' formulation can be correlated with family life as reflected in the Geniza documents. Eve Krakowski, in "Female Adolescence in the Cairo Geniza Documents" (PhD diss., University of Chicago, 2012) and *Coming of Age in Medieval Egypt: Women's Adolescence, Jewish Law, and Ordinary Culture* (Princeton, NJ: Princeton University Press, forthcoming), examines legal documents and responsa to understand how Jews in the Geniza community understood the transition of young women from puberty to first marriage. She shows that the classical rabbinic model defining female adolescence only partially accounts for women's real-life experience and men's own conception of their position. She claims that much of what we see in these documents reflects the impact of the environment, as represented in Islamic family law. Here and there, she points to places where the Mishneh Torah shows awareness of this acculturation, e.g., "Female Adolescence," 224 n. 483.

In her e-mail to me of May 6, 2014, Krakowski wrote: "In *Hilkhot ishut* (Laws of Marriage) 13:3, Maimonides asserts that a husband must provide his wife with lodging (*mador she-yoshevet bah*) as a basic condition of marriage. This is a legal innovation, which appears in neither classical rabbinic nor Gaonic sources; Maimonides justifies it by assimilating lodging to clothing (*kesut*), one of the three basic obligations that a husband owes to his wife under classical rabbinic law. In *Ishut* 14:3, he further states that a man with multiple wives may not compel them to live together in a single dwelling (*ḥaṣer*, here equivalent to Arabic *dār*), but must grant each a separate dwelling of her own. While neither of these ideas have clear rabbinic precedent, both directly echo Islamic jurists, who require husbands to provide each of their wives with private lodging separate from each other—and sometimes from their female in-laws—as part of their spousal maintenance (*nafaqa*, equivalent to rabbinic *mezonot*). (For detailed discussion of Ḥanafī jurists' treatment of this question, see Y. Meron, *L'obligation alimentaire entre époux en droit musulman hanéfite* [Paris: Librairie générale de droit et de jurisprudence, 1971], 202–209.) G. Libson therefore suggests that *Ishut* 14:3 simply borrows from Islamic law; see his *Jewish and Islamic Law*, 157. Geniza legal documents, however, tell a more complicated story: they suggest that Maimonides here is rather codifying contemporary *social* norms shared by Jews and Muslims alike, which understood women's access to private space not shared by other non-kin women in a jointly inhabited *dār* as integral to their personal honor. M. A. Friedman has identified a small corpus of marriage documents that reveal this shared norm by specifying that women entering a polygynous marriage must be granted separate lodging; see his discussion in *Ribbui nashim: Meqorot ḥadashim mi-gnizat Qahir* (*Jewish Polygyny in the Middle Ages: New Documents from the Cairo Geniza*) (Tel Aviv: Mossad Bialik, 1986). Other marriage documents contain similar clauses pertaining to women's co-residence with female in-laws; I discuss these documents and the conceptions that they reveal in my PhD thesis, 'Female Adolescence in the Cairo Geniza Documents' (University of Chicago, 2012), 202–226. Mordechai Friedman discusses 'Social Realities in Egypt and Maimonides' Rulings on Family Law,' in *Sobre la vida y obra de Maimonides*, ed. Jesús Peláez Rosal (Córdoba: Ediciones el Almendro, 1991), 177–186, referring to 'rulings' in his responsa though not in the Code."

# Works Cited


Abbot, Nabia. "Arabic Marriage Contracts Among Copts." *Zeitschrift der Deutschen Morgenländischen Gesellschaft* 95 (1941): 59–81.

Abraham b. Moses Maimonides. *Birkat Avraham*. Ed. Ber Goldberg. Lyck: 1859; repr., Jerusalem: n.p., 1960.

Abramson, Shraga. "From One of the Books of R. Samuel b. Ḥofni: B. from the Book of Acquisition?" (Hebrew). *Tarbiz* 18 (1946–1947): 34–45.

———. *'Inyanot be-sifrut ha-ge'onim*. Jerusalem: Mossad Harav Kook, 1974.

Ackerman-Lieberman, Phillip I. *The Business of Identity: Jews, Muslims, and Economic Life in Medieval Egypt*. Stanford, CA: Stanford University Press, 2014.

———. "Commercial Forms and Legal Norms in the Jewish Community of Medieval Egypt." *Law and History Review* 30 (2012): 1007–1052.

———. "Contractual Partnerships in the Geniza and the Relationship Between Islamic Law and Practice." *Journal of the Economic and Social History of the Orient* 54 (2011): 646–676.

———. "Legal Pluralism Among the Court Records of Medieval Egypt." *Bulletin d'Etudes Orientales* 63 (2014): 79–112.

———. "A Partnership Culture: Jewish Economic and Social Life Seen Through the Legal Documents of the Cairo Geniza." PhD diss., Princeton University, 2007.

———. "Revisiting Jewish Occupational Choice and Urbanization in Iraq Under the Early Abbasids." *Jewish History* 29 (2015): 113–135.

Adams, Robert McCormick. *Land Behind Baghdad: A History of Settlement on the Diyala Plains*. Chicago: University of Chicago Press, 1965.

Albeck, Shalom. "Rabbenu Tam's Attitude Toward the Problems of His Time" (Hebrew). *Zion* 19 (1954): 104–141.

Allony, Nehemya. *Ha-sifriya he-yehudit bimei ha-beinayim* (*The Jewish Library in the Middle Ages: Book Lists from the Cairo Geniza*). Ed. Miriam Frenkel and Haggai Ben-Shammai. Jerusalem: Makhon Ben-Zvi, 2006.

Al Saud, Torki Fahad Abdullah A. "Al-Qirqisānī and Maimonides' Polemics Against Islam: An Intercultural Study in Religion and Literature." PhD diss., Boston University, 2008.

Arabic Papyrology Database (APD). http://www.apd.gwi.uni-muenchen.de:8080/apd/project.jsp.

Ariel, Neri. "M anuals fo r Judges (ادب القضاة): A Study of Genizah Fragments of a

Judaeo-Arabic Monographic Legal Genre" (Hebrew). PhD diss., Hebrew University, forthcoming.

Ashburner, Walter. *The Rhodian Sea Law*. Oxford: Clarendon, 1909.

Ashtor, Eliyahu. "Un mouvement migratoire au haut Moyen Âge: Migrations de l'Irak vers le pays méditerranéens dans le haut Moyen Âge." *Annales: économies, sociétés, civilisations* 27 (1972): 185–214.

Ashur, Amir. "Protecting the Wife's Rights in Marriage as Reflected in Pre-Nuptials and Marriage Contracts from the Cairo Genizah and Parallel Arabic Sources." *Religion Compass* 6/8 (2012): 381–389.

———. "The Publications of Mordechai Akiva Friedman" (Hebrew). *Dine Israel* 26–27 (2009–2010): xix–xxxiii.

Badawi, Elsaid M., and Muhammad Abdel Haleem. *Arabic-English Dictionary of Qur'anic Usage*. Leiden: Brill, 2008.

Barak-Erez, Daphne. "Codification and Legal Culture: In Comparative Perspective." *Tulane European and Civil Law Forum* 13 (1998): 125–137.

Baron. Salo W. "The Economic Views of Maimonides." In *Essays on Maimonides: An Octocentennial Volume*, ed. Salo W. Baron. New York: Columbia University Press, 1941, 127–264.

Benedikt, Benjamin Zeev. *Ha-Rambam le-lo seṭiya min ha-talmud: Asufat ma'amarim* (*Maimonides, Without Swaying from the Talmud: Collected Articles*). Jerusalem: Mossad Harav Kook, 1985.

Ben-Menahem, Hanina. "The Second Canonization of the Talmud." *Cardozo Law Review* 28, 1 (2006): 37–51.

Ben-Sasson, Menahem. "The Jewish Community of Gabes in the 11th Century." In *Communautés juives des marges sahariennes du Maghreb*, ed. Michel Abitbol. Jerusalem: Makhon Ben-Zvi, 1982, 265–284.

———. "Maimonides' *Mishneh Torah*: On the Creation of a Canon During the Author's Lifetime" (Hebrew). In *Ha-qanon ha-samui min ha-'ayin: Ḥiqrei qanon u-geniza* (*The Hidden Canon: Studies in Canonization and Geniza*), ed. Menahem Ben-Sasson et al. Jerusalem: Scolion, 2010, 133–201.

———. "Remembrance and Oblivion of Religious Persecutions: On Sanctifying the Name of God (*Qiddush ha-Shem*) in Christian and Islamic Communities During the Middle Ages." In *Jews, Christians and Muslims in Medieval and Early Modern Times: A Festschrift in Honor of Mark R. Cohen*, ed. Arnold E. Franklin, Roxani Eleni Margariti, Marina Rustow, and Uriel Simonsohn (Leiden: Brill, 2014), 169–194.

———. "Remnants of the Book of Testimony and Formularies by R. Saadya Gaon" (Hebrew). *Shenaton ha-mishpaṭ ha-'ivri* 11–12 (1984–1986): 135–278.

———. *Ṣemiḥat ha-qehilla ha-yehudit be-arṣot ha-islam: Qayrawan, 800–1057* (*The Emergence of the Local Jewish Community in the Muslim World: Qayrawan, 800–1057*). Jerusalem: Magnes, 1996.

——— et al., eds. *Yehudei siṣilia 825–1068: Te'udot u-meqorot* (*The Jews of Sicily 825–1068: Documents and Sources*). Jerusalem: Makhon Ben-Zvi, 1991.

Blidstein, Gerald (Ya'akov). "*Halakhah*—the Governing Norm." *Jewish Political Studies Review* 8 (spring 1996): 37–90.

———. "Maimonides' *Taqqanah* Concerning Public Prayer." *Maimonidean Studies* 3 (1992–1993): 3–28.

———. Review of Twersky's *Introduction to the Code of Maimonides. Pe'amim* 11 (1982): 135–141.

———. "The Status of Islam in Maimonidean Halakha" (Hebrew). In *Rav-tarbutiyut bimdina demoqraṭit vi-yhudit* (*Multiculturalism in a Democratic and Jewish State*), ed. Menachem Mautner et al. Tel Aviv: Ramot, 1998, 465–476.

———. *Ha-tefilla be-mishnato ha-hilkhatit shel ha-Rambam* (*Prayer in the Halakhic Teaching of Maimonides*). Jerusalem: Mossad Bialik, 1994.

———. "Where Do We Stand in the Study of Maimonidean Halakhah?." In *Studies in Maimonides*, ed. Isadore Twersky. Cambridge, MA: Harvard University Press, 1990, 1–30.

Bloom, Jonathan. *Paper Before Print: The History and Impact of Paper in the Islamic World.* New Haven, CT: Yale University Press, 2001.

Botticini, Maristella, and Zvi Eckstein. *The Chosen Few: How Education Shaped Jewish History, 70–1492.* Princeton, NJ: Princeton University Press, 2012.

Boum, Aomar. *Memories of Absence: How Muslims Remember Jews in Morocco.* Stanford, CA: Stanford University Press, 2013.

Brody, Robert (Yeraḥme'el). *The Geonim of Babylonia and the Shaping of Medieval Jewish Culture.* New Haven, CT: Yale University Press, 1998.

———. *Ḥibburim hilkhatiyim shel Rav Saadya Gaon* (*Halakhic Works of Rav Saadya Gaon*). Jerusalem: Yad Ha-Rav Nissim, 2015.

———. "The Influence of Sa'adyah Gaon's Halakhic Monographs on Maimonides' *Mishneh Torah*" (Hebrew). In *Ha-Rambam: Shamranut, meqoriyut, mahapkhanut* (*Maimonides: Conservatism, Originality, Revolution*), 2 vols., ed. Aviezer Ravitzky. Jerusalem: Merkaz Zalman Shazar, 2008, 211–222.

———. "Maimonides' Attitude Towards the Halakhic Innovations of the Geonim." In *The Thought of Maimonides: Philosophical and Legal Studies*, ed. I. Robinson et al. Lewiston, NY: E. Mellen, 1990, 183–208.

———. "Were the Geonim Legislators?" (Hebrew). *Shenaton ha-mishpaṭ ha-'ivri* 11–12 (1984–1986): 290–304.

———, Carmiel Cohen, and Yehuda Zvi Stampfer, eds. *Oṣar he-ge'onim 'al Bava Meṣi'a.* Jerusalem: Ofeq Institute, 2012.

Brunschvig, Robert. "Le système de la preuve en droit musulman." In *Etudes d'Islamologie*, 2 vols. Paris: Maisonneuve et Larose, 1976, 2:201–218.

Choueka, Yaacov. "Computerizing the Cairo Genizah: Aims, Methodologies and Achievements." *Ginze Qedem* 8 (2012): 9–30.

Cohen, Amnon. *Jewish Life Under Islam: Jerusalem in the Sixteenth Century.* Cambridge, MA: Harvard University Press, 1984.

———. *A World Within: Jewish Life as Reflected in Islamic Court Documents from the Sijill of Jerusalem (XVIth Century).* 2 vols. Philadelphia: Center for Judaic Studies, University of Pennsylvania, 1994.

———, and Elisheva Simon-Pikali. *Yehudei Yerushalayim ba-me'ah ha-shesh-'esreh lefi te'udot turkiyot shel beit ha-din ha-shar'ī (Ottoman Documents on the Jewish Community of Jerusalem in the Sixteenth Century).* Jerusalem: Yad Izhak Ben-Zvi, 1976.

———. *Yehudim be-veit ha-mishpaṭ ha-Muslemi: Ḥevra kalkala ve-irgun qehillati bi-Yerushalayim ha-'Otmanit: ha-me'ah ha-sheva'-'esreh (Jews in the Moslem Religious Court: Society, Economy and Communal Organization in the XVIIth Century: Documents from Ottoman Jerusalem).* 2 vols. Jerusalem: Yad Izhak Ben-Zvi, 2010.

———. *Yehudim be-veit ha-mishpaṭ ha-Muslemi: Ḥevra kalkala ve-irgun qehillati bi-Yerushalayim ha-'Otmanit: ha-me'ah ha-tesha'-'esreh (Jews in the Moslem Religious Court: Society, Economy and Communal Organization in the XIXth Century: Documents from Ottoman Jerusalem).* Jerusalem: Yad Izhak Ben-Zvi, 2003.

———. *Yehudim be-veit ha-mishpaṭ ha-Muslemi: Ḥevra kalkala ve-irgun qehillati bi-Yerushalayim ha-'Otmanit: ha-me'ah ha-shemoneh-'esreh (Jews in the Moslem Religious Court: Society, Economy and Communal Organization in the XVIIIth Century: Documents from Ottoman Jerusalem).* Jerusalem: Yad Izhak Ben-Zvi, 1996.

———, *Yehudim be-veit ha-mishpaṭ ha-Muslemi: Ḥevra kalkala ve-irgun qehillati bi-Yerushalayim ha-'Otmanit: ha-me'ah ha-shesh-'esreh (Jews in the Moslem Religious Court: Society, Economy and Communal Organization in the XVIth Century: Documents from Ottoman Jerusalem).* Jerusalem: Yad Izhak Ben-Zvi, 1993.

Cohen, Boaz. *Jewish and Roman Law: A Comparative Study.* 2 vols. New York: Jewish Theological Seminary, 1966.

Cohen, Hayyim J. "The Economic Background and the Secular Occupations of Muslim Jurisprudents and Traditionists in the Classical Period of Islam (Until the Middle of the Eleventh Century)." *Journal of the Economic and Social History of the Orient* 13 (1970): 16–61.

Cohen, Mark R. "Correspondence and Social Control in the Jewish Communities of the Islamic World: A Letter of the Nagid Joshua Maimonides." *Jewish History* 1 (1986): 39–48.

———. "The 'Custom of the Merchants' in Gaonic Jurisprudence and in Maimonides' *Mishneh Torah.*" In *The Festschrift Darkhei Noam: The Jews of Arab Lands,* ed. Carsten Schapkow, Shmuel Shepkaru, and Alan T. Levenson. Leiden: Brill, 2015, 86–111.

———. "Defending Jewish Judicial Autonomy in the Islamic Middle Ages." In *Law and Religious Minorities in Medieval Societies: Between Theory and Praxis,* ed. Ana Echevarria et al. Turnhout: Brepols, 2016, 13–33.

———. "Geniza for Islamicists, Islamic Geniza, and the 'New Cairo Geniza.'" *Harvard Middle Eastern and Islamic Review* 7 (2006): 129–145.

———. *Jewish Self-Government in Medieval Egypt: The Origins of the Office of Head of the Jews, ca. 1065–1126.* Princeton, NJ: Princeton University Press, 1980.

———. "The Law of Power of Attorney in Maimonides' Code of Jewish Law." In *"From a Sacred Source": Genizah Studies in Honour of Professor Stefan C. Reif,* ed. Ben Outhwaite and Siam Bhayro. Leiden: Brill, 2010, 81–98.

———. "Maimonides and Charity in the Light of the Geniza Documents." In *The Trias of Maimonides/Die Trias des Maimonides*, ed. Georges Tamer. Berlin: De Gruyter, 2005, 65–81.

———. "Maimonides' Egypt." In *Moses Maimonides and His Time*, ed. Eric L. Ormsby. Washington, DC: Catholic University of America Press, 1989, 21–34.

———. "A Partnership Gone Bad: Business Relationships and the Evolving Law of the Cairo Geniza Period." *Journal of the Economic and Social History of the Orient* 56 (2013): 218–263.

———. *Poverty and Charity in the Jewish Community of Medieval Egypt*. Princeton, NJ: Princeton University Press, 2005.

———. *Under Crescent and Cross: The Jews in the Middle Ages*. Princeton, NJ: Princeton University Press, 1994; new ed., 2008.

———. *The Voice of the Poor in the Middle Ages: An Anthology of Documents from the Cairo Geniza*. Princeton, NJ: Princeton University Press, 2005.

———, and Yedida K. Stillman. "The Cairo Geniza and the Custom of Geniza Among Oriental Jewry: An Historical and Ethnographic Study" (Hebrew). *Pe'amim* 24 (1985): 3–35.

Cohn, Haim H. "Codificatory Method and Jewish Legal Theory." In *Maimonides as Codifier of Jewish Law*, ed. Nahum Rakover. Jerusalem: Library of Jewish Law, 1987, 31–43.

Constable, Olivia Remie. *Housing the Stranger in the Mediterranean World: Lodging, Trade, and Travel in Late Antiquity and the Middle Ages*. Cambridge: Cambridge University Press, 2003.

———. "The Problem of Jettison in Medieval Mediterranean Maritime Law." *Journal of Medieval History* 20 (1994): 207–220.

———. *Trade and Traders in Muslim Spain: The Commercial Realignment of the Iberian Peninsula 900–1500*. Cambridge: Cambridge University Press, 1994.

Cordes, Albrecht. "The Search for a Medieval *Lex Mercatoria*." *Oxford University Comparative Law Forum* 5 (2003), ouclf.iuscomp.org.

Danzig, Neil. "Lining in Holy Texts: The Source of a Halakha and Its Aftermath" (Hebrew). In *'Aṭara le-Ḥaim: Studies in Talmudic and Medieval Rabbinic Literature in Honor of Professor Haim Zalman Dimitrovsky*, ed. Daniel Boyarin et al. Jerusalem: Magnes, 2000, 283–359.

David ibn Abi Zimra. *Yeqar tif'eret 'al hilkhot sheluḥin ve-shutafin ve-hilkhot 'avadim*. Ed. Shemuel Barukh Werner. Jerusalem: Mossad Harav Kook, 1945.

Davidson, Herbert A. *Moses Maimonides: The Man and His Works*. Oxford: Oxford University Press, 2005.

Davis, Natalie Zemon. *The Gift in Sixteenth-Century France*. Madison: University of Wisconsin Press, 2000.

de Biberstein Kazimirski, A. *Dictionnaire Arabe-Français*. 2 vols. Paris: Maisonneuve, 1860.

Diem, Werner. *Arabische Briefe auf Papier aus der Heidelberger Papyrus-Sammlung*. Heidelberg: Universitätsverlag Winter, 2013.

———. *Arabische Briefe aus dem 10.–16. Jahrhundert.* Berlin: De Gruyter, 2011.

———. *Arabische Privatbriefe des 9. bis 15. Jahrhunderts aus der Österreichischen Nationalbibliothek in Wien.* Wiesbaden: Harrassowitz, 1996.

Dridi, Audrey. "Christian and Jewish Communities in Fusṭāṭ: Non-Muslim Topography and Legal Controversies in the Pre-Fatimid Period." In *The Late Antique World of Early Islam: Muslims Among Christians and Jews in the East Mediterranean*, ed. Robert Hoyland. Princeton, NJ: Darwin, 2015, 107–132.

Edelby, Néophyte. "The Legislative Autonomy of Christians in the Islamic world." In *Muslims and Others in Early Islamic Society*, ed. Robert Hoyland. Aldershot: Ashgate, 2004, 37–82.

Edwards, Jeremy, and Sheilagh Ogilvie. "Contract Enforcement, Institutions and Social Capital: The Maghribi Traders Reappraised." CESifo. Working Paper Series no. 2254 (2008).

———. "Contract Enforcement, Institutions, and Social Capital: The Maghribi Traders Reappraised." *Economic History Review* 65 (2012): 421–444.

Elon, Menachem. *Ḥerut ha-peraṭ be-darkhei geviyat ḥov ba-mishpaṭ ha-ʿivri* (*Freedom of the Debtor's Person in Jewish Law*). Jerusalem: Magnes, 1964.

———. *Jewish Law: History, Sources, Principles.* 4 vols. Trans. Bernard Auerbach and Melvin J. Sykes. Philadelphia: Jewish Publication Society, 1994.

Emon, Anver. *Religious Pluralism and Islamic Law: Dhimmīs and Others in the Empire of Law.* Oxford: Oxford University Press, 2012.

*Fatāwā al-lajna al-dā'ima li-buḥūth al-ʿilmiyya wa'l-iftā'.* Vol. 4. Riyadh, 2006.

Fattal, Antoine. "How Dhimmīs Were Judged in the Islamic World." In *Muslims and Others in Early Islamic Society*, ed. Robert Hoyland. Aldershot: Ashgate, 2004, 81–102.

———. *Le statut légal des non-musulmans en pays d'Islam.* Beirut: Imprimerie Catholique, 1958.

Fenton, Paul. "Maimonides—Father and Son: Continuity and Change." In *Traditions of Maimonideanism*, ed. Carlos Fraenkel. Leiden: Brill, 2009, 103–137.

Fischel, Walter J. *Jews in the Economic and Political Life of Mediaeval Islam.* London: Royal Asiatic Society, 1937.

Franklin, Arnold E. "More than Words on a Page: Letters as Substitutes for an Absent Writer." In *Jews, Christians and Muslims in Medieval and Early Modern Times: A Festschrift in Honor of Mark R. Cohen*, ed. Arnold E. Franklin, Roxani Eleni Margariti, Marina Rustow, and Uriel Simonsohn. Leiden: Brill, 2014, 287–305.

Frantz-Murphy, Gladys. Review of Ackerman-Lieberman's *The Business of Identity. Journal of Economic History* 75 (2015): 610–611.

Frenkel, Miriam. *Ha-ohavim veha-nedivim: ʿIlit manhiga be-qerev yehudei Alexandria bimei ha-beinayim* (*The Compassionate and Benevolent: The Leading Elite in the Jewish Community of Alexandria in the Middle Ages*). Jerusalem: Makhon Ben-Zvi, 2006.

Friedberg Genizah Project (FGP). https://fgp.genizah.org.

Friedell, Steven F. "Admiralty and the Sea of Jewish Law." *Journal of Maritime Law and Commerce* 27 (1996): 647–660.

Friedman, Mordechai A. "Abraham Maimonides on His Leadership, Reforms, and Spiritual Imperfection." *Jewish Quarterly Review* 104 (2014): 495–512.

———. "Abraham Maimuni's Prayer Reforms: Continuation or Revision of His Father's Teachings?." In *Traditions of Maimonideanism*, ed. Carlos Fraenkel. Leiden: Brill, 2009, 139–154.

———. "Division of the Marriage Gift into Immediate and Postponed Portions in the Cairo Geniza Documents" (Hebrew). In *Proceedings of the Sixth World Congress of Jewish Studies*, held in 1973. Jerusalem: World Union of Jewish Studies, 1977, 3: 377–387.

———. "Divorce upon the Wife's Demand as Reflected in Manuscripts from the Cairo Geniza." *Jewish Law Annual* 4 (1981): 101–127.

———. "The Monogamy Clause in Jewish Marriage Contracts." *Perspectives in Jewish Learning* 4 (1972): 20–40.

———. "New Fragments of Maimonides' Responsa from the Geniza" (Hebrew). In *Ḥiqrei 'ever va-'arav mugashim li-Yehoshu'a Blau (Hebrew and Arabic Studies Presented to Yehoshu'a Blau)*. Tel Aviv and Jerusalem: Tel Aviv University and the Hebrew University, 1993, 443–461.

———. "Quṣayr and the Documents on the Indian Ocean Trade." *Journal of the American Oriental Society* 126 (2006): 401–409.

———. *Ha-Rambam ha-mashiaḥ be-teiman veha-shemad (Maimonides, the Yemenite Messiah, and Apostasy)*. Jerusalem: Makhon Ben-Zvi, 2002.

———. "The Ransom-Divorce: Divorce Proceedings Initiated by the Wife in Medieval Jewish Practice." *Israel Oriental Studies* 6 (1976): 288–307.

———. "Social Realities in Egypt and Maimonides' Rulings on Family Law." In *Sobre la vida y obra de Maimonides*, ed. Jesús Peláez Rosal. Córdoba: Ediciones el Almendro, 1991, 177–186,

Gafni, Isaiah M. *Yehudei Bavel bi-tqufat ha-talmud: Ḥayyei ha-ḥevra veha-ruaḥ (The Jews of Babylonia in the Talmudic Period: A Social and Cultural History)*. Jerusalem: Merkaz Zalman Shazar, 1990.

Geoffrey, Eric. *Introduction to Sufism: The Inner Path of Islam*. Trans. Roger Gaetani. Bloomington, IN: World Wisdom, 2010.

Gerber, Haim. *Crossing Borders: Jews and Muslims in Ottoman Law, Economy and Society*. Istanbul: Isis, 2008.

Gil, Moshe. *Be-malkhut yishmael bi-tqufat ha-ge'onim (In the Kingdom of Ishmael)*. 4 vols. Tel Aviv and Jerusalem: Tel Aviv University, Mossad Bialik, and Ministry of Defense, 1997.

———. *Documents of the Jewish Pious Foundations from the Cairo Geniza*. Leiden: Brill, 1976.

———. *Ereṣ yisra'el ba-tequfa ha-muslemit ha-rishona (634–1099) (Palestine During the First Muslim Period [634–1099])*. 3 vols. Tel Aviv: Tel Aviv University and Ministry of Defense, 1983.

———. "The Rādhānite Merchants and the Land of Rādhān." *Journal of the Economic and Social History of the Orient* 17 (1974): 299–328.

———. "The Sughmar Family" (Hebrew). In *Ha-islam ve-'olamot ha-shezurim bo* (*The Intertwined Worlds of Islam: Essays in Memory of Hava Lazarus-Yafeh*), ed. Nahem Ilan. Jerusalem: Hebrew University, Institute of Asian and African Studies, Makhon Ben-Zvi, and Mossad Bialik, 2002, 149–170.

Ginzberg, Louis. *Gaonica*. 2 vols. New York: Jewish Theological Seminary, 1909.

Glickman, Mark. *Sacred Treasure—the Cairo Genizah: The Amazing Discoveries of Forgotten Jewish History in an Egyptian Synagogue Attic*. Woodstock, VT: Jewish Lights, 2011.

Goitein, S. D. "Abraham Maimonides and His Pietist Circle." In *Jewish Medieval and Renaissance Studies*, ed. Alexander Altmann. Cambridge, MA: Harvard University Press, 1967, 145–164.

———. "Documents on Abraham Maimonides and His Pietist Circle" (Hebrew). *Tarbiz* 33 (1964): 181–197.

———. "Formal Friendship in the Medieval Near East." *Proceedings of the American Philosophical Society* 115 (1971): 484–489.

———. "The Interplay of Jewish and Islamic Laws." In *Jewish Law in Legal History and the Modern World*, ed. Bernard S. Jackson. Leiden: Brill, 1980, 61–77.

———. *Letters of Medieval Jewish Traders, Translated from the Arabic*. Princeton, NJ: Princeton University Press, 1973.

———. "Maimonides, Man of Action: A Revision of the Master's Biography in Light of the Geniza Documents." In *Hommage à Georges Vajda*, ed. G. Nahon and Ch. Touati. Louvain: Peeters, 1980, 155–167.

———. *A Mediterranean Society: The Jewish Communities of the Arab World as Portrayed in the Documents of the Cairo Geniza*. 5 vols. plus index volume by Paula Sanders. Berkeley: University of California Press, 1967–1993.

———. "The Rise of the Near Eastern Bourgeoisie in Early Islamic Times." *Cahiers d'Histoire Mondiale* 3 (1956–1957): 583–604; repr., Goitein, *Studies in Islamic History and Institutions*, 217–241.

———. *Studies in Islamic History and Institutions*. Leiden: Brill, 2010 (1st ed., 1966).

———. "A Treatise in Defense of the Pietists by Abraham Maimonides" (Hebrew). *Journal of Jewish Studies* 16 (1965): 105–114.

———. "What Would Jewish and General History Benefit by a Systematic Publication of the Documentary Geniza Papers?." *Proceedings of the American Academy for Jewish Research* 23 (1954): 29–39.

———, and Mordechai A. Friedman. *India Traders of the Middle Ages: Documents from the Cairo Geniza* (*India Book*). Leiden: Brill, 2008.

———. *Sefer hodu I: Yosef al-Lebdi soḥer hodu ha-gadol: te'udot mi-gnizat qahir* (*India Book I: Joseph Lebdī Prominent India Trader: Cairo Geniza Documents*). Jerusalem: Makhon Ben-Zvi and Rabbi David and Amalia Rosen Foundation, 2009.

———. *Sefer hodu II: Maḍmūn negid ereṣ teman ve-saḥar hodu: te'udot mi-gnizat qahir* (*India Book II: Maḍmūn Nagid of Yemen and the India Trade: Cairo Geniza Documents*). Jerusalem: Makhon Ben-Zvi and Rabbi David and Amalia Rosen Foundation, 2010.

———. *Sefer hodu III: Avraham ben Yijū soḥer ve-yaṣran be-hodu: te'udot mi-gnizat qahir*

(*India Book III: Abraham Ben Yijū India Trader and Manufacturer: Cairo Geniza Documents*). Jerusalem: Makhon Ben-Zvi and Rabbi David and Amalia Rosen Foundation, 2010.

———, with the assistance of Amir Ashur. *Sefer hodu IV/B: Ḥalfon ha-soḥer ha-maskil ve-ha-nose'a ha-gadol: te'udot mi-gnizat qahir* (*India Book IV/B: Ḥalfon the Traveling Merchant Scholar: Cairo Geniza Documents*). Jerusalem: Makhon Ben-Zvi and Rabbi David and Amalia Rosen Foundation, 2013.

Goldberg, Jessica L. "Choosing and Enforcing Business Relationships in the Eleventh-Century Mediterranean: Reassessing the 'Maghribī Traders.'" *Past and Present* 216 (2012): 1–40.

———. "Geographies of Trade and Traders in the Eleventh-Century Mediterranean: A Study Based on Documents from the Cairo Geniza." PhD diss., Columbia University, 2005.

———. "On Reading Goitein's *A Mediterranean Society*: A View from Economic History." *Mediterranean Historical Review* 26 (2011): 171–186.

———. *Trade and Institutions in the Medieval Mediterranean: Geniza Merchants and Their Business World.* Cambridge: Cambridge University Press, 2012.

———. "The Use and Abuse of Commercial Letters from the Cairo Geniza." *Journal of Medieval History* 38 (2012): 127–154.

Goodblatt, David. "*Medinat Hayam:* The Coastal District" (Hebrew). *Tarbiz* 64 (1994–1995): 13–37.

Greif, Avner. "Contract Enforceability and Economic Institutions in Early Trade: The Maghribi Traders' Coalition." *American Economic Review* 83 (1993): 525–548.

———. "Contract Enforcement and Institutions Among the Maghribi Traders: Refuting Edwards and Ogilvie." CESifo. Working Paper Series no. 2350 (2008).

———. "Cultural Beliefs and the Organization of Society: A Historical and Theoretical Reflection on Collectivist and Individualist Societies." *Journal of Political Economy* 102 (1994): 912–950.

———. *Institutions and the Path to the Modern Economy: Lessons from Medieval Trade.* Cambridge: Cambridge University Press, 2006.

———. "The Maghribi Traders: A Reappraisal?." *Economic History Review* 65 (2012): 445–469.

———. "Reputation and Coalitions in Medieval Trade: Evidence on the Maghribi Traders." *Journal of Economic History* 49 (1989): 857–882.

Griffiths, John. "What Is Legal Pluralism?." *Journal of Legal Pluralism* 24 (1986): 1–55.

Grob, Eva Mira. *Documentary Private and Business Letters on Papyrus: Form and Function, Content and Context.* Berlin: De Gruyter, 2010.

Gulak, Asher. *Ha-sheṭarot ba-talmud* (*Legal Documents in the Talmud*). Trans. Ranon Katzoff. Jerusalem: Magnes, 1994.

———. *Das Urkundenwesen im Talmud im Lichte der griechisch-aegyptischen Papyri und des griechischen und roemischen Rechts.* Jerusalem: Rubin Mass, 1935.

Guo, Li. *Commerce, Culture, and Community in a Red Sea Port in the Thirteenth Century: The Arabic Documents from Qusair.* Leiden: Brill, 2004

———. "Quṣayr and the Documents on the Indian Ocean Trade." *Journal of the American Oriental Society* 126 (2006): 401–409.

Hacker, Joseph R. "Jewish Autonomy in the Ottoman Empire: Its Scope and Limits. Jewish Courts from the Sixteenth to the Seventeenth Centuries." In *The Jews of the Ottoman Empire*, ed. Avigdor Levy. Princeton, NJ: Darwin and Institute of Turkish Studies, 1994, 153–202.

Haim, Ofir. "Legal Documents and Persian Letters in Early Islamic Judaeo-Persian from Islamic Khurasan." MA thesis, Hebrew University, 2014.

———. "Letters from Afghanistan in the National Library" (Hebrew). *Ginze Qedem* 10 (2014): 9–28.

*Halakhot gedolot.* 2 vols. Ed. Ezriel Hildesheimer. Jerusalem: Mekize Nirdamim, 1971–1988.

Halbertal, Moshe. *Ha-Rambam: Rabbi Mosheh ben Maimon.* Jerusalem: Merkaz Zalman Shazar, 2009. English trans., *Maimonides: Life and Thought.* Trans. Joel Linsider. Princeton, NJ: Princeton University Press, 2014.

———. "Sefer Ha-Miṣvot of Maimonides: His Architecture of Halakha and Theory of Interpretation" (Hebrew). *Tarbiz* 59 (1989–1990): 457–480.

———. "What Is the Mishneh Torah? On Codification and Ambivalence." In *Maimonides After 800 Years: Essays on Maimonides and His Influence*, ed. Jay M. Harris. Cambridge, MA: Harvard University Press, 2007, 81–111.

Hallaq, Wael. *Authority, Continuity, and Legal Change in Islamic Law.* Cambridge: Cambridge University Press, 2001.

———. "Notes on the Term *Qarīna* in Islamic Legal Discourse." *Journal of the American Oriental Society* 108 (1988): 475–480.

———. *Sharīʿa: Theory, Practice, Transformations.* Cambridge: Cambridge University Press, 2009.

Havatselet, Meir. *Ha-Rambam veha-ge'onim (Maimonides and the Geonites).* Jerusalem: Sura, 1967.

Hayya ben Sherira. *Sefer ha-meqaḥ veha-mimkar.* Vienna: Joseph Hraschanzki, 1800.

———. *Sefer ha-sheṭarot le-rav Hayya b. Sherira Gaon.* Ed. Simḥa Assaf, supplement to *Tarbiz* 1 (1930).

———. *Sefer mishpeṭei shevuʿot (The Laws of Oaths).* Ed. Shraga Abramson and prepared for publication by Robert Brody and David Sklare. Jerusalem: Makhon Ben-Zvi, 2012.

*Ḥemda genuza.* Ed. Ze'ev Wolfensohn and Schneur Zalman Schneerson. Jerusalem: n.p., 1860.

Hezser, Catherine. *Jewish Travel in Antiquity.* Tübingen: Mohr Siebeck, 2011.

*Ḥiddushei Ha-RY Migash* (R. Yosef ha-Levi ibn Migash). Ed. Moshe Shmuel Shapira. Benei Beraq: Lippa Friedman, 1973.

Hodgson, Marshall G. S. *The Venture of Islam: Conscience and History in a World Civilization.* Vol. 1: *The Classical Age of Islam.* Chicago: University of Chicago Press, 1974.

Hoffman, Adina, and Peter Cole. *Sacred Trash: The Lost and Found World of the Cairo Geniza.* New York: Next Book /Schocken, 2011.

Ibn Rushd. *Bidāyat al-mujtahid* (*The Distinguished Jurist's Primer*). Trans. I. A. K. Nyazee. 2 vols. Reading: Garnet, 1994–1996.

Isaac ben Abba Mari. *Sefer ha-ʻiṭṭur*. Ed. Meir Yonah. 2 vols. Vilna-Warsaw, 1874–1885.

Islamic Law Materialized. http://cald.irht.cnrs.fr/php/ilm.php.

Jefferson, Rebecca. "The Historical Significance of the Cambridge Genizah Inventory Project." In *Language, Culture, Computation: Studies in Honour of Yaakov Choueka*, ed. Nachum Dershowitz and Ephraim Nissan. Berlin: Springer, 2014, 9–37.

Johansen, Baber. "The Valorization of the Human Body in Muslim Sunni Law." In Devin J. Stewart, Baber Johansen, and Amy Singer, *Law and Society in Islam*. Princeton, NJ: Markus Wiener, 1996, 71–112.

Judah ben Barzilai of Barcelona. *Sefer ha-sheṭarot*. Ed. S. J. Halberstam. Berlin: Itskovski, 1898.

Kadens, Emily. "The Myth of the Customary Law Merchant." *Texas Law Review* 90 (2012): 1153–1206.

Kahana, Isaac Zeev. "The Relationship Between Halakha and Minhag" (Hebrew). In *Mazkeret: Qoveṣ torani le-zekher Maran ve-Raban Yiṣḥaq Isaac ha-Levi Herzog* (*Mazkeret: Memorial Volume for Isaac Herzog*), ed. S. Y. Zevin and Z. Warhaftig. Jerusalem: Heikhal Shelomo, 1962, 554–564.

Kamali, Mohammad Hashim. *Principles of Islamic Jurisprudence*. Rev. ed. Cambridge: Islamic Texts Society, 1999.

Kamberg, Abraham. "Commercial Law According to the Talmud." *Commercial Law Journal* 38 (1933): 239–249.

Kaplan, Ilan. "*Qinyan Siṭumta* (The Custom of the Merchants): Its Validity and Meaning" (Hebrew). *Avnei Mishpaṭ* 2 (2003): 174–192.

———. "*Qinyan Siṭumta*: In the Case of Real Property and the Case of Objects That Do Not Exist" (Hebrew). *Avnei Mishpaṭ* 3 (2004): 168–184.

Kaplony, Andeas. *Fünfundzwanzig arabische Geschäftsdokumente aus dem Rotmeer-Hafen al-Quṣayr al-Qadīm (7./13. Jh.)*. Leiden: Brill, 2014.

———. "The Interplay of Different Kinds of Commercial Documents at the Red Sea Port al-Quṣayr al-Qadīm (13th c. CE)." In *Verbal Festivity in Arabic and Other Semitic Languages*, ed. Lutz Edzard and Stephan Guth. *Proceedings of the Workshop at the Universitätsclub Bonn on January 16, 2009*. Wiesbaden: Harrassowitz, 2010, 94–115.

Katz, Dov. "*Qinyan Siṭumta*" (Hebrew). *Morasha* 1 (1971): 79–86.

Katz, Jacob. *Exclusiveness and Tolerance: Studies in Jewish-Gentile Relations in Medieval and Modern Times*. New York: Schocken, 1961.

Khalilieh, Hassan. *Admiralty and Maritime Laws in the Mediterranean Sea (ca. 800–1050): The Kitāb akriyat al-sufun vis-à-vis the Nomos Rhodion Nautikos*. Leiden: Brill, 2006.

———. *Islamic Maritime Law: An Introduction*. Leiden: Brill, 1998.

Khan, Geoffrey. *Arabic Legal and Administrative Documents in the Cambridge Genizah Collections*. Cambridge: Cambridge University Press, 1993.

Kleinman, Ron S. *Darkhei qinyan u-minhagei misḥar ba-mishpaṭ ha-ʻivri* (*Methods of Acquisition and Commercial Customs in Jewish Law: Theory, Practice and History*). Ramat Gan: Bar-Ilan University Press, 2013.

Kraemer, Joel. *Maimonides: The Life and World of One of Civilization's Greatest Minds.* New York: Doubleday, 2008.

Krakowski, Eve. *Coming of Age in Medieval Egypt: Women's Adolescence, Jewish Law, and Ordinary Culture*. Princeton, NJ: Princeton University Press, forthcoming.

———. "Female Adolescence in the Cairo Geniza Documents." PhD diss., University of Chicago, 2012.

———, and Marina Rustow. "Formula as Content: Medieval Jewish Institutions, the Cairo Geniza, and the New Diplomatics." *Jewish Social Studies* 20 (2014): 111–146.

Krauss, Samuel. *Talmudische Archäologie*. 3 vols. Leipzig: G. Fock, 1910–1912.

Kuran, Timur. "The Economic Aspect of the Middle East's Religious Minorities: The Role of Legal Pluralism." *Journal of Legal Studies* 33 (2004): 475–515.

Lambert, Phyllis, ed. *Fortifications and the Synagogue: The Fortress of Babylon and the Ben Ezra Synagogue, Cairo.* London: Weidenfeld & Nicolson, 1994.

Lev, Yaacov. "Law and Society in Medieval Islam: A Review Article." *Jerusalem Studies in Arabic and Islam* 39 (2012): 423–436.

Levinger, Jacob. *Darkhei ha-maḥshava ha-hilkhatit shel ha-Rambam* (*Maimonides' Techniques of Codification: A Study in the Method of the Mishneh Torah*). Jerusalem: Magnes, 1965.

———. "Maimonides as Philosopher and Codifier." *Jewish Law Annual* 1 (1978): 133–145.

Levinthal, Israel H. "The Jewish Law of Agency." *Jewish Quarterly Review* 13 (1922): 117–191.

Levy-Rubin, Milka. *Non-Muslims in the Early Islamic Empire: From Surrender to Coexistence.* New York: Cambridge University Press, 2011.

Lewin, B. M., ed. *Oṣar ha-Ge'onim* (*Thesaurus of the Gaonic Responsa and Commentaries*). Vol. 2: *Shabbat*. Jerusalem: Warhaftig, 1930.

Lewis, Bernard, ed. and trans. *Islam: From the Prophet Muhammad to the Capture of Constantinople*. 2 vols. New York: Harper and Row, 1974.

Libson, Gideon. "Chapters of *Sefer ha-Mazranut* of R. Samuel b. Ḥofni Gaon" (Hebrew). *Tarbiz* 56 (1986–1987): 61–107.

———. "*Gezerta* and *Ḥerem Setam* in the Gaonic and Early Medieval Periods" (Hebrew). PhD diss., Hebrew University, 1979.

———. "Halakhah and Reality in the Geonic Period: Taqqanah, Minhag, Tradition and a Consensus: Some Observations." In *The Jews of Medieval Islam: Community, Society, and Identity*, ed. Daniel Frank. Leiden: Brill, 1995, 67–99.

———. "Islamic Influence on Medieval Jewish Law? Sefer Ha'Arevuth ('Book of Surety') of Rav Shmuel Ben Ḥofni Gaon and Its Relationship to Islamic Law." *Studia Islamica* 73 (1991): 5–23.

———. *Jewish and Islamic Law: A Comparative Study of Custom During the Gaonic Period.* Cambridge, MA: Harvard University Press, 2003.

———. "Legal Autonomy and the Recourse to Legal Proceedings by Protected Peoples, According to Muslim Sources During the Gaonic Period" (Hebrew). In *Ha-islam ve-'olamot ha-shezurim bo* (*The Intertwined Worlds of Islam: Essays in Memory of Hava*

*Lazarus-Yafeh)*, ed. Nahem Ilan. Jerusalem: Hebrew University, Institute of Asian and African Studies, Makhon Ben-Zvi, and Mossad Bialik, 2002, 334–392.

———. "Legal Status of the Jewish Woman in the Gaonic Period: Muslim Influence—Overt and Covert." In *Developments in Austrian and Israeli Private Law*, ed. Herbert Hausmaninger et al. Vienna: Springer, 1998, 213–243.

———. "Maimonides' Halakhic Writings Against the Background of Muslim Law and Jurisprudence of the Period" (Hebrew). In *Ha-Rambam: Shamranut, meqoriyut, mahapkhanut (Maimonides: Conservatism, Originality, Revolution)*, 2 vols., ed. Aviezer Ravitzky. Jerusalem: Merkaz Zalman Shazar, 2008, 1:247–294.

———. "Parallels Between Maimonides and Islamic Law." In *The Thought of Maimonides: Philosophical and Legal Studies*, ed. Ira Robinson et al. Lewiston, NY: E. Mellen, 1990, 209–248.

Lieberman, Saul. *Tosefet rishonim*. 4 vols. in 2. New York: Jewish Theological Seminary, 1999.

———, ed. *The Tosefta*. 5 vols. New York: Jewish Theological Seminary, 1955–1988.

———. *Tosefta Ki-fshuṭah*. 10 vols. New York: Jewish Theological Seminary, 1955–1988.

Liebersohn, Harry. *The Return of the Gift: European History of a Global Idea*. Cambridge: Cambridge University Press, 2011.

Mahmassani, S. *Falsafat al-tashrīʿ fī l-islām (The Philosophy of Jurisprudence in Islam)*. Trans. Farhat J. Ziadeh. Leiden: Brill, 1961.

Mallat, Chibli. *Introduction to Middle Eastern Law*. Oxford: Oxford University Press, 2007.

Mann, Jacob. "The Responsa of the Babylonian Geonim as a Source of Jewish History." *Jewish Quarterly Review* 7 (1917): 457–490; 8 (1918): 339–366; 9 (1918): 139–179; 10 (1919): 121–152 and 309–365; 11 (1921): 433–471.

Margariti, Roxani Eleni. *Aden and the Indian Ocean Trade: 150 Years in the Life of a Medieval Arabian Port*. Chapel Hill: University of North Carolina Press, 2007.

———. "*Aṣḥābunā l-tujjār*—Our Associates, the Merchants: Non-Jewish Business Partners of the Cairo-Geniza's India Traders." In *Jews, Christians and Muslims in Medieval and Early Modern Times: A Festschrift in Honor of Mark R. Cohen*, ed. Arnold E. Franklin et al. Leiden: Brill, 2014, 40–58.

Marglin, Jessica. "In the Courts of the Nations: Jews, Muslims, and Legal Pluralism in Nineteenth-Century Morocco." PhD diss., Princeton University, 2013.

———. "Jews in *Sharīʿa* Courts: A Family Dispute from the Cairo Geniza." In *Jews, Christians and Muslims in Medieval and Early Modern Times: A Festschrift in Honor of Mark R. Cohen*, ed. Arnold E. Franklin et al. Leiden: Brill, 2014, 207–225.

*Massekhet soferim B*. Ed. Michael Higger. New York: Debei-Rabbanan, 1937.

Masud, Muhammad Khalid, Rudolph Peters, and David S. Powers. "Qāḍīs and Their Courts: An Historical Survey." In *Dispensing Justice in Islam: Qadis and Their Judgements*, ed. Muhammad Khalid Masud et al. Leiden: Brill, 2006, 1–44.

Mauss, Marcel. *The Gift: The Form and Reason for Exchange in Archaic Societies*. Trans. W. D. Halls. London: W. W. Norton, 2002.

Mazor, Amir. "Maimonides' Conversion to Islam: New Evidence" (Hebrew). *Pe'amim* 110 (2007): 5–8.

Meron, Ya'akov. *L'obligation alimentaire entre époux en droit musulman hanéfite*. Paris: Librairie générale de droit et de jurisprudence, 1971.

Messick, Brinkley. "Commercial Litigation in a Sharī'a Court." In *Dispensing Justice in Islam: Qadis and Their Judgements*, ed. Muhammad Khalid Masud et al. Leiden: Brill, 2006, 195–218.

*The Mishnah*. Trans. Herbert Danby. Oxford: Oxford University Press, 1933.

Modarressi, Hossein. "The Legal Basis for the Validity of the Majority Opinion in Islamic Legislation." In *Under Siege: Islam and Democracy*, ed. Richard W. Bulliet. New York: Middle East Institute of Columbia University, 1994, 81–92.

Morony, Michael. "Commerce in Early Islamic Iraq." *Asien Afrika Lateinamerika* 20 (1993): 699–720.

Moses Maimonides. *The Code of Maimonides*. 14 vols. New Haven, CT: Yale University Press, 1949.

———. *Mishna 'im perush rabbenu Moshe ben Maimon*. Ed. and trans. Joseph Kafiḥ. 6 vols. Jerusalem: Mossad Harav Kook, 1963–1968.

———. *Mishneh Torah*. Ed. Shabse Frankel. 15 vols. Jerusalem: Hoṣa'at Shabse Frankel, 1975–2007.

———. *Sefer Mishneh Torah* (Maimonides' *Mishneh Torah*, published for the first time according to Yemenite manuscripts accompanied with a comprehensive commentary). 23 vols. Kiryat Ono: Makhon Mishnat Ha-Rambam, 1984–1996.

Mueller, Christian. "Non-Muslims as Part of Islamic Law: Juridical Casuistry in a Fifth/Eleventh-Century Law Manual." In *The Legal Status of Ḏimmī-s in the Islamic West*, ed. Maribel Fierro and John Tolan. Turnhout: Brepols, 2013, 21–63.

Müller, Joel, ed. *Ḥilluf ha-minhagim bein benei bavel li-vnei ereṣ yisra'el*. Vienna: n.p., 1878.

Nachalon, Aharon. *Qahal ve-taqqanot qahal be-toratam shel ha-ge'onim* (*The Kahal and Its Enactments in the Gaonic Period*). Jerusalem: Institute for Research in Jewish Law, Hebrew University of Jerusalem, 2001.

Nethanel al-Fayyūmī. *Bustān al-'uqūl*. Ed. and trans. Joseph Kafiḥ. Kiryat Ono: Agudat Halikhot Am Yisra'el, 1984.

Niazi, Liaquat Ali Khan. *Islamic Law of Contract*. Lahore: Research Cell, Dyal Sing Trust Library, n.d.

Nuland, Sherwin B. *Maimonides*. New York: Next Book/Schocken, 2005.

Nyazee, Imran A. K. *Islamic Law of Business Organization: Partnerships*. Islamabad: International Institute of Islamic Thought, 1999.

Ostersetzer, J. "The דיוקני [*diyoqne*] in Legal Documents in Talmudic Jurisprudence" (Hebrew). *Tarbiz* 11 (1940): 39–55.

Oulddali, Ahmed. "Recevabilité du témoignage du *ḏimmī* d'après les jurists mālikites d'Afrique du Nord." In *The Legal Status of Ḏimmī-s in the Islamic West*, ed. Maribel Fierro and John Tolan. Turnhout: Brepols, 2013, 275–292.

Passamaneck, Stephen M. "Caravan Custom in Early Rabbinic Sources." *Revue d'histoire du droit* 36 (1968): 73–88.

———. "Traces of Rabbinical Maritime Law and Custom." *Revue d'histoire du droit* 34 (1966): 525–551.

Patai, Raphael. "Ancient Jewish Seafaring and Riverfaring Laws." In *By Study and Also by Faith: Essays in Honor of Hugh W. Nibley on the Occasion of His Eightieth Birthday*, ed. Stephen D. Ricks and John Lundquist. Salt Lake City: Desert Book Company and Foundation for Ancient Research and Mormon Studies, 1990, 389–416.

Paul, Jürgen. "*Khidma* in the Social History of Pre-Mongol Iran." *Journal of the Social and Economic History of the Orient* 57 (2014): 392–422.

Payne, Richard E. "Christianity and Iranian Society in Late Antiquity, ca. 500–700 CE." PhD diss., Princeton University, 2010.

Pedersen, Johannes. *The Arabic Book.* Trans. Geoffrey French. Princeton, NJ: Princeton University Press, 1984.

Popper, William. *The Censorship of Hebrew Books.* New York: Burt Franklin, 1899.

Princeton Geniza Project (PGP). http://etc.princeton.edu/genizaproject.

al-Qattan, Najwa. "Dhimmīs in the Islamic Court: Legal Autonomy and Religious Discrimination." *International Journal of Middle East Studies* 31 (1999): 429–444.

Rāġib, Yūsuf. *Marchands d'étoffes du fayyoum au IIIe/IXe siècle d'après leurs archives (actes et lettres) II: La correspondance administrative et privée des Banū 'Abd al-Mu'min.* Cairo: Institut Français d'Archéologie Orientale, 1985.

Rakover, Nahum. "Maimonides as Codifier of Jewish Law. In *Sobre la vida y obra de Maimonides*, ed. Jesús Peláez Rosal. Córdoba: Ediciones el Almendro, 1991, 414–421.

———. *Ha-shelihut veha-harsha'a ba-mishpaṭ ha-'ivri* (*Agency and Legal Proxy in Jewish Law*). Jerusalem: Mossad Harav Kook, 1972.

———, ed. *Maimonides as Codifier of Jewish Law.* Jerusalem: Library of Jewish Law, 1987.

Ravitzky, Aviezer, ed. *Ha-Rambam: Shamranut, meqoriyut, mahapkhanut* (*Maimonides: Conservatism, Originality, Revolution*). 2 vols. Jerusalem: Merkaz Zalman Shazar, 2008.

Ravitzky, Aviram. "Saadya Gaon and Maimonides on the Logic and Limits of Legal Inference in Context of the Karaite-Rabbanite Controversy." *History and Logic of Philosophy* 32 (2011): 29–36.

Reif, Stefan C. *A Jewish Archive from Old Cairo: The History of Cambridge University's Genizah Collection.* Richmond, Surrey: Curzon, 2000.

Rivlin, Joseph. *Shiṭre qehillat al-Yusanah min ha-me'ah ha-aḥat-'esreh* (*Formularies of the Community of Lucena from the Eleventh Century*). Ramat Gan: Bar-Ilan University Press, 1994.

Russ-Fishbane, Elisha. "Between Politics and Piety: Abraham Maimonides and His Times." PhD diss., Harvard University, 2009.

———. *Judaism, Sufism, and the Pietists of Medieval Egypt: A Study of Abraham Maimonides and His Times.* Oxford: Oxford University Press, 2015.

———. "The Maimonidean Legacy in the East: A Study of Father and Son." *Jewish Quarterly Review* 102 (2012): 190–223.

Rustow, Marina. "At the Limits of Communal Autonomy: Jewish Bids for Intervention from the Mamluk State." *Mamlūk Studies Review* 13 (2009): 134–159.

———. "Benefaction (Niʿma): Gratitude (Shukr): and the Politics of Giving and Receiving in Letters from the Cairo Geniza." In *Giving in Monotheistic Religions*, ed. Miriam Frenkel and Yaakov Lev. Berlin: De Gruyter, 2009, 365–390.

———. "Formal and Informal Patronage Among Jews in the Islamic East: Evidence from the Cairo Geniza." *Al-Qanṭara* 29 (2008): 341–382.

Saadya Gaon ben Yosef. *Kitāb al-mawārīth*. Ed. Joel Müller. Paris: Ernest Leroux, 1897.

Salaymeh, Lena. "Every Law Tells a Story: Orthodox Divorce in Jewish and Islamic Legal Histories." *UC Irvine Law Review* 4, 1 (2014): 19–63.

Samuel ben Ḥofni Gaon. *Kitāb al-sharika wa'l-muḍāraba* (*Book on Partnership and Commenda*). Ed. B. M. Lewin and Israel Friedlander. *Ginze Kedem* 6 (1944): 41–73.

al-Sarakhsī. *Al-mabsūṭ*. 30 vols. Cairo: Maṭbaʿat al-Saʿadah, 1906–1913.

Schacht, Joseph. *Introduction to Islamic Law*. Oxford: Clarendon, 1964.

Schepansky, Israel. *Ha-taqqanot be-yisra'el*. 4 vols. New York and Jerusalem: Michael Scharf Publication Trust and Mossad Harav Kook, 1991–1993.

Schlossberg, Eliezer. "Maimonides' Attitude Toward Islam" (Hebrew). *Peʿamim* 42 (1990): 38–60.

Schwartz, Seth. "Historiography on the Jews in the Talmudic Period (70–640 CE)." In *The Oxford Handbook of Jewish Studies*, ed. Martin Goodman. Oxford: Oxford University Press, 2002, chap. 5.

*Sefer ha-ʿiṭṭur*. Ed. Meir Yonah. 2 vols. Vilna-Warsaw, 1864–1885.

al-Shāfiʿī. *Kitāb al-umm*. 8 vols. Cairo: Maktabat al-Kulīyāt al-Azharīya, 1961.

Shaham, Ron. "Jews and the Sharīʿa Court in Modern Egypt." *Studia Islamica* 82 (1995): 113–136.

Shailat, Isaac, ed. *Iggerot ha-Rambam* (*Letters and Essays of Moses Maimonides*). 2 vols. Maʿaleh Adumim: Yeshivat Birkat Mosheh, 1988.

*She'elot u-teshuvot R. Yiṣḥaq Alfasi*. Ed. Wolf Leiter. Pittsburgh: Makhon Ha-Rambam, 1954.

*She'elot u-teshuvot R. Yosef ha-Levi ibn Migash*. Ed. Simḥa Ḥasida. Jerusalem: Makhon Lev Sameaḥ, 1991.

Silver, Daniel Jeremy. *Maimonidean Criticism and the Maimonidean Controversy, 1180–1240*. Leiden: Brill, 1965.

Simonsohn, Shlomo. *The Jews in Sicily*. Vol. 1: *383–1300*. Leiden: Brill, 1997.

Simonsohn, Uriel I. *A Common Justice: The Legal Allegiances of Christians and Jews Under Early Islam*. Philadelphia: University of Pennsylvania Press, 2011.

Sinai, Yuval. "Maimonides' Commentary on the Mishna" (Hebrew). In *Mi-birkat Moshe* (*Essays on the Teachings of the Rambam in Honor of R. Naḥum Eliezer Rabinovitz*), 2 vols., ed. Zvi Heber and Carmiel Cohen. Maʿaleh Adumim: Maʿaliyot, 2011, 2:200–262.

Singer, Amy. *Charity in Islamic Societies*. Cambridge: Cambridge University Press, 2008.

Sklare, David. *Samuel ben Ḥofni Gaon and His Cultural World: Texts and Studies*. Leiden: Brill, 1996.

Sokoloff, Michael. *A Dictionary of Jewish Babylonian Aramaic of the Talmudic and Gaonic Periods*. Baltimore: Johns Hopkins University Press, 2002.

Soloveitchik, Haym. "Can Halakhic Texts Talk History?" *AJS Review* 3 (1978): 153–196; repr., idem, *Collected Essays*. Oxford: Littman Library of Jewish Civilization, 2013, 1:169–223.

———. *Collected Essays*. 2 vols. Oxford: Littman Library of Jewish Civilization, 2013.

———. "Pawnbroking: A Study in *Ribbit* and of the Halakhah in Exile." In idem, *Collected Essays*. Oxford: Littman Library of Jewish Civilization, 2013, 1:57–166.

———. "Religious Law and Change: The Medieval Ashkenazic Example." *AJS Review* 12 (1987): 205–221; repr., idem, *Collected Essays*. Oxford: Littman Library of Jewish Civilization, 2013, 1:239–257.

———. "'Religious Law and Change' Revisited." In idem, *Collected Essays*. Oxford: Littman Library of Jewish Civilization, 2013, 1:258–277.

———. *Ha-yayin bimei ha-beinayim: Yein nesekh—Pereq be-toledot ha-halakha be-Ashkenaz* (*Wine in Ashkenaz in the Middle Ages: Yein Nesekh—a Study in the History of Halakha*). Jerusalem: Merkaz Zalman Shazar, 2008.

———. *Yeinam: Saḥar be-yeinam shel goyim 'al gilgulah shel halakha be-'olam ha-ma'aseh* (*Principles and Pressures: Jewish Trade in Gentile Wine in the Middle Ages*). Tel Aviv: Alma-Am Oved, 2003.

Sperber, Daniel. "*Nautica* in Talmudic Palestine." In *Seafaring and the Jews*, ed. Nadav Kashtan. London: F. Cass, 2001, 29–46.

———. *Nautica Talmudica*. Ramat Gan and Leiden: Bar-Ilan University Press and Brill, 1986.

Stampfer, Y. Zvi. "An Influence of Islamic Law of Divorce on Rav Samuel b. Ḥofni Gaon and Maimonides" (Hebrew). In *'Alei 'asor: Proceedings of the Tenth Conference of the Society for Judaeo-Arabic Studies*, ed. Daniel J. Lasker and Haggai Ben-Shammai. Beer Sheva: Ben-Gurion University of the Negev Press, 2008, 309–316.

———. "Maimonides *Hilkhot ha-yerushalmi* on Tractate Ketubbot" (Hebrew). In *Mi-birkat Moshe* (*Essays on the Teachings of the Rambam in Honor of R. Naḥum Eliezer Rabinovitz*), 2 vols., ed. Zvi Heber and Carmiel Cohen. Ma'aleh Adumim: Ma'aliyot, 2011, 1:12–108.

———, ed. *Sefer ha-gerushin (Kitāb al-Ṭalāq) le-Rav Shmuel ben Ḥofni Geon Sura* (*Laws of Divorce [Kitāb al-Ṭalāq] by Samuel ben Ḥofni Gaon*). Jerusalem: Makhon Ben-Zvi, 2009.

Stern, Samuel. "The Constitution of the Islamic City." In *The Islamic City: A Colloquium*, ed. Albert Hourani and Samuel M. Stern. Oxford: Cassirer; Philadelphia: University of Pennsylvania Press, 1970, 25–50.

Stewart, Devin J., Baber Johansen, and Amy Singer. *Law and Society in Islam*. Princeton, NJ: Markus Wiener, 1996.

———. "Three Petitions of the Fatimid Period." *Oriens* 15 (1962): 172–209.

Stillman, Norman A. *The Jews of Arab Lands: A History and Source Book*. Philadelphia: Jewish Publication Society, 1979.

Stroumsa, Sarah. *Maimonides in His World: Portrait of a Mediterranean Thinker*. Princeton, NJ: Princeton University Press, 2009.

al-Ṭaḥāwī. *Al-shurūṭ al-ṣaghīr*. Ed. Rawḥī Ūzjān. 2 vols. Baghdad: Ri'āsat Dīwān al-Awqāf, 1974.

Ta-Shma, Israel. *Creativity and Traditions: Studies in Medieval Rabbinic Scholarship, Literature, and Thought.* Cambridge, MA: Harvard University Press, 2006.

*Teshuvot ge'onei mizraḥ u-ma'arav.* Ed. Joel Müller. Berlin: P. Deutsch, 1888.

*Teshuvot ha-ge'onim.* Ed. Abraham Eliyahu Harkavy. Berlin: Itskovski, 1887.

*Teshuvot ha-ge'onim.* Ed. Simha Assaf. Jerusalem: Darom, 1929.

*Teshuvot ha-ge'onim.* Ed. Simḥa Assaf. Jerusalem: Makhon le-Madda'ei Ha-yahadut 2, 1927.

*Teshuvot ha-ge'onim.* Ed. Simḥa Assaf. Jerusalem: Mekize Nirdamim, 1942.

*Teshuvot ha-ge'onim.* Ed. Ya'akov Mussaphia. Lyck: Rudolph Siebert, 1864.

*Teshuvot ha-ge'onim.* Ed. Naḥman Nathan Coronel. Vienna, 1871; repr., Jerusalem, 1967.

*Teshuvot ha-ge'onim sha'arei ṣedeq.* Salonika, 1792; repr., Jerusalem: Kelal U-Ferat, 1966.

*Teshuvot ha-Rambam.* Ed. Joshua Blau. Vols. 1–3. Jerusalem: Mekize Nirdamim, 1957–1961; vol. 4, Jerusalem: Rubin Mass, 1986.

*Teshuvot Rabbenu Avraham ben ha-Rambam* (Abraham Maimuni Responsa). Ed. A. H. Freimann. Trans. S. D. Goitein. Jerusalem: Mekize Nirdamim, 1937.

*Teshuvot Rav Naṭronai bar Hilai Gaon.* Ed. Robert (Yeraḥme'el) Brody. 2 vols. Jerusalem: Ofeq Institute, 1994.

Tillier, Mathieu. "Dispensing Justice in a Minority Context: The Judicial Administration of Upper Egypt Under Muslim Rule in the Early Eighth Century." In *The Late Antique World of Early Islam: Muslims Among Jews and Christians in the East Mediterranean*, ed. Robert G. Hoyland. Princeton, NJ: Darwin, 2015, 133–156.

Twersky, Isadore. "The Beginnings of *Mishneh Torah* Criticism." In *Biblical and Other Studies.* Ed. Alexander Altmann. Cambridge: Cambridge University Press, 1963, 161–83.

———. *Introduction to the Code of Maimonides (Mishneh Torah).* New Haven, CT: Yale University Press, 1980.

———. *Rabad of Posquières, a Twelfth-Century Talmudist.* Cambridge, MA: Harvard University Press, 1962.

Tykocinski, Chaim. *Taqqanot ha-ge'onim.* Trans. Meir Havatselet. Jerusalem and New York: Sura and Yeshiva University, 1960.

Udovitch, A. L. "At the Origins of the Western Commenda: Islam, Israel, Byzantium?." *Speculum* 37 (1972): 198–207.

———. "Bankers Without Banks: Commerce, Banking, and Society in the Islamic World of the Middle Ages." In *The Dawn of Modern Banking*, ed. Fredi Chiapelli. New Haven, CT: Yale University Press, 1979, 255–273.

———. "Credit as a Means of Investment in Medieval Islamic Trade." *Journal of the American Oriental Society* 87 (1967): 260–264.

———. "An Eleventh-Century Islamic Treatise on the Law of the Sea." *Annales Islamologiques* 27 (1993): 37–54.

———. "Formalism and Informalism in the Social and Economic Institutions of the Medieval Islamic World." In *Individualism and Conformity in Classical Islam*, ed. Amin Banani and Speros Vryonis. Wiesbaden: Harrassowitz, 1977, 61–81.

———. "The 'Law Merchant' of the Medieval Islamic World." In *Logic in Classical Islamic Culture*, ed. G. E. von Grunebaum. Wiesbaden: Harrassowitz, 1970, 113–130.

———. *Partnership and Profit in Medieval Islam*. Princeton, NJ: Princeton University Press, 1970.

———. "A Tale of Two Cities: Commercial Relations Between Cairo and Alexandria During the Second Half of the Eleventh Century." In *The Medieval City*, ed. David Herlihy et al. New Haven, CT: Yale University Press, 1977, 143–162.

———. "Time, the Sea and Society: Duration of Commercial Voyages on the Southern Shores of the Mediterranean During the High Middle Ages." In *La Navigazione Mediterranea nell'alto Medioevo*. Spoleto: Presso la sede del Centro, 1978, 2:503–563.

Urbach, Ephraim. *Ba'alei ha-tosafot*. Jerusalem: Mossad Bialik, 1968.

Vogel, Frank E. "Contract Law of Islam and the Arab Middle East." *International Encyclopedia of Comparative Law* (2006), vol. 7, chap. 7.

Voguet, Élise. "Les communautés juives du Maghreb central à la lumière des *fatwā*-s mālikites de la fin du Moyen Âge." In *The Legal Status of Ḏimmī-*s *in the Islamic West*, ed. Maribel Fierro and John Tolan. Turnhout: Brepols, 2013, 295–306.

Wakin, Jeanette A. *The Function of Documents in Islamic Law: The Chapters on Sales from Ṭaḥāwī's Kitāb al-shurūṭ al-kabīr*. Albany: State University of New York Press, 1972.

al-Wansharīsī, Aḥmad ibn Yaḥyā. *Al-mi'yār al-mu'rib wa'l-jāmi' al-mughrib 'an fatāwī 'ulamā' ifrīqīya wa'l-andalus wa'l-maghrib*. Vol. 10, ed. Muḥammad Ḥajjī. Beirut: Dār al-Gharb al-Islāmī, 1981.

Watson, Alan. *Legal Transplants: An Approach to Comparative Law*. Edinburgh: Scottish Academic Press, 1974.

———. *Society and Legal Change*. Edinburgh: Scottish Academic Press, 1977.

———. "Society's Choice and Legal Change." *Hofstra Law Review* 9 (1980–1981): 1473–1484.

Westreich, Elimelech. "Elements of Negotiability in Talmudic and Gaonic Sources." *Jewish Law Association Studies* 29 (2008): 247–274.

Wieder, Naphtali. *Hashpa'ot islamiyot 'al ha-pulḥan ha-yehudi* (*Islamic Influences on the Jewish Worship*). Oxford: East and West Library, 1947.

Zinger, Oded. "Women, Gender and Law: According to Documents from the Cairo Geniza." PhD diss., Princeton University, 2014.

Zysow, Aron. "The Problem of Offer and Acceptance: A Study of Implied-in-Fact Contracts in Islamic Law and the Common Law." *Cleveland State Law Review* 34 (1985–1986): 69–77.

# Index

# Acknowledgments

As with most ambitious projects taking long to complete, I am indebted to many institutions and people. A grant from the National Endowment for the Humanities (2007–2008) provided the initial impetus to the research. A delightful month spent that spring as a short-term Meymandi Fellow at the National Humanities Center offered a robust intellectual environment for my research and writing. I spent fruitful time during two subsequent spring terms (2013 and 2014) as a fellow of the Sackler Institute for Advanced Studies at Tel Aviv University. I put the finishing touches on the manuscript while I was a Polonsky Visiting Fellow at the Oxford Centre for Hebrew and Jewish Studies in June 2016.

I was fortunate in having many opportunities to share my work-in-progress with colleagues during the course of preparing the book: a lecture early on in the Program in Medieval Studies at my university, Princeton; a conference celebrating the retirement of Stefan C. Reif from directorship of the Taylor-Schechter Genizah Research Unit at Cambridge University Library; conferences of the Society for Judaeo-Arabic Studies, one in Israel, one in Córdoba, Spain, and one in Nashville, Tennessee; a conference on documents in medieval Jewish history held in Oxford, UK; a lecture at the Consejo Superior de Investigaciones Cientificas in Madrid; the conference "Trade and Legal Pluralism in the Era of the Geniza" at Tel Aviv University Law School; a seminar presentation to the students in Dean Ron Harris's course "Law and History" at the same institution; a conference at Yale University on the Cairo Geniza documents; a lecture before Columbia University's Institute for Israel and Jewish Studies; a faculty and graduate-student seminar at Yale; a conference in Córdoba on law and minorities sponsored by the RELMIN (Religious Minorities) Project of the University of Nantes, directed by John Tolan; a presentation to faculty and students at NYU Abu Dhabi; and a faculty and graduate-student workshop at the University of Haifa. On all these occasions, I benefited from questions and other responses that helped me refine the argument of the book. Responsibility for any errors remaining in the book are my own.

Many colleagues and research students were kind enough to read parts or all of the manuscript in progress and offer their critique. They are Phillip Ackerman-Lieberman, Neri Ariel, Gerald Blidstein, Robert Brody, Miriam Frenkel, Jessica Goldberg, Moshe Halbertal, Eve Krakowski, Roxani Eleni Margariti, Jessica Marglin, Intisar Rabb, Joseph Rivlin, Amichai Rosenfeld, Elisha Russ-Fishbane, Marina Rustow, Lena Salaymeh, Raymond Scheindlin, Uriel Simonsohn, Haym Soloveitchik, Zvi Stampfer, Avrom Udovitch, Elimelech Westreich, and Oded Zinger. The comments of the two anonymous readers of my manuscript for the University of Pennsylvania Press were very helpful. I thank Jerry Singerman, Senior Humanities Editor at the University of Pennsylvania Press, and the faculty editorial board for having confidence in what some may see as a challenging, new interpretation of Maimonides' Mishneh Torah. For her meticulous copyediting, I thank Janice Meyerson.

Along the way, I published several articles that made their way, partially or in whole, into the book. My chapter "The 'Custom of the Merchants' in Gaonic Jurisprudence and in the *Mishneh Torah* of Maimonides," in *The Festschrift Darkhei Noam: The Jews of Arab Lands*, forms part of Chapter 2. Chapters 5–6 include portions of my "A Partnership Gone Bad: Business Relationships and the Evolving Law of the Cairo Geniza Period." in the *Journal of the Economic and Social History of the Orient*. Chapter 7 represents a slightly revised version of my "The Law of Power of Attorney in Maimonides' Code of Jewish Law," in *"From a Sacred Source": Genizah Studies in Honour of Professor Stefan C. Reif.* Portions of Chapter 9 are echoed in my essay "Defending Jewish Judicial Autonomy in the Islamic Middle Ages," in *Law and Religious Minorities in Medieval Societies: Between Theory and Praxis.* I thank all the publishers for permission to draw upon these pieces here.

It remains for me to acknowledge and thank my wife, Linda Charet, who has been at my side during the entire period of the writing of this book, constantly encouraging me. Though her specialty as a lawyer is unrelated to the subject of this book, she has been a stalwart listener and critic, always giving me the benefit of her keen legal mind.